Library of
Davidson College

NEW YORK CITY'S CHANGING ECONOMIC BASE

NEW YORK CITY'S CHANGING ECONOMIC BASE

Edited by Benjamin J. Klebaner

PICA PRESS

New York

Published in the United States of America in 1981 by
PICA PRESS
Distributed by Universe Books
381 Park Avenue South, New York, N.Y. 10016
© 1981 by Universe Books

All rights reserved. No part of this publication may be reproduced, stored in a retrieval system, or transmitted, in any form or by any means, electronic, mechanical, photocopying, recording, or otherwise, without the prior permission of the publishers.

Library of Congress Cataloging in Publication Data
Main entry under title:
New York City's changing economic base.

   1. New York (N.Y.)—Economic conditions—Addresses, essays, lectures. 2. New York (N.Y.)—Industries—Addresses, essays, lectures. I. Klebaner, Benjamin Joseph, 1926-
HC108.N7N33   330.9747'1043   81-40498
ISBN 0-87663-731-4   AACR2

Dedication

In memory of Harry Schwager, CCNY 1911, whose generosity made possible this and previous conference volumes sponsored by the Department of Economics of the City College of the City University of New York

The views expressed herein do not necessarily represent those of the organizations with which the authors are associated.

Contents

INTRODUCTION: THE DECLINE AND TESTING OF NEW YORK CITY'S ECONOMY
    Benjamin J. Klebaner   1

1. SOME PERSPECTIVES ON THE NEW YORK CITY ECONOMY IN A TIME OF CHANGE
    Samuel M. Ehrenhalt   6
2. THE APPLE'S CORE: New York City's Export Industries
    Matthew P. Drennan   23
3. THE ROLE OF NATIONAL CORPORATIONS IN NEW YORK CITY'S ECONOMY
    Regina Belz Armstrong   33
4. NEW YORK CITY AND THE SERVICES TRANSFORMATION
    Thomas M. Stanback, Jr.   48
5. THE ROLE OF NEW YORK CITY'S FOREIGN EXPORTS IN LOCAL MANUFACTURING
    Maurice B. Ballabon   57
6. NEW YORK CITY'S FINANCIAL INDUSTRY: Just How Captive Is It?
    Thomas J. Spitznas   72
7. THE COMMERCIAL PRINTING INDUSTRY: Is It Still Made In New York?
    Emanuel Tobier and Mark A. Willis   81
8. NEW YORK CITY'S COMPETITIVE POSITION: A Review of Selected Manufacturing and Service Industries
    Pearl Kamer and Dennis Young   92
9. URBAN INDUSTRIAL PARKS VERSUS THE EXODUS OF MANUFACTURING
    Edwin P. Reubens   110
10. REGIONAL ECONOMIC DEVELOPMENT STRATEGY
    Marilyn Rubin and Ilene Wagner   124
11. NEW YORK CITY AFTER THE 1970s: A Case for Guarded Optimism
    William J. Lawrence   132
12. STRATEGIES FOR NEW YORK CITY ECONOMIC DEVELOPMENT
    Irving Leveson   142
13. THE FUTURE OF MANHATTAN
    Boris S. Pushkarev   156
14. NEW YORK CITY'S FISCAL SITUATION
    Herbert J. Ranschburg   185
15. NEW YORK IN THE NATIONWIDE SLOWDOWN OF 1980–81
    George P. Roniger   188

    CONTRIBUTORS   192

INTRODUCTION
THE DECLINE AND TESTING OF NEW YORK CITY'S ECONOMY

Benjamin J. Klebaner

"New York City continues to have a vital economy," Eli Ginzberg insisted in early 1972. The manpower expert's message that the city was "very much alive" was incorporated in the title of a volume of studies by his Conservation of Human Resources staff. Readers were assured that "New York is thriving as an economic center."[1]

The shrinkage in local employment in 1970–71 was attributed to recession in the national economy, and there was "good reason to hope" that the 1970s would be an easier decade for the city than the 1960s.[2] Three years later, however, the Empire City was on the brink of bankruptcy, in part because of a deteriorating economic base.

In 16 of the 20 years between 1950 and 1969, employment in the city exceeded the preceding year's total (Table 1). Total employment declined only in the recession years 1954, 1958, and 1961, as well as in 1963. The prior record of 1953 was surpassed in 1956 and 1957. Not until 1964, however, was the 1957 level reached again. And by 1969, peaking at 3.8 million jobs, employment was 6.7% above the 1957 level. Private-sector employment declined in every year in which total employment fell, as well as in 1952. Thus, private employment exceeded the preceding year's in 15 of the 20 years prior to 1970. Yet it took 11 years for the 1957 level to be surpassed. Only five cities had a slower growth of private-sector employment than did New York in the 1960s.[3]

Private-sector employment in 1969 was a record 3.25 million, 3% above the 1956 level. Growth in finance, insurance, and real estate (FIRE), as well as in services, more than offset declines in the rest of the private sector. By 1980, however, only services had more employees than in 1969. Although 1979 and 1980 showed some improvement, private-sector jobs in 1980 were 14.4% below the 1969 peak. As with total employment, only an incurable optimist would project a return to the 1969 private employment total by the year 2000.

Federal, state, and local government employment at 574,000 in 1974 was more than 50% above the 1950 total. Subsequent attrition, however, brought the 1980

TABLE 1
EMPLOYMENT IN NEW YORK CITY, 1950-80
(in thousands)

	Government	Private	Total
1950	374.4	3,093.8	3,468.2
1951	391.5	3,117.8	3,509.3
1952	406.5	3,113.9	3,520.4
1953	400.8	3,123.3	3,524.1
1954	393.9	3,055.4	3,449.3
1955	390.0	3,086.2	3,476.2
1956	396.0	3,151.7	3,547.7
1957	399.6	3,160.1	3,559.7
1958	404.8	3,074.4	3,479.2
1959	402.8	3,115.6	3,518.4
1960	408.2	3,130.2	3,538.4
1961	414.8	3,111.7	3,526.5
1962	428.9	3,130.4	3,559.3
1963	439.8	3,093.1	3,532.9
1964	448.3	3,111.5	3,559.8
1965	461.9	3,115.4	3,577.3
1966	483.8	3,130.5	3,614.3
1967	504.5	3,157.0	3,661.5
1968	526.0	3,195.7	3,721.7
1969	547.0	3,250.7	3,797.7
1970	563.2	3,182.3	3,745.5
1971	570.1	3,041.7	3,611.8
1972	565.7	3,000.4	3,566.1
1973	575.9	2,964.7	3,540.6
1974	583.7	2,862.4	3,446.1
1975	573.8	2,712.5	3,266.3
1976	522.3	2,687.4	3,209.7
1977	507.8	2,680.1	3,187.9
1978	520.8	2,715.8	3,236.6
1979	520.1	2,758.7	3,278.8
1980	516.6	2,781.8	3,298.4

SOURCE: U.S. Bureau of Labor Statistics, Middle Atlantic Region.

INTRODUCTION

total back to the 1968 level (11.5% below the 1974 peak), whereas private-sector employment was almost 13% below 1968's.[4]

Unavailability of job opportunities has kept the city's labor force participation rate well below the national average.[5] This ratio of those at work or actively seeking employment to the noninstitutional population aged 16 or over reached new highs in the nation as the 1970s unfolded. Not so in New York City, where even in 1969 the rate was 4 percentage points below the national average (Table 2). The gap widened to more than 8 percentage points by the late 1970s. Whereas the national trend was upward from 1970 through 1980, the city's participation rate ranged from 54.4% to 56.4%.

Before 1970, the unemployment rate of New York residents was almost always below the national average. Since 1970, however, New York City has been consistently above — as much as 3.5 percentage points higher in 1976. At 9.2% in the first seven months of 1981, the incidence of unemployment was more than double the rate of 1969.

In view of the discouraging labor market developments in New York City, it is not surprising that per capita personal income has declined relative to the nation. In 1929, the city had enjoyed a per capita income 95% above the national average; even in 1950 it was 43% higher.[6] By the late 1960s, however, New York City was only about one-fourth above the U.S. average, and a decade later it was barely above it. As living costs in New York City are well above the national average, in real terms New Yorkers today suffer from below-average real personal income, despite the fact that transfer payments are well above average for the nation.

Adjusted for inflation, in 1978 the value of production for export from the city to the rest of the world was 8.3% less than in 1968, while total production in the city also was 8.3% less.[7]

Measures of employment, output, and income all reveal a deterioration of New

TABLE 2
NEW YORK CITY UNEMPLOYMENT RATES, 1970-80
(percentages)

Year	Rate
1970	4.8
1971	6.7
1972	7.0
1973	6.0
1974	7.2
1975	10.6
1976	11.2
1977	10.0
1978	8.9
1979	8.7
1980	8.6

SOURCE: U.S. Bureau of Labor Statistics, Middle Atlantic Region, Release, May 8, 1981.

York City's economy unanticipated by previous forecasts. Thus, although a major study completed at the end of the 1950s projected total employment in 1975 as 8% above the 1956 level, it actually turned out to be 7% below that level. For 1985 employment was expected to be 13% above 1956's, and almost 5% more than the 1975 projected total.[8] The metropolis, contrary to Ginzberg's 1972 assessment, is not thriving.

More recent projections forecasted a decline in 1980 relative to the mid-1970s, with shrinkage at a reduced rate until 1985. By 1985 private employment would be 4% below 1976, according to the Temporary Commission on City Finances, while the Center for Urban Policy Research predicted a level almost 5% below its estimate for 1975.[9]

Early in 1980, two elaborate econometric models produced gloomy forecasts: Wharton's anticipated no growth in employment in the 1980s. Chase Econometrics ranked New York at the bottom of all 108 major areas in terms of employment growth: By 1990 the area was expected to lose 4% of its jobs, with an even greater decline for New York City.[10]

Despite such negative projection's, doom is not inevitable. The federal government's General Accounting Office made a fair assessment in October 1979: There was "little hope for real growth unless the City implements a comprehensive plan to improve its stagnating economic base."[11] Much the same message came from the final report submitted by Mayor Beame's Temporary Commission on City Finances in mid-1977: "in the next decade the decline of the local economy can be slowed significantly and perhaps even halted," provided "substantial public investment would make New York a more attractive location for business activity."[12]

A vision of New York as "the global marketplace for business, finance, communications, the professions, and the arts" was offered by a Twentieth Century Fund task force reporting near the end of 1979.[13] This "potentially" bright long-run transformation of New York into the "future world capital"[14] is a very ambitious but not impossible goal.

For the fading Empire City to become World City, all levels of government must make a long-term commitment to sound public policies. The studies in this volume indicate that such a transformation will not be accomplished easily.

Notes

1. Eli Ginzberg, *New York is Very Much Alive* (New York: McGraw-Hill, 1973), pp. 283, 276; see also pp. 274, 78. Richard Knight mentioned the "vitality" of the city's economy; Ibid., p. 7.

2. Ibid., pp. 70, 79.

3. Pittsburgh, Newark, Philadelphia, and St. Louis did worse than New York. Ibid., p. 24.

4. The federal government had 117,500 employees in New York City in 1958 but only 84,700 in 1978. "Employment and Earnings: States and Areas, 1939– 78," *Bureau of Labor Statistics Bulletin,* 1370– 13 (1979). In 1980 the figure was 87,900.

5. A substantial underground economy may be another factor. Rona B. Stein, "New York City's Economy in 1980," Federal Reserve Bank of New York *Quarterly Review,* Spring 1981, p. 5.

6. *Economics and Demographic Trends in New York City: The Outlook for the Future* (Temporary Commission on City Finances, 13th Interim Report, New York, May 1977), p. 96. Between 1962 and 1973 inflation-adjusted labor personal income of city residents, after payments of social insurance contributions, had increased by only 13%. Meanwhile, transfer payments had more than doubled. Ibid., p 14.

INTRODUCTION

7. Mathew Drennan and Georgia Nanopoulous-Stergiou, "The Local Economy and Local Revenues," in Raymond D. Horton and Charles Brecher (eds.), *Setting Municipal Priorities 1980* (Montclair, N.J.: Allanheld, Osmun; New York: Universe, 1979), p. 12. Because of productivity gains, employment declined by 13.4% between 1968 and 1978.

8. Raymond Vernon, *Metropolis 1985* (Cambridge, Mass.: Harvard University Press, 1960), pp. 234–37. The table gives 1956 employment at 3.9 million, but the latest BLS statistics show 3.55 million.

9. *The City in Transition: Prospects and Policies for New York* (New York: Temporary Commission on City Finances, 1978), p. 99. The projections were prepared by Karen Gerard and George Roniger. Their 1976 actual estimate was 22,000 below the latest BLS figures. The Center for Urban Policy Research gave 2.93 million for private employment in 1975; subsequently the BLS reported 2.71 million. Employment in 1980 was 2.78 million — 42,000 less than the estimates in James W. Hughes and George Sternlieb, *Jobs and People: New York City, 1985* (New Brunswick, N.J.: Rutgers University Center for Urban Policy Research, 1978), p. 120.

10. *The New York Times,* January 21, 1980, p. B1; March 28, 1980.

11. "New York City's Fiscal Problems: A Long Road Still Lies Ahead," U.S. General Acccounting Office Report GGD 80–5, p. 24.

12. *The City in Transition,* pp. 95, 129. An analysis by David Grossman of public investments is in the report of the Twentieth Century Fund Task Force on the Future of New York City, *New York – World City* (Cambridge, Mass.: Oelgeschlager, Gunn & Hain, 1980), pp. 175-217. Mr. Grossman discussed this topic at a conference on May 15, 1980 sponsored by the Department of Economics of the City College of New York.

13. *New York – World City,* p. 5. However, Masha Sinnreich's accompanying background paper stated that the city faces an uneviable and uncertain future (p. 138).

14. Ibid., p. 5.

1

SOME PERSPECTIVES ON THE NEW YORK CITY ECONOMY IN A TIME OF CHANGE

Samuel M. Ehrenhalt

Our focus is on time and on change. The past decade saw a substantial reshaping of the New York economy. The changes came swiftly, accelerating long-term trends, imposing adjustments on New York City's people, its government, and its institutions that were more difficult in a highly condensed time frame.

Widespread and severe job losses during the first seven years of the 1970s were most pronounced in the goods-producing sector. The subsequent recovery resulted almost entirely from gains in service-producing activities. The rapid rise in the importance of this sector brought with it a further shift to white-collar, knowledge-oriented jobs and declines in the importance of blue collar and all other occupations.

The economic crisis that began in 1969 and lasted for eight years marked a sharp, for many industries decisive, break with the past, followed by a significant but quite partial recovery. The present economic scene in New York may be viewed in some respect as the most favorable in well over a decade.

The city weathered the 1980 national recession well after suffering disproportionately severe job losses in the prior two economic downturns. The downtrend which prevailed during most of the last decade was reversed in the period 1977–1980. Private-sector employment growth exceeded 100,000. This 3.8% rise from 1977 about matched the rate of increase for the last half of the 1960s when private employment rose at a pace unequaled since the beginning of our records in 1950. The city's competitive position relative to other areas has improved, as reflected in a lower-than-national inflation rate and indications that recent earnings increases in New York have been below those in the rest of the country. Yet even a cursory review of some topside indicators points up major underlying weaknesses in the New York City labor market.

The city continues to suffer long-term problems of inadequate economic development, problems deeply rooted in the experience of the past two decades. The proportion of the city's population with jobs remains substantially below the national average. It would take over one third of a million jobs to raise it to the national ratio. The jobless rate for 1980 was one fifth above the national. So the pattern of higher local unemployment evident for most of the 1970s continues unbroken.

The city's job recovery of 1977–80 was accompanied by further losses in manufacturing and no gains in the trade-and-transportation and public utilities sectors. The increases were strong in the service industries, for the most part reflecting gains in business and professional services. There were also advances in the finance, insurance, and real estate and construction sectors. Reflecting a pickup in the rate of long-term factory job decline in this three-year period, by 1980 the city had less than half the more than one million manufacturing jobs it had in 1950. The 40,000 factory-job loss of the 1977–80 period was of particular concern since this sector has traditionally been an important source of jobs for the city's sizeable resident blue-collar work force.

In addition, recent figures suggest that there has been no reversal of the long-term outflow of corporate headquarters offices which are of significance in generating economic activity in the city's service-based economy. Employment in administrative offices of manufacturing firms, the only sector for which data are available, dropped for the eleventh consecutive year in 1980.

Virtually all of the private-sector job gain since 1977 has been in Manhattan, which accounts for about two-thirds of the city's employment. The outer boroughs continue to experience difficulty in attracting new jobs. The centralization of employment and the geographic concentration of job increases in the recent recovery underscore the importance of a well-functioning public transit system to bring people to their jobs.

Recent CPI figures for this area suggest that the city may be losing some of the competitive advantage that emerged during the last half of the 1970s. Although the 1980 inflation rate for the greater New York–Northeastern New Jersey area remained lower than the national rate for the fourth consecutive year, the gap was the smallest since 1976. During the first quarter of 1981, it was smaller yet.

Impact of recession

National economic developments are among the forces that shape New York City's economic posture. Perhaps one of the best-advertised recessions in history came in early 1980, marking the seventh national economic downturn in the post-World War II period. At the end of 1980, the national jobless rate was 7.4%, seasonally adjusted, remaining in a narrow band of 7.4%–7.6% prevailing since May. The national jobless rate for December was about one fifth higher than the 6.2% rate at the beginning of the year, representing nearly 1.3 million more unemployed.

The city's employment performance over the last decade was characterized by a changing sensitivity to shifts in the national business cycle. Prior to the 1969–70 recession, New York was able to ride out national economic downturns better than other parts of the country, reflecting a much smaller local concentration of cyclically sensitive goods-producing industries. This strength was notably absent in the 1970s. Of greater importance, there was no participation in the national job recoveries of 1971–73 and after 1975.

ANNUAL CHANGES IN PAYROLL EMPLOYMENT, NEW YORK CITY, 1968-80

1

(NUMBERS IN THOUSANDS)

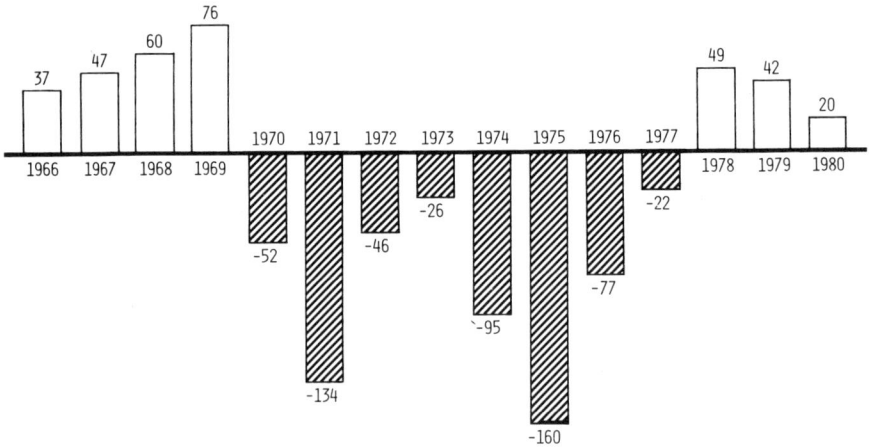

The 1969–70 national recession plunged the city into an economic crisis that saw eight consecutive years of job loss totaling more than 6000,000 (Chart 1). An outgrowth of this debacle was the financial crisis of the mid-1970s and some fundamental changes in the city's economy. The job recovery from 1977 to 1980, significant as it is, represents only a fraction of the jobs lost earlier in the 1970s.

In the 1969–70 recession, the job loss in the city totaled more than 100,000, and in the 1973–75 downturn, over 200,000. The rate of decline for the city in each of these two recessions was about triple the national rate. Between 1970 and 1973, a period of national recovery which saw 7.6 million jobs added to the nation's nonfarm payrolls, the city lost another 176,000 jobs.

The 1969–77 job loss for the city was pervasive. Six of seven major industry sectors experienced substantial employment cutbacks. Nearly half of the decline reflected a loss of 287,000 manufacturing jobs. There were also sizeable declines of 129,000 in trade employment; 66,000 in transportation and public utilities; 50,000 in finance, insurance, and real estate; and 42,000 in contract construction. Only the service industries remained little changed during this period.

By 1977, the city had lost nearly 40 out of every 100 contract construction jobs it had in 1969 and 35 of every 100 factory jobs. About 20 of every 100 jobs in trade and transportation and public utilities jobs were lost and 10 of every 100 in finance, insurance, and real estate.

On the unemployment side, the city's jobless rate peaked at 11.2% in 1976, about 3.5 times the 3.1% rate in 1968. The number of unemployed more than tripled, from 104,000 to 344,000. In 1968, the city's jobless rate was below the national average of 3.6%, but by 1976 it was nearly 1.5 times the national figure of 7.7%. Among ten major cities across the country for which data are available, New

York City's jobless rate was second lowest in 1968, with only Dallas registering a lower rate. By 1976, the city's rate was fourth highest.

It was widely expected by private economic forecasters that in the event of a national recession in late 1979 or early 1980, New York City would be much more seriously affected than the rest of the country. In contrast with these somber predictions, from the start of the recession in January 1980 through the end of the year, the city did not experience the employment dislocations which occurred in other parts of the country. From January through July, the nation suffered a 1.2-million reduction in the number of nonfarm payroll jobs, then recovered the loss by December. In New York City, disregarding the April transit strike which caused a temporary drop in payroll jobs, employment was hardly affected, holding steady at about the 3.3-million mark.

Looking at the year as a whole, the payroll job total in New York City rose by 20,000 in 1980, the third consecutive year of increase. Strong gains in the services and finance, insurance, and real estate sectors were partially offset by a significant loss of 20,000 jobs in manufacturing and a 6,000 decline in trade. The overall 1979–80 job rise was less than half the increases of over 40,000 in each of the two prior years. But an advance during a recession year was notable, particularly in light of the experiences of the past decade.

While the national jobless rate rose sharply over 1980, there was little change in New York City. The city's jobless rate averaged 8.6% for all of 1980, about unchanged from 8.7% in 1979. Nationally, the jobless rate went from 5.8% in 1979 to 7.1% in 1980. With the sharp national rise and no increase in the city, the local–national jobless rate gap for 1980 was the smallest since 1971.

Relative prices and pay

The strong performance in the 1980 national recession and the upward momentum of job growth from 1977 to 1980 may be related to improvements in the competitive position of New York City as compared to other parts of the country (Chart 2). Despite a second consecutive year of double-digit consumer price rise in 1980, the 11.3% advance in New York–Northeastern New Jersey was below the national increase of 13.5%. This marked the fourth consecutive year that the inflation rate for the area was below the national, a dramatic turnaround from the early part of the 1970s when local increases exceeded the national by as much as a third.

Among 23 major areas across the country, the New York–Northeastern New Jersey 11.3% consumer price rise for 1980 was the lowest, along with the Minneapolis–St.Paul area. The steepest 1979–80 rises were recorded in the Dallas–Fort Worth area, 16.9%, and the Seattle–Everett area, 16.6%, each about 1.5 times this area's increase.

A further indication of improved competitive advantage is reflected in changes in relative wage position. The historical competitive disadvantage of high wages in this region compared to other parts of the country appears to be abating, as earnings increases here have been lower in recent years than those in other major labor markets. A number of earnings measures indicate a downtrend in pay relative to other areas. This development can be seen in data for both private- and public-

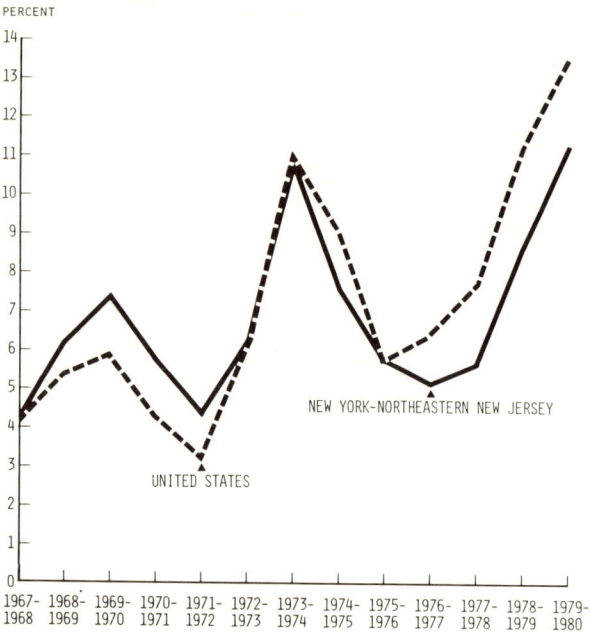

CHANGES IN THE CONSUMER PRICE INDEX, NEW YORK-NORTHEASTERN NEW JERSEY AND UNITED STATES, 1967-80

sector jobs, and for white-collar professional and clerical as well as blue-collar workers.

During the latter part of the 1970s, pay data for the private sector show a turnaround in the rate of increase in New York City as compared with all metropolitan areas across the country (Chart 3). Average earnings of office clerical workers employed in New York City rose at a 5.8%-a year rate between 1975 and 1979, about one-fifth lower than the 7.2% average for all areas. In the prior seven years for which data are available, 1967–74, the yearly increase in New York City was higher—6.3% compared to 5.8% nationally.

For nonproduction blue-collar workers, a similar shift is evident. The 1975–9 annual rates of increase in pay for skilled maintenance and unskilled plant workers in New York City were 7.1% and 7.9%, each below corresponding national rates of 8.6% and 8.4%. In the 1967–74 period, local increases for both groups exceeded the national.

For Dallas–Fort Worth, one of the nation's fastest-growing major areas, the differential since 1975 was quite pronounced. Office clerical pay in the Dallas area rose by 34.3% between 1975 and 1979, a third more than the New York rise. Increases in Dallas were also markedly sharper than in New York City for electronic data-processing jobs, skilled maintenance trades, and unskilled plant workers.

As a result of generally lower earnings increases, a significant shift in New York City's relative pay position took place. In office clerical jobs, New York City pay

ANNUAL RATE OF PERCENT CHANGE IN AVERAGE EARNINGS OF PRIVATE SECTOR WORKERS, UNITED STATES ALL METROPOLITAN AREA AVERAGE AND NEW YORK CITY, 1967-79

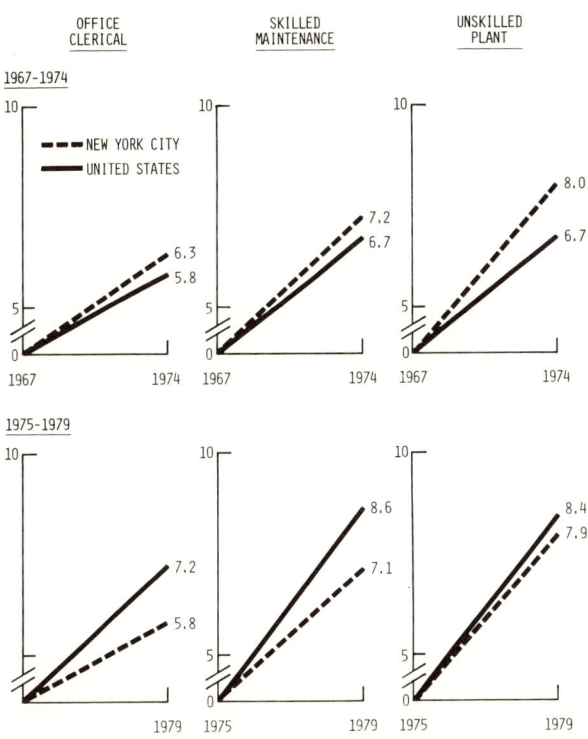

levels moved down from third highest among 30 major areas in 1964 — 75 to 13th place in 1978. For skilled maintenance trades, New York City's position went from 18th to 27th place.

For professional occupations, indications are that earnings increases in New York have likewise been lower than in the rest of the country. Among five professional and administrative occupations for which data are available, including accountants, auditors, attorneys, job analysts, and engineers, earnings of workers employed in New York City rose an average 20% between 1976 and 1979, one-fifth below the corresponding national increase of 25%. In contrast, from 1970 to 1976, the average increase in New York City was 46% compared with 44% nationally.

Union wage scales of construction workers, historically higher in New York City than in other cities, have also increased more slowly. In 1970, local pay averages for journeyman building-trades workers were 12% above the national average. By 1980, the gap narrowed to 2%.

The pattern of earning increases for factory production workers in New York City as compared to other major manufacturing centers differed in the 1970s from

PERCENT CHANGE IN AVERAGE HOURLY EARNINGS OF FACTORY PRODUCTION WORKERS, FIFTEEN AREA AVERAGE AND NEW YORK CITY, 1960-79   4

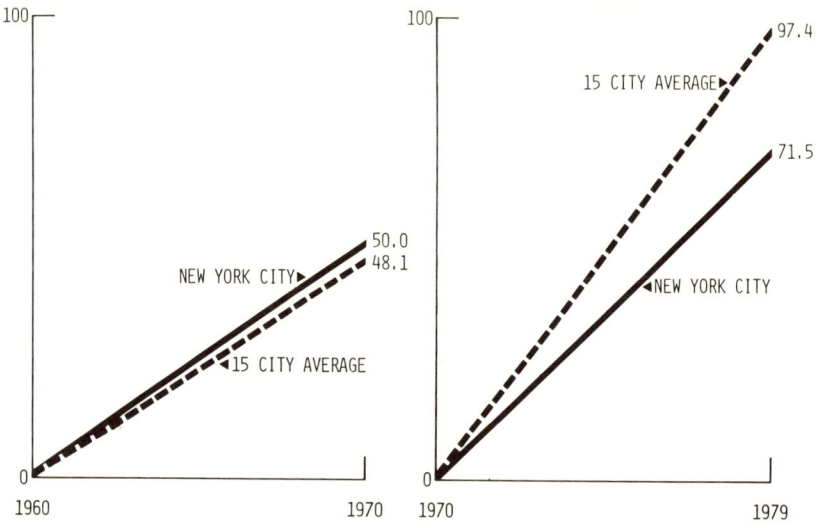

Note: Fifteen area average includes Anaheim-Santa Ana-Garden Grove, Boston, Chicago, Cleveland, Dallas-Ft. Worth, Detroit, Houston, Los Angeles-Long Beach, Milwaukee, Minneapolis-St. Paul, Philadelphia, Pittsburgh, St. Louis, San Francisco-Oakland and San Jose.

the prior decade (Chart 4). Among fifteen areas across the country with 200,000 or more manufacturing workers in 1979, the increase in average hourly earnings in New York City for 1970–79, was next to the lowest. From 1960 to 1970, the New York City rise ranked sixth highest among fifteen areas for which data are available. New York City's increase was slightly above the 15-area average between 1960 and 1970, but substantially lower in the decade of the 1970s.

For New York City municipal government workers, indications are that although average pay levels remain higher than in a number of other cities, there has been some narrowing of the gap. Between the mid and late 1970s, public-safety pay averages rose more slowly in New York than in 20 of the 21 other major cities for which we have data. For sanitation workers, pay rose more slowly in New York City than in 16 of the 18 other cities for which data are available, and for janitorial workers more slowly than 14 of 20.

The pattern of smaller wage increases in New York City relative to other parts of the country in recent years is part of a broader regional pattern of reduction in the higher wage position traditionally held by workers in the older major industrial areas of the Northeast. Employment growth in the Northeast has lagged behind each of the other regions, with the largest increases in the West and the South. Reflecting the tighter labor markets of these regions, increases in average earnings of private-sector white- and blue-collar workers exceeded those in the Northeast during the last half of the 1970s.

By mid-1979, among 63 white-and blue-collar occupational work levels, the Notheast exceeded the pay averages in the other three regions for only one, executive secretaries. Northeast earnings levels in mid-1979 were below the national averages for most of the jobs. Among other regions, the highest pay was found in the North Central region and the West, which exceeded averages in the Northeast for 95% of the work levels studied. For 13 of the 63 work-level categories, Northeast pay fell below the South, an historically low-wage region relative to other parts of the country.

Sources of job recovery

A further look at employment developments from 1977 to 1980 points up the important role played by business in the city's economy, a notably different environment from the 1960s. The growth in the city's job base since 1977 has been almost entirely concentrated in the private sector. Of the 111,000 increase in payroll employment between 1977 and 1980, 102,000, or 92%, was in the private sector. The increase in private-sector employment for these three years followed eight years of loss totaling 571,000 and exceeded the 89,000 net increase for the prior two decades for which data are available. The 34,000-a-year average advance for 1977–80 equaled that of 1965–69 which saw an unprecedented increase of 135,000 private-sector jobs during the four-year recession-free period.

The bulk of the 111,000 employment rise between 1977 and 1980 was due to an increase of about 100,000 jobs in services, with particularly strong gains in business services, including advertising, management consulting, personnel supply services, and computer and data-processing, for example (Charts 5 and 6). There were significant increases in such professional activities as legal, accounting, engineering, and architectural services. There were also sizeable advances in finance, insurance, and real estate and in contract construction. These were partially offset by sharp declines, totaling 40,000 in manufacturing. About half of the three-year manufacturing job loss occurred in 1980.

A waning edge

As a result of the job growth of the late 1970s and the strong performance in the 1980 recession, some have begun to speak of New York City as thriving, prosperous, recession-proof. Yet, serious long-term economic development problems remain much in evidence. Further, recent figures suggest that some of the improvements in the competitive price postion of the area may be eroding.

The 1977–79 national CPI increase was about one-third higher than the area's. Between 1979 and 1980 the gap narrowed to about one-fifth. By March 1981, the national over-the-year increase of 10.6% was less than one-tenth higher than the 9.8% New York–Northeastern New Jersey rise.

Among eighteen major areas across the country for which March 1981 CPI data are available, the 9.8% over-the-year increase for New York–Northeastern New Jersey ranked eleventh highest, along with the Washington, D.C. area, exceeding

CHANGES IN NONFARM PAYROLL EMPLOYMENT, NEW YORK CITY, 1977-80   5

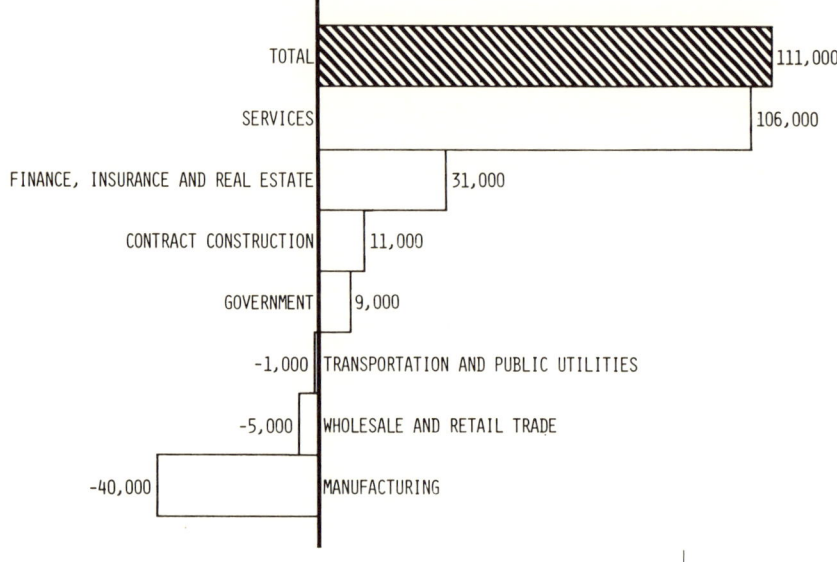

DISTRIBUTION OF EMPLOYMENT CHANGE IN SERVICE SECTORS, NEW YORK CITY, 1977-80   6

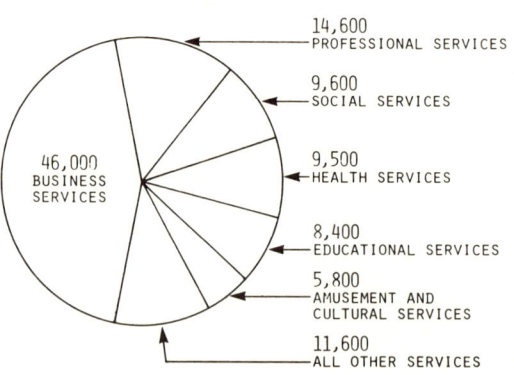

increases in the Miami, Los Angeles – Long Beach, St. Louis, Anchorage, Cincinnati, and Portland, Oregon areas. A year earlier, the increase for the New York – Northeastern New Jersey area was the smallest among the eighteen areas, with the sole exception of Anchorage, Alaska.

Unemployment continues higher

Although 1980 labor-force developments appear favorable, particularly in light of the deterioration nationally during the 1980 recession, the city has continued to run a higher-than-national unemployment rate since 1971, and the proportion of the population employed remains sharply below the national average (Charts 7 and 8). The 8.6% 1980 jobless rate for New York City was one-fifth higher than the national average, and the proportion of the working age population with jobs, at 50.8%, was nearly ten perentage points below the national figure of 59.3%.

Jobless rates in New York City, except for blacks, are significantly above the national average for all major population groups. The proportion of the working-age population with jobs is lower for each major group: whites and blacks, adults and youth, and men and women. To match the national employment-population ratio, taking into account variations in the age structure of the population, New York City would need one-third of a million more jobs.

The youth-employment situation remains a problem of substantial magnitude. The 1980 unemployment rate for 16– 19-year-olds in New York City was 28.3%, more than 1.5 times the national average of 17.7%. The proportion of the teenage population employed in New York City, at 22.0%, is less than half the national figure of 46.8%.

Manufacturing decline accelerates

A major sector of weakness in the city's employment picture is manufacturing. With some 300,000 production jobs, the city's factories have traditionally been an important source of entry-level blue-collar jobs and generate substantial economic activity in a number of other sectors.New York City has lost more than half of the 1,073,000 manufacturing jobs that existed in 1947.

In 1980 alone, manufacturing employment in the city dropped by 20,000 to 499,000, representing an acceleration in the attrition of recent years (Chart 9). In 1979, the decline was 14,000 and in 1978, 7,000. In the first half of the 1970s, the losses had averaged 48,000 a year.. These losses were in contrast with a better-than-100,000 increase in services as well as advances in finance, insurance, and real estate and in contract construction that provided the basis for the city's 1977– 80 job recovery. The city's nonfactory job total was up by more than 150,000 since 1977, rising 40,000 in 1980 alone.

The decline between 1977 and 1980 was widespread. Among 20 major manufacturing industry sectors, 18 experienced job cutbacks. The apparel industries now employ 140,000 in New York City, down 13,000 since 1977, yet apparel manufacturing continues to be one of New York City's largest employers. The job total in printing and publishing was up by 4,000 between 1977 and 1980, with

ANNUAL AVERAGE UNEMPLOYMENT RATES, 1968-80

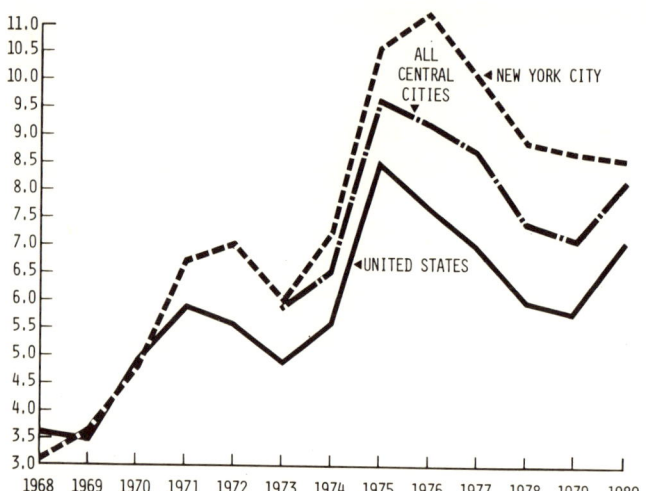

XI = export income component of an industry (i) in the year it (t) for a region

ANNUAL AVERAGE EMPLOYMENT-POPULATION RATIOS, 1968-80

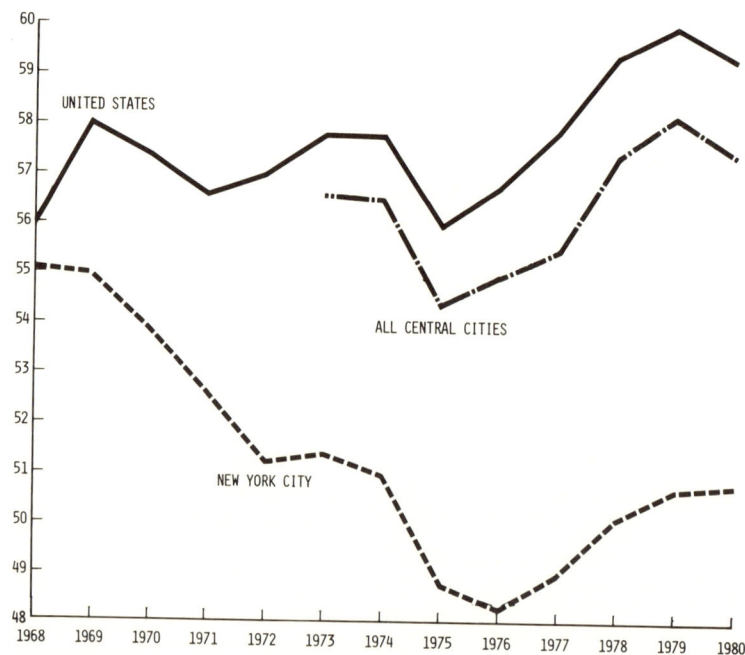

ANNUAL CHANGES IN MANUFACTURING EMPLOYMENT, NEW YORK CITY, 1968-80
(NUMBERS IN THOUSANDS)

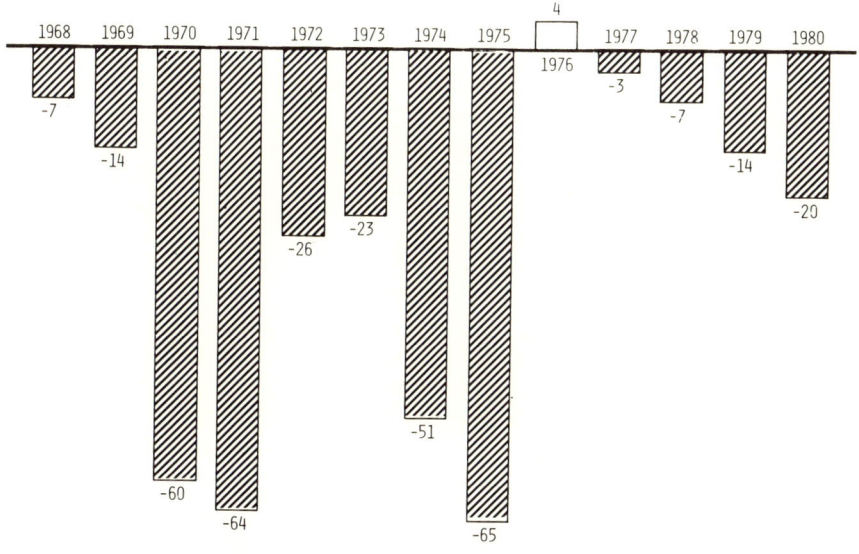

about half of the increase in the periodicals sector.

The decade of the 1970s saw a loss of 267,000 manufacturing jobs. This decline followed a 181,000 drop between 1960 and 1970 and a 1950– 60 loss of 92,000. In percentage terms, the 35% rate of decline for the 1970s was nearly double the 19% rate for the prior decade and about quadruple the 1950– 60 rate of 9%.

The total loss of 540,000 jobs in the last thirty years has reduced the city's manufacturing jobs by half. Nearly two-fifths of the decline reflected a 200,000 loss in the apparel sector. With 140,000 jobs in 1980, the city's apparel industry had lost six of every ten jobs it had had in 1950. Other sectors with substantial declines included food and kindred products, down 70,000 since 1950, and miscellaneous manufacturing, down 41,000.

The 267,000 drop in factory employment from 1970 to 1980 accounted for nearly three-fifths of the city's 447,000 net job loss for the decade. Between 1970 and 1977, the city's overall job total was down 558,000, with a 227,000 manufacturing job loss. Since 1977, while the city's overall job total has risen by 111,000, the continued downtrend in manufacturing brought the total 1970– 80 loss in this sector to 35 jobs for every 100 in 1970.

The long-term declines caused manufacturing employment in the city to drop from about 30% of the city's payroll job total in 1950 to 15% in 1980. Despite this, New York remains one of the country's major centers of manufacturing. Although the city has never been a predominantly factory town, in 1979, the latest year for which comparable data are available, New York City's manufacturing job total ranked forth highest among the nation's metropolitan areas after the Los Angeles–Long Beach, Chicago, and Detroit metropolitan areas.

Recovery limited to Manhattan

That there was virtually no net job recovery in the four outer boroughs between March 1977 and March 1980 suggests the necessity for a more comprehensive citywide look at job development needs.

Based on data for workers covered by New York State unemployment insurance, private-sector employment rose 6.5% in Manhattan and less that 1% in the rest of the city since 1977. The four outer boroughs, with 938,000 private-sector jobs in 1980, showed a gain of less than 6,000 jobs since 1977. The number of jobs was up 8,000 in Queens for a gain of 2.2%. An increase of 5,000 jobs raised the total in Staten Island by 13% to 43,000. Private-sector jobs declined by nearly 4,000 in the Bronx and by over 3,000 in Brooklyn.

The Manhattan-based New York City recovery partially reflects the borough's industrial composition. Manhattan has a higher proportion of the city's jobs in services and finance, insurance, and real estate, the principal sources of recent job growth in the city. Manhattan accounts for nearly 70% of the city's service jobs and 87% of its finance, insurance, and real estate employment. Together, employment in these two sectors rose by 135,000 citywide between March 1977 and March 1980, with 110,000 of the rise in Manhattan. However, Manhattan has a lower proportion of the city's manufacturing industries which have continued to decline in all five boroughs.

The number of jobs in services was up in each borough, although the increase of 28,000, or 12%, for the outer boroughs lagged behind a 79,000 or 15%, increase for Manhattan. In finance, insurance, and real estate, employment rose by 31,000 in Manhattan, but was down 3,000 in the other four boroughs between March 1977 and March 1980. Similarly, small advances in Manhattan in the trade-and-transportation and public utilities sectors contrasted with downward movement in the outer boroughs.

Employment in the city's manufacturing industries, a citywide sector of long-term weakness, is less concentrated in Manhattan, and from 1977 to 1980 its rate of loss was below that of the rest of the city. Manufacturing employment declined citywide between March 1977 and March 1980, decreasing by 4.7% in Manhattan and 7.2% in the four other boroughs combined.

Workers and jobs– the transit connection

While Manhattan accounts for nearly two-thirds of the city's private-sector jobs, it accounts for only 20% of the overall resident work force. Thus, substantial numbers of workers must commute to their jobs, not only from other boroughs, but from other parts of the region. Public transportation is more significant in New York City's job picture than in any other major area in the country.

More than two-fifths of all workers residing in New York City and in Nassau, Suffolk, Westchester, and Rockland counties use public transportation to get to their jobs, based on Census surveys conducted in the mid-1970s. Partially reflecting the concentration of the region's employment in Manhattan, this proportion is by far the largest among 26 large areas for which data are available. The second largest proportion, 18%, was in the Chicago area, followed by 16% in the Boston and San Francisco – Oakland areas, 15% in Philadelphia, and 14% in Washington, D. C. For 15 of the 26 areas the proportion was less than 10% and in seven areas (including Detroit, Houston, St. Louis, and Dallas), it was under 5%.

Front office exodus

The continued job downtrend in administrative offices of manufacturing firms located in New York City is troubling. The deterioration in this key sector may be suggestive of how corporate offices in the broader sense view New York City as a front-office location in terms of competitive advantage.

New York City employment in administrative offices of manufacturing companies declined by 3,500 in 1980, the sharpest drop in five years, and followed an almost equally sharp 3,200 loss in the prior year. These losses are especially disturbing against the backdrop of job recovery. While the number of jobs in the New York City economy was up by over 100,000 since December 1976, employment in manufacturing administrative offices dropped by 8,300, or 14%, to 50,900. During the preceding seven years, the exodus of manufacturing front-office jobs totaled 27,000. The 31% loss in this sector was nearly double the 16% decline in the city's overall job total. By the end of 1980, employment in the headquarters sector of the New York City economy was down 41% from its 1969 peak of 86,000.

The continued weakness in the city's ability to hold and attract headquarters office jobs is of concern for its economic development and its national economic image. These headquarters jobs are significant for the city's economic vitality. Administrative offices generate economic activity in a number of the city's important employment sectors including finance, communications, transportation, advertising, and other business-services industries.

In contrast, employment in administrative offices of manufacturing companies in the five neighboring suburban counties (Nassau, Suffolk, Westchester, Rockland, and Putnam) inched up by 200 after rising by 1,800 in the prior year. At 26,500 in 1980, employment was at a record high. From 1976 to 1980, 4,400 suburban front-office jobs were added. The number of such jobs tripled since 1962, the first year for which data are available. Yet, New York City employment was down by one-third, with significant shifts to locations outside the region.

New York, the nation's prime front-office city, has traditionally enjoyed a competitive advantage as a location for home offices. Although advantages of being situated in the hub continue, corporate headquarters in the age of the computer and jet plane are now substantially more free to choose their location. This is an especially important consideration in light of the city's three-year job recovery, which is centered in the business and professional service and finance sectors. These industries, to a significant extent, serve broad national and international markets and have flexibility in locational preference.

The issue of competitive advantage and how firms view the New York City business environment and the general quality of life is closely related to the key issue of job development. New employment opportunities depend on encouraging a hospitable climate for economic expansion for the spectrum of industries that have an affinity for the metropolis, the world city, that is New York. The city's attractiveness as a place to do business depends strongly on how firms and people view it as a place to work and live. Consequently the health of the city's art galleries, museums, and theaters, the security of the streets, the quality of schools, and a variety of other quality of life factors are important elements determining the city's economic strength.

Ongoing transformation

The direction of future change in the New York City economy is in some respects clear. A starting point is a recognition of its structure and changes that have taken place in its industrial center of gravity in the past decade.

New York City's economy has been and continues to be in transition — from goods to services, from blue collar to white collar, from skill to knowledge orientation. A review of the record of the past thirty years points up significant elements of both continuity and change. Although New York City has traditionally had a more service-oriented economy than other parts of the country, the tide has been running more strongly in recent years. This reflects principally the accelerated pace of job loss in the factory sector in the 1970s and centralization of the employment recovery from 1977 to 1980 in the service-producing sector. In 1980, 82.6% of the city's jobs were in service-producing industries compared with 71.5% nationally. Three decades ago, 66.4% of its jobs were in the service-producing sector compared with 59.1% nationally.

A look at some specifics brings the transformation into sharper focus. Chart 10 looks at New York City's largest employers in 1960, 1970, and 1980. The ten industries shown (two-digit industries in the standard classification scheme) had the largest job totals for these three periods, accounting for about half of the jobs in the city, some 1.7 million in 1980. Their relative importance increased from 47% in 1960 to 52% in 1980.

Interestingly, eight of the ten largest employing industries in all three periods were in the service sector. Only two — apparel and printing and publishing — were in manufacturing and in the picture consistently, ranking third and fifth among the top ten in 1960 but slipping to sixth and eighth in 1980. Taken together, in 1960 they had nearly 400,000 jobs, about one-quarter of the combined total for the top ten. Now these two industries have less than 250,000 jobs, representing only 14% of the total employment of the top ten.

The eight service-producing industries on the list show some significant growth overall, from just over 1.25 million in 1967 to nearly 1.5 million in 1980. Despite substantial continuity, the listing shows some significant changes as well. Insurance, ninth in 1960, is no longer among the top ten, having been replaced by banking, which has grown to become the fifth largest employer in the city, with over 150,000 jobs in 1980. Local government went from second place in 1960 to

New York City industries with largest job totals, 1960, 1970 and 1980

(numbers in thousands)

Rank	Industry	1960	Industry	1970	Industry	1980
1	Wholesale trade	315	Local government	415	Local government	376
2	Local government	268	Wholesale trade	302	Wholesale trade	246
3	Apparel manufacturing	268	Apparel manufacturing	204	Business services	241
4	Business services	135	Business services	198	Health services	194
5	Printing and publishing	127	Health services	150	Banking	152
6	Eating and drinking places	125	Banking	132	Apparel manufacturing	140
7	Federal government	116	Printing and publishing	121	Eating and drinking places	113
8	Real estate	104	Eating and drinking places	118	Printing and publishing	94
9	Insurance	102	Federal government	108	Federal government	88
10	Health services	97	Insurance	96	Real estate	83

first place in 1970 and 1980, yet, its 376,000 employees numbered some 40,000 less than a decade earlier. Health services just made the top ten in 1960 with 97,000 jobs and now ranked fourth, in 1980, having doubled its employment to 194,000. Business services moved up from fourth place (135,000 employees in 1960) to third (240,000) in 1980. An important growth industry in recent years, it was already a major source of jobs two decades ago.

Several industries have slipped in relative importance. Wholesale trade, once number one, with 315,000 jobs, now ranks second, having lost some 70,000 jobs. Restaurants — eating and drinking places — were sixth in 1960, and seventh today with 113,000 employees. The federal government, seventh in 1960 with 116,000 employees, moved down to ninth place in 1970, with 108,000. Having cut back another 20,000 jobs in the 1970s, it is in ninth place with 88,000 employees. Real estate activities declined from eighth place in 1960 to tenth in 1980, with 83,000 jobs.

New York City may be expected to move further in the direction of a service-oriented economy in the years ahead, but its success will depend in a major way on its ability to retain and capitalize on its demonstrated competitive advantages, to improve the quality of life for those who work and live in the city, and to hold on to its status as a national and international economic center. The recent record shows some substantial weaknesses and some real strengths. The city has come a long was from the mid-1970s, when the apocalyptic notion gained some currency that New York City was beyond hope. But it is also far from the state of flourishing prosperity and well-being suggested by some recent comments. The economy has a long way to go. It will need the perseverance and stamina of a marathon runner — it's not in a sprinter's race.

2

THE APPLE'S CORE: NEW YORK CITY'S EXPORT INDUSTRIES

Matthew P. Drennan

Conceptually, the necessary condition for the emergence of an urban agglomeration that is not self sufficient is production of a surplus available for export. Specialization in economic activities for which a comparative advantage exists vis-à-vis the rest of the world is the source of that surplus. The existence and growth of an urban agglomeration lead to the development of economic activities that are supportive in character. If the supportive activities were swept away by some act of God, they could spring up again. If the comparative advantage disappeared, there is no assurance that a new one would develop. If none did, the urban area would eventually wither away.

That, in distilled form, is the export-base theory. Econonists find the logic of the theory most compelling. The economic activities that are the source of the export surplus are referred to as basic or export activities. The supportive activities are referred to as local. In economic base models, the only variables within the system or region that are exogenous (independent) are the measures of activity in the export sector such as output, employment, and income. The export sector is assumed to respond to forces outside the region, chiefly changes in demand for export-sector products in the rest of the world. As in national macro models, where net investment and government expenditures are exogenous variables, the exogenous sector, exports, determines the level of income, output, and employment in the entire region through a multiplier effect. The size of the multiplier is chiefly determined by the propensity to consume and the propensity to import goods and services from the rest of the world.

Identifying city export industries and measuring their output

In empirical studies that flow from the export-base theory of urban economic development and growth, two major problems are confronted. The first is the identification of the export sector and its magnitude. The second is the choice of a measure of output in both the export and local sectors.

Considering the first problem, the best way to identify the export sector is by a large-scale survey of firms in the area to determine where their output is shipped (i.e., how much is sold within the region and how much outside). Aside from the difficulties of cost, time, response rates, and reliability of such information, the critical flaw is that it is valid only for the survey year. A regional econometric model requires time-series data on the export and local sectors. The only method available for developing such time series is the use of location quotients. Location quotients for a region can be calculated for each industry (i) and for each year (t) as follows:

$$LQ_{it} = \frac{RO_{it} / \Sigma RO_{it}}{NO_{it} / \Sigma NO_{it}}$$

where

LQ_{it} = location quotient for region's industry i in year t

RO_{it} = region's output in industry i in year t

ΣRO_{it} = region's output in all industries in year t

NO_{it} = national ouput in industry i in year t

ΣNO_{it} = national output in all industries in year t

The location quotient compares a specific industry's relative share of total regional output to that same industry's relative share of total national output. If a region's industry, such as retail trade, was 7% of total regional output and at the national level retail trade was also 7% of national output, then the location quotient for retail trade in the region would be 1.0 (i.e., 7%/7%). If the steel industry in the Pittsburgh area was 10% of regional output and nationwide the steel industry was 2% of the U.S. total output, then the location quotient for steel in the Pittsburgh area would be 5.0 (i.e., 10%/2%).

Any regional industry for which the locatio quotient exceeds 1.0 is assumed to be an export industry, that is, producing more than what would be required locally, assuming local requirements are relatively (in percentage terms) the same as national requirements. Any regional industry for which the location quotient is equal to or less than 1.0 is assumed to be a local industry, producing the same as or less then what is required locally.

The next step is to split the output of each export industry (i.e., an industry with a location quotient greater than one) into that part which is assumed to be for export and that part which is assumed to be for local requirements. The export component is calculated as follows:

$$X_{it} = RO_{it} - \xi RO_{it} \left(\frac{NO_{it}}{\xi NO_{,it}} \right)$$

X_{it} = export component of region's industry i output in year t.

$$VAPE_{it} = \frac{NI_{it}/IPD_t}{NE_{it}}$$

Because the export component and the local component together make up the total output, as stated above, then the local component (L) can be calculated as:

$$L_{it} = RO_{it} - X_{it}$$

The total export output of the region is, then, ΣX_{it}

Thus location quotients provide a means, albeit crude, for identifying the export sector (i.e., estimating which industries are export oriented) and estimating its magnitude.

The second problem, noted above, is the choice of an appropriate measure of output. Physical output is not good because there are usually no such measures available for trade and services. Dollar measures of output for a region, such as value added, are available annually only for manufacturing industries and then only for the larger metropolitan areas. Consequently, the measure usually settled for is employment, because employment data by industry are widely available for metropolitan areas. The major shortcoming of using employment data is that, across industries, there is an implicit assumption that all jobs are equal (i.e., each makes the same contribution to output), which is far from true. Over time, the shortcomings of using employment data are that they fail to take into account growth in productivity. An industry with no change in total employment over ten years can have a marked increase in output due to growth in productivity.

To avoid those shortcomings of using regional employment data as a proxy for output, an income measure for each regional industry has been computed in the Drennan–CHR model. The method was first devised by Richard Knight.[1] In the U.S. National Income Accounts, detailed industry data on national income originating (value added less depreciation) and corresponding industry employment data are published annually. From those data, value added per employee (hereafter VAPE) in each industry for each year can be calculated. Then making the assumption that national VAPE in a given industry and year is the same as the unobserved *regional* VAPE in that industry and year, it is possible to compute regional income for that industry and year by multiplying VAPE by regional employment in that industry. The calculation is set forth as follows:

$$RI_{it} = RE_{it} (VAPE_{it})$$

where

$VAPE_{it}$ = value added per employee, in constant dollars, for the United States in industry i and year t

NI_{it} = U.S. national income in industry i and year t

IPD_{it} = implicit price deflator for U. S. GNP, 1972 = 100

NE_{it} = U.S. employment in industry i and year t

RI_{it} = estimated regional income, in constant dollars, in industry i and year t

RE_{it} = regional employment in industry i and year t

The estimated regional income (RI) is a measure of productive activity or value added in the industry within the region. The sum of RI over all industries is comparable to national income (i.e., net national product valued at factor prices), not personal income. To the extent that the region's true but unobserved value added per employee (VAPE) in any industry differs from the national VAPE in that industry, then the estimates of industry regional income are off. Such differences between the true and the estimated VAPE must certainly exist because of (a) differences in the industry mix within any two-digit industry, and (b) differences in hours worked. Given the present state of regional published data, there is no avoiding that problem.

Nonetheless, the important point is that interindustry differences in VAPE are doubtless far greater than interregional differences in VAPE within the same industry. Thus the value of this method is that it explicitly recognizes differences in VAPE across industries. That is, it does not assume all jobs are equal. Some jobs generate more value added than others. The method also explicitly takes into account the fact of increasing productivity over time.

The method described above has been used to estimate annual time-series data on regional income (in constant dollars) for each industry. The extent of industry detail was limited by the regional employment data.

Using the estimated city income by industry and national income by industry-time-series data described above, location quotients were calculated. That was done for each industry and each year for New York City. The purpose is to identify the export industries and to compute the magnituude of total export income over time. The calculation is represented as follows:

$$LQ_{it} = \frac{RI_{it} / \Sigma RI_{it}}{NI_{it} / \Sigma NI_{it}}$$

As noted above, RI is regional income in a specific industry (i) and a specific year (t). ΣRI is the total regional income (all industries) in that year. NI and ΣNI are the corresponding national income measures. Since all industries' income was deflated by the same price index (the GNP implicit price deflator, 1972=100), there is no need to represent it in the calculation of the location quotient.

Time series estimates of the constant dollar value of exports for each city industry were calculated as follows:

$$XI_{it} = RI_{it} - \Sigma RI_{it} \frac{\left(\frac{NI_{it}}{\Sigma NI_{it}}\right)}{}$$

Any regional industry for which XI is consistently positive and significantly above zero is thus identified as an export industry. All other regional industries are thus identified as local industries (i.e., those industries for which XI is consistently negative or for which XI randomly fluctuates around zero).

Shifts in the composition of the city's export sector

The methodology described above has been used in the Drennan–CHR model to develop time series on income (or value added) in constant dollars in each of 54 industries in New York City, 1958–79. Each industry has been classified as export or local, and the export component has been computed for each export industry over time.

It must be stressed that the chief reason for calculating the export component of a city industry's income is to determine which industries are export-oriented. Because of the naive assumptions underlying the use of location quotients, little attention is devoted in the following analysis to the export components of export industries. Instead, the *total* income of the export industries is used as the base for analysis. But before presenting detailed industry data, it is informative to consider the aggregate export component for all city export industries compared with total city income, shown in Table 1.

The export component of total city income runs under 30%, or, put another way, the average export multiplier is about 3.5. The marginal export multiplier, estimated by regression in the model, is about 2.5. The export component is more volatile than total city income.

Also shown in Table 1 is the total income of all city export industries (column 3), which of course is larger than the export component of all city export industries (column 2). An example can clarify the distinction between the two series.

City Industry	Total income, 1978	Export Component of Income, 1978
Apparel	1,132	762
Wholesale trade	3,560	898

Shown above are total income and the export component of that income (in millions of 1972 dollars) for two city export industries in 1978. Column 3 of Table 1 includes the total income of those two export industries and all the other export

TABLE 1

N.Y.C. INCOME, 1958-79
(in billions of 1972 dollars)

Year	N.Y.C. Income or Value Added		Income of N.Y.C. Export Industries
	Total	Export	
1958	34.3	9.6	19.0
1968	43.1	12.6	24.8
1969	43.2	12.5	25.0
1970	41.9	11.6	23.9
1971	41.4	11.5	23.8
1972	41.7	11.7	24.3
1973	41.9	11.6	24.4
1974	39.0	10.7	22.9
1975	37.2	10.2	21.9
1976	37.9	10.9	22.8
1977	38.5	11.3	23.6
1978	39.3	11.6	24.3
1979	39.0	11.7	24.4
Average Annual Percentage Change			
1958-68	+2.3	+2.8	+2.7
1968-75	-2.1	-3.0	-1.8
1975-79	+1.2	+3.5	+2.7
1958-79	+0.6	+1.0	+1.2

SOURCE: Drennan-CHR Econometric Model of New York.

industries. Column 2 of Table 1 includes the export components only of all city export industries.

The model disaggregates the city's economy into 53 industries (the two-digit Standard Industrial Classification industries, with a few consolidations). Of those 53 industries, 21 have been identified as export industries. Grouping the 21 export industries into broad sectors (manufacturing, services, etc.), Table 2 shows the shifting composition of the city's export base over time. The most striking change is the declining importance of goods production. Manufacturing's share of city export income dropped from 25% in 1958 to 14% in 1979. In contrast, the service sector's share rose from 16% to 25%.

Table 1 reveals that the income of all city export industries (column 3) peaked in 1969, then hit a low in 1975 and has since been recovering. The 1969 high has not yet been exceeded. Table 2 reveals that the composition of the export base has changed. A detailed examination of trends in the 21 export industries is necessary to understand that past and to formulate realistic expectations about the future.

Growth performance of the export industries

A logical scheme for grouping the 21 export industries of New York has been devised which reveals distinctly different patterns of performance. Those different patterns have implications for public policy that should be aimed at stimulating (or not hampering) the strong parts of the export base.

Table 3 presents total income (not the export component) of each of the 21 export industries, grouped into three sets, for 1958, 1968, 1975, and 1979. The six export industries included in the category "Production and Distribution of Goods" have collectively been the most laggard part of the city's export base. In the 1958–68 expansion, that part had the slowest growth (summarized below) of 1.3% per year. In the long contraction, 1968–75, the goods production and distribution set suffered the sharpest decline: −3.4% per year. In the 1975–1979

TABLE 2

COMPOSITION OF N.Y.C. EXPORT BASE, 1958 AND 1979
(in percentage shares of export income)

	1958	1979
Manufacturing	24.9	13.8
Transportation, communications, and public utilities	11.7	14.9
Wholesale trade	12.2	8.7
Finance, insurance, real estate	35.0	37.5
Services	16.2	25.1

SOURCE: Drennan-CHR Econometric Model of New York.

TABLE 3

THE N.Y.C. EXPORT INDUSTRIES
(in millions of 1972 dollars)

N.Y.C. Export Industries, Grouped by Activity	Income of N.Y.C. Export Industries			
	1958	1968	1975	1979
Production & Distribution of Goods				
Apparel	1,581	1,622	1,018	1,101
Printing	1,252	1,538	1,113	1,225
Leather	187	251	108	114
Miscellaneous manufacturing	641	695	461	503
Wholesale trade	3,399	3,980	3,859	3,494
Water transportation	668	706	356	330
Totals	7,728	8,792	6,915	6,767
Consumer Services to the Region				
Health services*	883	1,409	1,878	1,969
Educational services*	193	468	393	615
Totals	1,076	1,877	2,271	2,584
Corporate Services				
Banking	1,215	1,821	1,704	1,605
Security & commodity brokers	783	2,288	1,275	1,406
Insurance carriers	707	925	742	924
Insurance agents & brokers	313	389	372	480
Real estate, investment & holding companies	2,781	1,999	1,747	2,523
Business services	1,239	1,846	1,762	2,177
Legal services	538	825	966	1,047
Miscellaneous services	600	963	850	1,005
Communication	953	1,408	1,501	1,648
Air transportation	286	705	744	987
Transportation services	180	267	254	358
Nonprofit membership organizations	382	509	612	631
Motion pictures	148	227	149	227
Totals	10,185	14,172	12,678	15,018
Totals, all export industries	18,989	24,841	21,864	24,369

*Private sector only.

recovery, the manufacturing industries included showed small gains, more than offset by further shrinking in wholesale trade (which nonetheless continues to be New York's single largest export industry).

	Average Annual Percentage Change		
Production & distribution	*1958–68*	*1968–75*	*1975–79*
of goods	1.3	−3.4	−0.5
Consumer services	5.7	2.8	3.3
Corporate services	3.4	−1.6	4.3
Totals	2.7	−1.8	2.7

Thus by 1979, goods production and distribution accounted for only 27.8% of export industries' income, down from 40.7% in 1958. A resurgence for that part of the export base is simply not in the cards. The costs associated with manufacturing in the city, including congestion costs, argues against any strong expansion. The decline of wholesale trade primarily reflects the simple fact that the greater New York–Northeastern New Jersey area has lost 850,000 people since about 1970. Wholesale trade in New York, as in most cities, is primarily a region-serving industry, not a national industry. Water transportation, which has dropped by half since 1958, is a casualty of technological change. Containerization of ocean freight shifted most port activity to the New Jersey side of the port where the required open space was readily available.

Consumer services to the regions, the health and education export industries, together showed the strongest growth of the three export groups during the 1958–68 expansion. Fueled by federal dollars, the health industry was impervious to the general economic decline in the city, 1968–75, but education services did fall. Both expanded in the 1975–79 recovery. Because health and education services, like wholesale trade, primarily serve the region, their future growth is importantly tied to the size of the region. In addition, health is linked to a noneconomic factor, namely government funding. The demographic outlook does not favor educational services as a growth industry. Thus consumer services to the region cannot be expected to expand in the future as they have in the past. Also, as only 10.6% of all export industries' income in 1979, that part of the export base can have only a marginal impact on the future course of the city's economy.

The best hope for the future economic viability of New York rests with the largest and strongest part of its export base: corporate services. The thirteen industries in that set accounted for 62% of export industries' income in 1979, up from 54% in 1958. In the 1968–75 decline, that group dropped 1.6% per year much less severe than the decline in goods-producing and -distributing export industries, which fell 3.4% per year. In the recovery since 1975, the corporate services group expanded at a faster rate than the consumer services industry.

The corporate service group is not strongly tied to the size of the region because it it serving a national and international market. It is the dominant part of what I have called in an earlier work the corporate headquarters complex in New York. The other parts are the corporate headquarters themselves and the ancillary services to that complex: restaurants, hotels, and entertainment. Corporate services in New York flourish because of a national and world economy increasingly dominated by large private corporations and large public enterprises and increasingly tied together by trade and international investment. New York is the international center of corporate services, and the central issue for the future viability of the New York economy is to maintain that position of dominance.

Local public policy and the future of New York's export industries

It should be clear from the above analysis that industrial parks are not the route for strengthening New York's export base. Given the national and even global character of the demand forces upon corporate services in New York, the beginning of wisdom about local policy is the recoginition that it can be effective only at the margin. There are some things city government and perhaps state government can do which in the long run would contribute to the efficiency and thus competitiveness of corporate services in New York. I offer the following list, which has one unifying theme: reducing the cost, in money and time, of providing corporate services from a New York location.

1. Improve passenger transit to and from the Manhattan central business district in terms of time, dependability, and pleasantness.

2. Improve access to and from the region's major airports.

3. Expand airport capacity.

4. Institute a review of the office-building operation codes of the city aimed at throwing out rules which add to operating costs without providing significant benefits.

5. Purge the construction code of featherbedding rules.

6. Insure that a New York City high school diploma truly certifies employability at entry-level clerical jobs.

7. Reduce the progressivity of the state personal income tax.

Note

1. Richard Knight, *Employment Expansion and Metropolitan Trade* New York: Praeger, 1973).

3

THE ROLE OF NATIONAL CORPORATIONS IN NEW YORK CITY'S ECONOMY

Regina Belz Armstrong

With cutbacks proposed in parts of the federal budget upon which New York City and its social welfare needs are dependent, and with the city's fiscal condition pronounced serious, it is incumbent upon us to consider which aspects of structural change in New York's economic base are more or less cyclically reponsive. Some lessons can be learned from an examination of New York's performance in the 1974-75 recession by type of business organization, and implications can be drawn for policy formation and the future. To do so requires us to look at the role of national corporations vis-à-vis small businesses and the public – nonprofit sector, each of which is a cornerstone of an increasingly pluralistic city economy. This paper takes as its task a brief review, as well as a discussion of what the national headquarters component means from the perspective of New York's control over national resources, and the impact of corporate location or investment decisions on the city's economy and built environment.

Sizing up New York's corporate complex

New York City has long been recognized as the corporate capital or premier city for private enterprise headquarters in the Unitied States. Of late, its world-class function has grown, as officers of foreign parent corporations and direct foreign investment joined international divisions of domestic corporations and export– import merchants in a nexus of foreign trade and finance that has come to represent about one tenth of the gross city product. The magnate or base upon which this increasingly elite and global-market white-collar economy has evolved is New York City's complex of major American corporations. At times perceived to be on the wane — buffeted by periods of intense headquarters relocation, chronicled by the long slide of Fortune's 500 industrials from 136 in the late 1960s to 78 in the late 1970s — the national corporate sector remains a highly visible but eminently unknown factor in the measure of the city's economy.

For this analysis, the three-year period 1972–75 is taken as a reference point. Then, the number of Fortune 500 headquarters in New York showed its steepest decline, 115 to 90, in a twelve-year loss of 58 major industrials. Yet expanding the data base from Fortune's 500 to the 3,500 publicly traded corporations that account for the bulk of gross domestic corporate product in the nation, New York City's complex of national corporate head offices increased in number to 369, or 1 in 10 major headquarters in 1975. Included were Fortune's 90, 55 of the second 500 industrials, 75 smaller manufacturers, and 149 nonmanufacturing corporations. Between 1972 and 1975, headquarters losses among these numbered 47, offset by 11 gains.

Several hundred other major domestic corporations were present in New York City, to some significant degree as production or office activities, although their corresponding headquarters were located elsewhere. New York's suburban environs, stretching 100 miles into New York State, New Jersey, and Connecticut, housed chief executive offices of 307 major corporations, or 1 in 12 national headquarters. Suburban locations accessible to the city's support services and other externalities have proven to be a more competitive draw on resident front offices — attracting 27 of the moveouts — than major business centers outside the region.

New York's *own 500* — the corporate complex represented by headquarters, production, and nonheadquartered office activity of all publicly traded firms in the nation — accounted for 11% of citywide employment in 1975. Corporate facilities in the city averaged about 700 employees per firm. By comparison, 180,000 establishments of small corporations, partnerships, and proprietorships represented small business in New York with less than 13 employees each, while 10,000 nonprofit services of slightly larger scale and more than 500,000 federal, state, and local government workers comprised the voluntary and public sectors. Respectively, 65%, 8%, and 16% of citywide employment were associated with population- and business-related functions, serving essentially local market consumption.

Chart 1 portrays the sharp divergence between establishments and the distribution of employment by type of enterprise in New York City. As a measure of gross city product, the contrast is stretched further. Strong productivity advantages

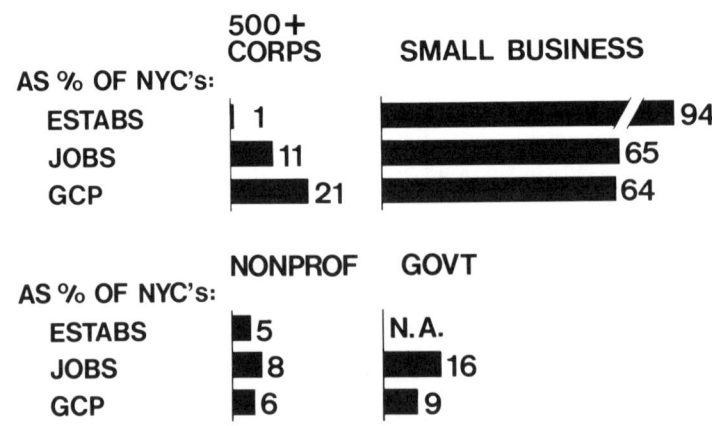

conferred on large corporations by the intensity and profitability of their capital in use, separate the production performance of national market firms from that of small business and the public/nonprofit sector. Goods and services produced by New York's *own 500,* at headquarters, production, or other office sites and as a share of profit returns to management from international operations, accounted for 21% of output in New York City. Small for-profit businesses produced 64% of gross city product, while government and the nonprofit services contributed 15% of the total.

Aside from such positive returns to scale that characterize national corporations and extend to the urban economies of which they are a part, other implications of their location require more insight into the makeup of New York's corporate complex. Chief among them, the 369 headquartered firms, were comprised of 129 nondurables, 78 durables, and 13 mining industrials, 45 financial institutions and conglomerates, 40 trade, 33 service, and 31 regulated utilities including transport and communications. Though the region as a whole retains a stronger hold on manufacturing-related national corporations than on nonmanufacturers, this bias is not evident among the city's headquarters component. With 10% of the total, an equal 10% of mining-manufacturing and nonmanufacturing corporate front offices were in residence.

Specialization and diversification become apparent beneath the broad distinction in goods and service production. Conglomerates lead city headquarters in share of national firms with nearly one-quarter of total, followed by communications, transportation, and services, each half again more specialized than headquarters activity as a whole. The pattern of specialization is mirrored in a diversified mix of banks, insurers, holding companies, telecommunications and broadcasting firms, airlines, shipping, hotels, and business service corporations. Many of these firms, like the soft-goods manufacturers that comprise nearly two-thirds of New York's industrial front offices, directly service consumer demands. But unlike population-related activities that are underrepresented in the city's headquarters complex — such as retailing, construction, or electric utilities — many giant consumer-product corporations monitor and promote a national market from a more centralized New York location.

As important as product line specialization and diversification is the size stratification of New York's corporate complex. The 369 city headquarters are drawn from the largest-scaled corporate operations in the nation. Company sales averaged $1 billion in 1975, whereas corporations headquartered in the suburbs sold in the $400-million range and those located ouside the region at the $700-million scale, on an average. New York also attracts head offices of the largest corporations measured in terms of employment rolls. With an average work force of 16,300 per firm in corporatewide operations, companies headquartered in the city are twice as large as those in the suburbs, and even larger than major corporations elsewhere in the nation.

Scale, diversity, and industry specialization are features of New York's corporate complex that assure more stability in a period of economic decline and should position the city advantageously to attract future headquarters growth. Though manufacturing accounts for the larger share of central administrative office employment nationally, since the late 1950s nonmanufacturing headquarters have grown more rapidly. In absolute terms, the two classes were generating a roughly equal number of new front-office opportunities into the mid-1970s, but nonmanufacturers were more selective as to where growth occurred.[1]

Nonmanufacturing headquarters expansion characterizes office-oriented and balanced urban economies across a range of metropolitan scale, but it consistently excludes business centers of traditional production areas, such as Philadelphia or Detroit. In all probability, headquarters growth of the industrials will be further overshadowed by relative and absolute gains in service-corporation head offices, as a reflection of the underlying structural shift in the American economy away from goods to service consumption. Because New York holds attraction for manufacturing offices that are not solely linked to its production base, and equally for nonmanufacturers that are not strictly population-related, its economy is comparatively advantaged to compete for future headquarters activity. Whether it can retain these jobs, from the lure of the suburbs, is quite a separate issue.

Controlling corporate output in the nation

The benefits of a major corporate complex can be indirectly measured by the control that headquarters exert over national and regional resources, and directly by the contribution all corporate facilities make to production in the city's economy.

The 369 corporations with head offices in New York City directed a nationwide network of establishments that produced $166.6 billion, 18% of gross domestic corporate product and one-tenth of GNP in 1975.[2] As such, they exercised administrative control over the production of nearly as much output as originated at all levels of government nationwide. Net sales, including semifinished products, amounted to $367 billion in 1975, out of which they purchased $200 billion in materials and services from other business enterprises. Six million persons, or about one in every twelve American workers, were in their employ. The aggregate payroll of $86.6 billion comprised 14% of all corporate compensation in the nation, placing their employees 28% ahead of the average private-sector salary.

Compared to all corporate productivity in domestic operations, the headquartered firms generated over one-fourth more value of output per dollar of labor input. This margin enabled them to earn $35.9 billion in pretax profits from operations, about 30% of gross domestic corporate earnings in 1975. Measured as a rate of return, or after-tax profits as a share of net sales, New York's 369 national firms earned nearly 5%, considerably above the 3.5% earnings rate of corporations headquartered elsewhere in the nation.

Although New York's headquarters comprise one-tenth of publicly traded corporations in the nation, they issued 27% of all corporate dividend payments, or $8 billion, and retained 24% of all undistributed corporate profits, or $9 billion in 1975. Companywide taxes on profits, paid from the head office address and including foreign payments, amounted to $19 billion, or 38% or the profit-tax liability of all domestic corporate operations in the nation. Combined with indirect business taxes and payroll taxes, the headquartered corporations in New York City contributed $40 billion to government, or one-twelfth of all government revenues from personal and business sources nationwide.

As the locus of ownership and management for one-tenth of the nation's productive capacity, New York's 369 headquarters are decision-making centers for an even larger share of new investment activity. In 1975, their corporatewide business savings from depreciation allowances and adjusted earnings amounted to $22 billion, 13% of all private producers funds for investment in the nation. Capital expenditures were $32 billion on domestic and international operations. Assuming that one-quarter of foreign investment flowed from them, domestic capital outlays were $24 billion, or one in six dollars of all nonresidential expenditures on structures and equipment in the nation. With so much leverage over capital funds and capital stock, these firms can effectively redistribute a significant share of the factors of production between regions by channeling their savings, replacement, and net investment through a slow process of disinvestment in less productive operations, or through a rapid expansion in cost-competitive areas.

Chart 2 depicts the significance of New York's headquarters by the corporate share of the industry market in gross national product (GNP) and gross regional product (GRP) in 1975. Nine communications firms, led by American Telephone & Telegraph, are the most concentrated, controlling 75% of telephone, broadcasting, and other communications output from a headquarters in New York City. Apparel, publishing, petroleum, chemical, and other sales by the city's 129 nondurable manufacturers comprised 36% of all soft-goods production in the nation, while 78 durable manufacturers produced 15% of the total. An equivalent share of heavy-industry output was administered from suburban locations.

IN 1975, 369 NYC HDQTRS CONTROLLED:

	PERCENT	
	GNP	GRP
MIN	12	74
CONST	1	1
MFG	24	17
Dur	15	0
Nondur	36	22
TRANSP	12	23
COMM	75	29
UTIL	10	44
W/T	1	1
R/T	5	6
F.,I.,R.E.	9	11
SERV	1	2
PRIV GROSS PROD	13	11

Thirty-seven major banks and insurers provided 26% of financial corporate output with 11% of labor payments in the nation. As a share of the combined finance, insurance, and real estate sector, which includes the imputed value of owner-occupied housing in GNP, the city's relatively few financial institutions still accounted for 9% of total. High corporate productivity among banks and insurers ranks second only to the unit-cost labor output of seven national electric-gas utility systems with parent headquarters in New York City. Nondurable goods, communications, and mining firms are also highly productive, while the more profitable corporations are the nondurables, banks and insurers, utilities and mining concerns, ranked by order of pretax profit per unit-cost of labor. Regulated industries and petroleum mining corporations exhibit the highest capital ratios of gross investment to labor payments.

Tables 1 and 2 summarize gross corporate product of the corporations headquartered in New York City, by the industry and income contributions of production to national (corporatewide) and regional output. Between 1972 and 1975, changes in the value of gross corporate product reflected changes in real output, price changes, and 36 net headquarters relocations.

Linking New York City with a regional economy

If the 369 New York City headquarters controlled $166.6 billion of national output, with $90.3 billion in manufacturing in 1975, they contributed disproportionately less and a more diverse share of private gross product in the New York – New Jersey – Connecticut economy. Regional output measured $17.1 billion, or 10% of corporatewide production and 11% of private GRP, compared to 13% of GNP excluding government. As such, the companies allocated somewhat less corporate activity to the region, than the region accounted for in private GNP (11.7%), and this share can be seen to fall perceptibly for those firms that remained in place over the 1972–75 period.

Unlike national output controlled by New York City headquarters, regional production is dominated by nonmanufacturing. Transportation and utilities, finance, services, and construction are least geographically diversified, siting from one-fifth to two-fifths of corporate activity in the region, while a scant 2% of conglomerate and 5% of durable-goods national-market production is located here. Within the region, the tendency is also for headquartered firms, particularly nonmanufacturers, to concentrate the bulk of other operations in New York City. Chart 2 shows the contribution of the city's 369 headquartered corporations to industry output in the region, indicating highest shares in mining, the regulated industries, and nondurable manufacturing. Dominance of the small-business form of organization is apparent in construction, trade, and services, while durable-goods production is drawn to suburban headquarters locations when in the region, and from industrials headquartered elsewhere as the major processed commodities imported by the regional economy.

Although the spin-off of corporate back offices to the suburbs is increasing, particularly among more standardized clerical and computer operations of white-

TABLE 1

GROSS CORPORATE PRODUCT OF CORPORATIONS HEADQUARTERED IN N.Y.C.:
THE INDUSTRIAL ORIGIN OF OUTPUT IN THE REGION AND NATION BY INDUSTRY, 1972 AND 1975
(hundreds of thousands of dollars)

Industrial Origin of Output	Gross Corporate Product in Nation 1972	Gross Corporate Product in Nation 1975	Gross Corporate Product in Region 1972	Gross Corporate Product in Region 1975
Mining	1,615.2	2,854.4	134.8	197.8
Construction	135.8	242.2	63.1	39.0
Manufacturing	83,386.2	90,328.3	5,807.7	6,566.9
Durable goods	41,127.3	32,230.8	1,862.9	1,670.0
Nondurable goods	42,258.9	58,097.5	3,944.8	4,896.9
Transportation	5,474.9	6,633.2	1,254.2	1,537.6
Communications	27,626.6	30,221.5	1,471.2	1,669.6
Utilities	2,796.5	4,068.6	1,155.7	1,811.8
Wholesale trade	1,409.6	1,668.3	133.9	138.1
Retail trade	7,873.7	7,983.9	913.8	907.7
Finance, insurance, real estate	7,231.2	11,467.6	2,450.6	3,464.8
Selected services	2,197.0	2,450.2	413.6	519.7
Conglomerates	7,099.0	8,653.8	158.1	210.7
Gross corporate product	146,845.7	166,572.0	13,956.7	17,063.7
Number of corporate headquarters	405	369		

SOURCE: Based on a table in Regina B. Armstrong, Regional Accounts: Structure and Performance of the New York Region's Economy in the Seventies (Bloomington: Indiana University Press, 1980).

TABLE 2
GROSS CORPORATE PRODUCT OF CORPORATIONS HEADQUARTERED IN N.Y.C.:
THE DISTRIBUTIVE SHARES OF INCOME IN THE REGION AND NATION, 1972 AND 1975.
(hundreds of thousands of dollars)

Distributive Shares of Income	Gross Corporate Product in Nation 1972	Gross Corporate Product in Nation 1975	Gross Corporate Product in Region 1972	Gross Corporate Product in Region 1975
Net sales	276,057.6	367,076.4	---	---
plus: inventory change	1,439.6	192.1	---	---
equals: total value of production	277,547.2	367,268.5	---	---
less: cost of purchased materials & services	130,661.5	200,696.5	---	---
equals: output for final demand by income	146,885.7	166,572.0	---	---
Output for final demand by income	---	---	13,956.7	17,063.7
Payments by producers to individuals	96,631.4	104,391.6	9,641.3	10,992.9
Labor income	78,725.7	82,164.1	7,939.6	8,702.0
Net interest, rent	10,261.4	14,307.5	1,081.8	1,598.6
Dividends	7,644.3	7,920.0	619.9	692.3
Income retained by producers	18,389.4	21,763.5	1,471.0	2,098.1
Capital consumption allowances	12,725.2	14,658.6	847.8	1,018.9
Undistributed profits	7,319.8	8,995.7	732.1	1,183.4
Inventory valuation adjustment	-1,654.6	-1,890.8	-108.9	-104.2
Tax & nontax payments to government	31,821.9	40,416.9	2,844.4	3,972.7
Taxes on profits	12,276.9	18,999.2	928.2	1,541.1
Indirect business taxes	14,916.9	16,991.0	1,494.7	1,958.5
Payroll taxes	4,628.1	4,426.7	421.5	473.1
Gross corporate product	146,845.7	166,572.0	13,956.7	17,063.7
Number of corporate headquarters	405	369	---	---

SOURCE: Based on a table in Regina B. Armstrong, Regional Accounts: Structure and Performance of the New York Region's Economy in the Seventies (Bloomington: Indiana University Press, 1980).

collar industry corporations, the city's national headquarters retain their strongest regional ties to suburban goods handling facilities of the firm and to suburban headquarters of complementary corporations. As such, the 369 concerns accounted for about 8% of private output and wages and 5% of private employment in the suburbs. Because New York-based corporations are larger and make a greater relative as well as absolute commitment to the region's economy than corporations headquartered in the suburbs or elsewhere, the outward extension of their activity has twice the impact on suburban output and employment than suburban headquarters exert on New York City.

A corollary relationship between New York City headquarters activity and suburan well-being can be identified from journey-to-work flows. Over 600,000 suburban residents hold jobs in New York City, chiefly in higher-paid white-collar occupations (74% of total). The large net outflow of labor payments amounted to $11 billion in 1975, or 23% of total wages and benefits paid by New York City producers. Probably the national corporations accounted for one-third or more of this commuter income. In the suburbs, city-based earnings represented significant shares of all personal income received by residents, or 21% in suburban New York, 7% in New Jersey, and 8% in Connecticut.

Lastly, national corporations headquartered in New York have, at times, viewed the region's suburban environs as alternative locations that offer benefits of increased employee productivity, lower corporate taxes, and a cleaner, safer environment, while allowing corporations to retain existing ties to central-city support services, the market, and amenities by ease of access. Over the decade preceding 1975, New York lost, on balance, 38 of the Fortune 500 headquarters, or 30% of its total; 25 head offices moved to the suburbs and 13 left the region entirely. Between 1972 and 1975, headquarters flight to other regions accelerated but remained below suburban relocation. Several independent studies of mover-firm income statements — including those of the Regional Plan Association and Karen Gerald, deputy mayor of New York City — have shown that the majority of corporations moving from New York City to the suburbs tend not to reveal any subsequent financial enhancement. Tables 3 and 4 depict the gross corporate product originating by industry and income shares in the 47 headquarters that moved out and the 11 that moved into the city between 1972 and 1975.

Stabilizing the New York City economy

How New York City's economy will perform in a rebound from another recession depends in part on whether the existing corporations will repeat their relatively buoyant past performance and on whether a new rash of headquarters relocations can be averted. In 1975, New York's corporate complex accounted for $7 billion, or one-seventh, of all labor compensation to the city work force and about $4 billion or nearly one-quarter of all producer taxes paid to local, state, and federal governments. In the measure of profits and other income retained by producers for investment, the city's *own 500* headquarters, production, and other office activity generated $5 billion in pretax earnings and $2.5 billion in business savings, or respectively 43% and 27% of New York's total in 1975. Yet net interest

TABLE 3

GROSS CORPORATE PRODUCT OF CORPORATIONS WITH HEADQUARTER MOVES INTO AND OUT OF N.Y.C.:
THE INDUSTRIAL ORIGIN OF OUTPUT IN THE REGION AND NATION, 1972 AND 1975
(hundreds of thousands of dollars)

Industrial Origin of Output	Gross Corporate Product in Nation 1972	Gross Corporate Product in Nation 1975	Gross Corporate Product in Region 1972	Gross Corporate Product in Region 1975
Mining	4.1	---	0.4	---
Construction	---	---	---	---
Manufacturing	15,269.0	586.3	715.2	133.9
Durable goods	10,820.8	567.4	317.3	92.7
Nondurable goods	4,448.2	18.9	397.9	41.2
Transportation	---	---	---	---
Communications	3,750.4	---	173.8	---
Utilities	---	---	---	---
Wholesale trade	15.9	---	3.4	---
Retail trade	2,698.0	---	199.9	---
Finance, insurance, real estate	---	---	---	---
Selected services	51.3	12.9	5.3	0.9
Conglomerates	---	---	---	---
Gross corporate product	2,788.7	599.2	1,018.0	134.8
Number of headquarter moves	47	11		

SOURCE: Based on a table in Regina B. Armstrong, Regional Accounts: Structure and Performance of the New York Region's Economy in the Seventies (Bloomington: Indiana University Press, 1980).

TABLE 4

GROSS CORPORATE PRODUCT OF CORPORATIONS WITH HEADQUARTER MOVES INTO AND OUT OF N.Y.C.:
THE DISTRIBUTIVE SHARES OF INCOME IN THE REGION AND NATION, 1972 AND 1975
(hundreds of thousands of dollars)

Distributive Shares of Income	Gross Corporate Product in Nation 1972	Gross Corporate Product in Nation 1975	Gross Corporate Product in Region 1972	Gross Corporate Product in Region 1975
Payments by producers to individuals	17,131.9	506.0	763.3	105.5
Labor income	14,109.4	459.8	659.7	90.2
Net interest, rent	2,265.4	42.1	70.9	14.3
Dividends	757.1	4.1	32.7	1.0
Income retained by producers	2,286.5	52.0	93.4	14.2
Capital consumption allowances	1,715.4	37.9	71.6	9.3
Undistributed profits	684.8	7.2	26.1	-2.9
Inventory valuation adjustment	-113.7	6.9	-4.3	7.8
Tax & nontax payments to government	2,370.4	41.2	161.3	15.1
Taxes on profits	1,017.7	18.2	43.4	3.7
Indirect business taxes	1,352.7	23.0	81.2	6.9
Payroll taxes	n.a.	n.a.	36.7	4.5
Gross corporate product	21,788.7	599.2	1,018.0	134.8
Number of headquarter moves	47	11	---	---

SOURCE: Based on a table in Regina B. Armstrong, Regional Accounts: Structure and Performance of the New York Region's Economy in the Seventies (Bloomington: Indiana University Press, 1980).

transactions were more concentrated than any other factor payment: fully $3 billion, or three-fifths, of all interest charges in local production originated in national corporations, reflecting their much higher level of demand for capital.

Capital is used more intensively by the corporate complex, and the benefits of this accrue not only to after-tax profit margins, but also to government and labor in the form of greater tax liabilities and higher average labor payments. Per unit of output, less labor input is required in this sector than among small businesses, the voluntary nonprofits, or government. For these reasons — as well as for their control over national markets, their product-line diversification, and other factors — the corporations that were continuously located in the city throughout the 1972–75 period performed far better than the rest of New York's economy in the recession of the mid-1970s. Tables 5 and 6 portray the rate of change in average gross corporate product in the region and nation for the 358 headquartered corporations that remained in New York City.

The cyclical contraction of New York City's economy was really confined to small for-profit businesses. Their real output expressed in constant dollars declined by 14% over the 1972–75 period, compared to a growth of 6% in the corporate complex and virtual stability in the public/nonprofit sector. The decline of small businesses was half again steeper in the city than in the region as a whole, while for corporations — particularly those headquartered firms in place — the rate of growth was twice as fast. Although the national firms also showed period gains in productivity, real profit, and business savings, in contrast to small-business losses across-the-board, the corporations nonetheless accounted for some of New York's employment decline. But these losses were roughly one-tenth the scale of the one hundred thousand jobs lost annually in the private sector of the city's economy, and they could be attributed mainly to the accelerated relocation of corporate headquarters. Chart 3 depicts the relative performance of 358 headquartered corporations that stayed in New York over the 1972–75 period and compares the impact of corporate moveouts on production control nationally and in the region.

The 47 corporations that shifted headquarters to the rest of the region or nation over the three-year period represented 15% of the $146.8 billion in national output administered from a New York City-headquartered address in 1972. Of this $22 billion, $15.3 billion in output value originated in manufacturing; durable goods, hardest hit at $10.8 billion, registered a 9% loss of control over national markets annually. Unlike those corporations that stayed, the movers had vested only half the share of national production in regional operations, making a 5% commitment of the total, which accounts for the relatively lower impact of out-movement on New York City's and the New York region's gross corporate product in 1972. The movers, 27 of whom relocated to the suburbs, also tended to be below average for their industry in terms of productivity, profitability, and subsequent rates of growth.

The 358 firms that kept their headquarters in New York City increased their output and profits much faster than their peers both within the region and nationally. The chart shows that this advantage was 3 percentage points ahead of gross domestic corporate product growth in the nation, 2 percentage points ahead of the increase in output by all eleven hundred publicly traded corporations in the

TABLE 5

THE COMPONENTS OF CHANGE IN AVERAGE CORPORATE PRODUCT OF CORPORATIONS HEADQUARTERED IN AND MOVED INTO AND OUT OF N.Y.C. BETWEEN 1972 AND 1975: THE INDUSTRIAL ORIGIN OF OUTPUT IN THE REGION AND NATION PER FIRM (hundreds of thousands of dollars)

Industrial Origin of Output	Gross Corporate Product in Nation Average per Firm that Remained			Average Moved Out	Average Moved Into	Gross Corporate Product in Region Average per Firm that Remained			Average Moved Out	Average Moved Into
	1972	1975	% 1972-75			1972	1975	% 1972-75		
Mining	123.9	219.6	77.2%	4.1	---	10.3	15.2	47.6%	0.4	---
Construction	45.3	80.7	78.1	---	---	21.0	13.0	-38.1	---	---
Manufacturing	345.8	455.5	31.7	449.1	58.6	25.9	32.7	26.3	21.0	13.4
Durable goods	439.2	458.9	4.5	601.2	63.0	22.4	22.9	2.2	17.6	10.3
Nondurable goods	295.4	453.7	53.6	278.0	18.9	27.7	37.9	36.8	24.9	41.2
Transportation	365.0	442.2	21.2	---	---	83.6	102.5	22.6	---	---
Communications	2,652.9	3,357.9	26.6	1,875.2	---	144.2	185.5	28.6	86.9	---
Utilities	399.5	581.2	45.5	---	---	165.1	258.8	56.8	---	---
Wholesale trade	107.2	128.3	19.7	15.9	---	10.0	10.6	6.0	3.4	---
Retail trade	191.7	295.7	54.3	539.6	---	29.4	33.6	14.3	24.0	---
Finance, insurance, real estate	195.4	309.9	58.6	---	---	66.2	93.6	41.4	---	---
Selected services	67.1	76.2	13.6	12.8	12.9	12.8	16.2	26.6	1.3	0.9
Conglomerates	1,419.8	1,730.8	21.9	---	---	31.6	42.1	33.2	---	---
Gross corporate product	349.3	463.6	32.7%	463.6	54.5	36.1	47.3	31.0%	21.7	12.3
Number of corporate headquarters	358	358	358	47	11	---	---	---	---	---

SOURCE: Based on a table in Regina B. Armstrong, Regional Accounts: Structure and Performance of the New York Region's Economy in the Seventies (Bloomington: Indiana University Press, 1980).

TABLE 6

THE COMPONENTS OF CHANGE IN AVERAGE CORPORATE PRODUCT OF CORPORATIONS HEADQUARTERED IN AND MOVED INTO AND OUT OF N.Y.C. BETWEEN 1972 AND 1975: THE DISTRIBUTIVE SHARES OF INCOME IN THE REGION AND NATION PER FIRM
(hundreds of thousands of dollars)

Distributive Shares of Income	Gross Corporate Product in Nation Average per Firm		That Remained % 1972-75	Average Mover		Gross Corporate Product in Region Average per Firm		that Remained % 1972-75	Average Mover	
	1972	1975		Out	Into	1972	1975		Out	Into
Payments by producers to individuals	222.1	290.2	30.7%	364.5	46.0	24.8	30.4	22.6%	16.2	9.6
Labor income	180.5	228.2	26.4	300.2	41.8	20.3	24.1	18.7	14.0	8.2
Net interest, rent	22.3	39.8	78.5	48.2	3.8	2.8	4.4	57.1	1.5	1.3
Dividends	19.3	22.1	14.5	16.1	0.4	1.7	1.9	11.8	0.7	0.1
Income retained by producers	45.0	60.6	34.7	48.6	4.7	3.8	5.8	52.6	2.0	1.3
Capital consumption allowances	30.8	40.8	32.5	36.5	3.4	2.2	2.8	27.3	1.5	0.8
Undistributed profits	18.5	25.1	35.7	14.6	0.7	2.0	3.3	65.0	0.6	-0.3
Inventory valuation adjustment	-4.3	-5.3	23.3	-2.4	0.6	-0.3	-0.3	0.0	-0.1	0.7
Tax & nontax payments to government	82.3	112.8	37.1	50.4	3.8	7.5	11.1	48.0	3.4	1.4
Taxes on profits	31.5	53.0	68.3	21.7	1.7	2.5	4.3	72.0	0.9	0.3
Indirect business taxes	37.9	47.4	25.1	28.8	2.1	3.9	5.5	41.0	1.7	0.6
Payroll taxes	12.9	12.4	-3.9	n.a.	n.a.	1.1	1.3	18.2	0.8	0.4
Gross corporate product	349.3	463.6	32.7%	463.6	54.5	36.1	47.3	31.0	21.7	12.3
Number of corporate headquarters	358	358	358	47	11	---	---	---	---	---

SOURCE: Based on a table in Regina B. Armstrong, Regional Accounts: Structure and Performance of the New York Region's Economy in the Seventies (Bloomington: Indiana University Press, 1980).

region, and 7 percentage points faster than New York's *own 500's* increase in production. Had the city held on to at least those corporations that relocated to the suburbs, its control over corporate output nationwide would have been 10% higher in 1975.

Conclusions

Sudden shifts of the magnitude suggested by the 15% decline in New York-headquarters control over national corporate resources underscore the point that, without careful attention, other unfavorable circumstances can further dismantle the complex of corporate decision-making, despite the apparent benefits firms receive in being in the city. Retaining this complex is of paramount importance to the city's economy. Their presence assures a qualitative difference in the commitment of resources locally; they spearhead export activity that is dominated by the outflow of white-collar administrative, financial, and professional services; and their vast capital resources are essential to implementing improvements in productivity.

In 1975, a year of disinvestment in the region and particularly in New York City, the national corporations accounted for the only source of net expansion in productive capacity. Small businesses and households replaced less capital stock than they depreciated, while corporations invested at twice the rate. Half of the region's household and business savings for investment flowed out to fund opportunities elsewhere, balancing on capital account a current account deficit in the region's balance of payments. These commodity trade payments rose sharply during the recession, not as a result of increased demand but as the response of substitution for decline in the local production of certain manufactured products.

The national corporations can be expected to remain quite stable as New York employers during another national recession. The greater danger is their subsequent relocation to the suburbs or elsewhere, as the perceived quality of life — especially the condition of basic public services and infrastructure — erodes with declining real resources or competing social needs in local governments. Maintaining the corporate capital of private enterprise in the United States requires not only the skills, the private capital, the support services, the face-to-face communication among competing and complementary firms, but also the image and prestige of a thriving cosmopolitan environment.

Notes

1. Regina B. Armstrong, "National Trends in Office Construction, Employment and Headquarter Location in US Metropolitan Areas," in P. W. Daniels (ed.), *Spatial Patterns of Office Growth and Location* (Chichester: Wiley, 1979).

2. Nationally, the share of income and product originating in foreign affiliates could not be separated from domestic operations of the headquarterd corporations. One measure would place income on equity abroad at about 13% of corporate pretax profits. References to respective shares of gross domestic corporate product should be taken as approximate. See Regina B. Armstrong, *Regional Accounts: Structure and Performance of the New York Region's Economy in the Seventies* (Bloomington: Indiana University Press, 1980). All six tables included in this article are reproduced, with permission, from this book.

4

NEW YORK CITY AND THE SERVICES TRANSFORMATION

Thomas M. Stanback, Jr.

Since World War II New York City has experienced a dramatic series of changes during which it has lost a major share of manufacturing jobs, gained sharply in service employment, encountered severe financial crises, and emerged as the major city in a rapidly growing world economy. These changes are part of a massive transformation from goods to service employment throughout the nation which has dramatically impacted the entire urban system.

The growth of services in the U.S. economy

The transformation in the U.S. economy that resulted in an increase in service employment from 57% to roughly two-thirds during the period 1948 – 77 has been largely misinterpreted as simply a shift toward consumption of public-sector and market services and away from a primary orientation toward goods.[1,2] Behind this misinterpretation lies a failure to observe how very different the services are and how very different are the forces that have propelled their growth. In particular, there has been a failure to observe that in the private sector it is the intermediate services — those which assist production, not consumer services — that are the most important and that have played the major role in the changing nature of work.

Let's look briefly at the record since just after the war (1948).[1,2] First, there are certain well-recognized changes. In primary production, largely agriculture, the share of employment declined from about 11% to 6% in 1977 while manufacturing dropped from 32% to 24%. In the not-for-profit sectors, government rose from 14% to almost 20%, and nonprofit services, largely health and education, from less than 3% to more than 6%.

The rest of the story is not well understood. The distributive services (transportation, communications, utilities, wholesale, retail) — broadly conceived as all those activities focusing mainly on transporting and distributing goods and providing communications — have remained roughly unchanged in terms of share of employment (about 26%). Producer services — those activities devoted largely to assisting business through finance, insurance, and a variety of administration, developmental, and housekeeping functions (e.g., legal, advertising, R & D, consulting, building maintenance) — have grown rapidly, however, rising from 6% to 12%.

The most striking observation, in view of the widespread assumption that we as individuals are shifting rapidly to services, is that the freestanding consumer services — personal services, hotels, amusements, motion pictures, domestic services, etc. — declined from almost 8% to 5%. This decline is traceable principally to the drop in employment of domestic servants. Some consumer services have increased in importance; but the consumer services (even if we exclude domestic employment) have shown decidedly "soft" growth.

In order to highlight the forces that have propelled the growth of services it is helpful to distinguish between those changes that involve what we produce — changes in final demand — and those associated with how we produce. In terms of what we produce, government and the nonprofit services, conventionally regarded as final outputs of our economy, have increased in importance in response to the public's desire for more adequate health and educational services in an economy that has been growing in terms of population and per capita income. They have been abetted on the one hand by the development of nonprofit institutions (e.g., voluntary hospitals and Blue Cross–Blue Shield) and on the other by radical changes in demographic composition.

At the same time there have been dramatic changes in the marketplace that were part cause, part result, of changes in how we produce and distribute goods and services. The postwar era has seen the development of mass national and international markets and the breakdown of local and regional barriers, which has led only superficially to a homogenization of consumption patterns. More fundamental has been an increase in product differentiation and in the segmentation of markets according to income and taste.

Producing firms have found it increasingly important to target marketing strategy to particular segments of the population, to develop, brand, and promote a stream of new products and services. At the same time consumers have shifted from emphasis on products and services that provide for basic necessities and comfort and toward those that appeal in terms of realizing preferred style of life and of enhancing self-identity. This has been taking place across a broad spectrum of income.

Historically, the goods-production processes have lent themselves most readily to application of physical capital and incorporation of new science-based technology, allowing the substitution of high technology embodied capital for labor in these activities. As plant processes have been routinized and brought under control, management has focused increasingly on exploiting the growth of markets, developing and promoting new products and services, responding to increasing regulation, and coping with its own internal administration.

The result of this shift in functional emphasis has been the rise of producer services, both freestanding and in-house, and the growth of the large corporation. Companies have increasingly made use of producer services to provide expertise in a variety of fields, including R & D, advertising, marketing, accounting, financing, community and governmental relationships. At the same time they have increased the size and importance of their headquarters and divisional staffs.

The growth of producer services must not be regarded as related entirely to large corporations, however. With their own markets expanding, producer-service firms have found it advantageous to reach out to smaller firms as well, making available expertise not previously affordable and facilitating the birth and development of young firms with new, innovative products and services to sell.

It is important to recognize how large this group of intermediate services has become. Independent producer-service firms today account for 12% of total employment and a much larger share, 20%, of GNP (value added).[1,2] In-house producer services (service activities carried on within the firm) account for at least another 5% of employment and GNP. Thus, total producer services (provided independently and in-house), the most rapidly growing segment of the American economy, account for more than one-sixth of employment and roughly one-fourth of national product in the U.S. economy!

The services transformation and the urban system

In large measure, this transformation in the U.S. economy has involved an urban transformation. Although the earlier industrialism favored a concentration of manufacturing employment in cities, more recent developments have favored diffusion. Production employment has declined, and plants have tended to disperse to the suburbs and to smaller towns and cities, particularly to locations in the new fast-growing areas of the South and Southwest.

Services, on the other hand, have favored cities. To understand this, we must distinguish between those activities that are essentially residential and those that are largely export-oriented. We must also recognize the strong forces of agglomeration and complementarity among services. Residentiary services are those for which the nature of demand and the economies of scale and market size permit them to be provided close to people wherever they dwell. Export-type services require larger markets or are specialized to meet the needs of organizations that are reaching out to broad markets. Moreover, export-type services tend to be complementary and to require location close to each other.

Analysis of the employment structure of metropolitan places indicates that some cities are heavily specialized in the provision of a variety of distributive and producer services and of corporate headquarters or divisional head-office activities, while others tend to be more restricted in their specialization, with principal focus given to educational, health, resort, or governmental activities. Some remain heavily specialized in manufactures; some combine manufacturing and service specialization. Many are in transition.

In order to visualize how metropolitan areas have responded to the changes at work in the national economy it is useful to think of the hierarchy of urban places as a three-tier system.[3] The first tier includes roughly 35 SMSAs with a population above 1 million; the second, about 100 with a population range from a quarter-million to one million; and the third, the 125 smallest SMSAs and non-SMSA urban areas.[4]

In the first tier we include not only the major cities of thirty or forty years ago — New York, Chicago, San Francisco, Los Angeles, Philadelphia, Pittsburgh, Cleveland, etc. — but also cities such as Atlanta, Houston, Dallas, and Phoenix, which have more recently grown into the top echelon. The difference in the experience of these two groups of places is chiefly that whereas the former have strengthened their roles as service centers largely by a painful process of shifting specialization — losing industrial and gaining service jobs — the latter have developed more by simply becoming focal points for providing distributive and producer services to their growing hinterlands. Taken as a group the top-echelon places are clearly the major providers of exportable services. Together they account for 60% of all employment in corporate-administrative and producer-services activities (the corporate-complex services), although they account for 45% of total U.S. employment.

The experience of New York City is remarkable when seen from this perspective. Its specialization in corporate headquarters, producer services, and distributive services (excluding retail) is by far the greatest, accounting for 42% of its total employment as compared with 32% for Chicago, 34% for San Francisco, 34% for Houston.

Moreover, in spite of the fact that New York's shift toward a service base began much earlier, dating back into the prewar era, the extent of its transformation during the postwar years has been as wrenching as, and greater than most, major cities in the nation.

The experience of the second tier is more diverse. One group is composed of places that are developing as dynamic regional service centers (e.g., Charlotte, Memphis, Indianapolis, Tulsa), although some retain sizeable manufacturing sectors. A second group remains strongly dominated by manufacturing. Some of these places have become increasingly more service-oriented over the years as they serve as hosts to corporate headquarters or divisional offices; while others, largely in the old industrial belt, have failed to move away from their manufacturing specialization and are encountering difficulties. A third group includes a number of fast-growing places that specialize in government, resort, or retirement activities or as medical and educational centers.

The lower tier of the urban hierarchy includes a number of places whose export strength lies in specialized services, but it also includes a large number of places in both the old industrial areas and in the Sunbelt states that are specialized in manufacturing activities.

What is the most important lesson for New York City that can be learned from this brief, highly simplified analysis? I believe it is that New York City is increasingly in competition with other cities as the nation grows and the urban system develops. Although it is by far the largest and its transformation to a service base the most advanced, it accounts for a decreasing share of the nation's exportable services. In 1959, 15% of the nation's employment in corporate-complex activities was found within the New York SMSA; today it is only 10%. As cities which were previously middle-sized join the top echelon and even smaller places advance to the intermediate level, scale-of-market thresholds are overcome, and it becomes feasible for their service firms to deliver sophisticated advanced services that previously had to be sought only in the major metropolises, especially in New York. Moreover, there is an increasing abundance of highly trained talent available throughout the land, as state and regional schools of business, law, medicine, and engineering attain increasingly higher levels of excellence.

New York as a super service center: opportunities and problems

New York's competitive strength must then lie in being the most advanced and sophisticated among the service centers. As the national and world economies become larger and operations of firms and public sector and nonprofit organizations become more complex and demanding, New York must continuously improve and broaden its expertise and reach out to a developing world market.

Just how the city may accommodate to change is illustrated by its recent experience as a corporate headquarters center and as a major center in international business.

In 1959, 137 of Fortune 500 firms were located in New York City. By 1977 the number had dropped to 100. Clearly, the net loss of 37 major firms was serious, yet there were a number of compensating developments.[5,6] First, most of the firms that left relocated within the greater New York region and continued to make use of producer services within the city. Second, those firms that remained included the most dynamic in terms of their emphasis on development of international business. Third, the expansion of producer-service firms and the in-migration of foreign corporations more than filled the void and tilted the city even further toward a preeminent role as an international service center.

Multiple specialization and interdependence

Thus far we have stressed the importance of the complex of corporate offices and producer services. Yet the nature of the city's economy can be comprehended only when it is recognized how truly multipronged is its economic base. New York is not simply a center of corporate headquarters, business services, and financial activities. It is a center of the arts, of fashion and interior decoration, of education and health services, of tourism. Moreover, and often overlooked, it is the major city most closely linked with Washington. Unlike the other major cities of the world that are centers of business and culture as well as capital cities, New York is separated from the seat of government. Yet it has created a vital link with the nation's capital through airlines that daily and quickly ferry thousands of persons back and forth.

It is not by accident that New York is a city of multiple specializations, for there are forces of agglomeration at work which are very powerful. They lie principally in the fact that each specialized activity finds ready at hand the great market of the metropolis; that it is able to draw upon the city's huge, diversified pool of labor and infrastructure of transportation, housing, commercial facilities, government services, and cultural and recreational amenities. Moreover, to a large extent specialized activities depend upon each other — corporate headquarters upon producer services, finance upon the entire business community, the business community upon the theater, the arts, hotels, restaurants, and so on. The linkages are almost numberless — some subtle, some clear-cut. Taken as a whole, they are vital. The success of the city's economy depends upon the clocklike functioning of an incredibly complex mechanism.

What, then, can be said about the nature of developmental policy? In a metropolis so large, so multifaceted, yet so beset by financial constraints in the public sector, what is an appropriate strategy for assuring vitality to its economy and equity to its people? Is a developmental policy that addresses first the needs of the corporate complex appropriate for so varied an economy?

I believe that it is. Moreover, I believe that such a policy is likely to favor the development of the city across a wide range of activities. Let me illustrate by calling attention to the importance of flows of people into and out of the city and the kinds of action that can be taken to facilitate such flows.

Unlike a manufacturing center where people simply move daily from home to work, New York is a city into which and out of which thousands of people also flow daily from and to distant places in order to transact business and to visit. Of an estimated 17.5 million people who visited New York City in 1979, more than 5 million came on business and over 2 million for conventions.[5] Putting the corporate complex first means facilitating this flow of people. It means close attention to air transport. Matthew Drennan and Georgia Nanopoulous-Stergiou estimate that the export component of "other transportation" (largely airports) constitutes 5.4% of total value of exports of the city.[7] It means also attention to assuring personal safety, to improving the environment (e.g., cleaning the streets), and to enriching the amenities (e.g., encouraging waterfront development for restaurants and recreation).

Such a set of priorities does not focus narrowly. What favors the flow of persons who come and go to transact business also favors tourism and conventions, the arts, the theater, the universities and medical centers, and through many lines of linkage, restaurants, hotels, and retail stores.

The same argument can be applied across the broad range of possible actions by the public sector: a tax structure that does not garner revenues by undue levies on particular types of firms and that does not discourage innovative firms or small businesses (many firms among both the producer services and the consumer services will be small), building codes that do not add unnecessary costs or bring about unnecessary delays, a transportation system that permits the city's workers to move readily and cheaply from home to work.

Employment problems in a service-based economy

But there is another area that is fundamental to any consideration of developmental priorities: the provision of suitable employment. Here the basic premise is that the economic base of any city influences the kinds of work that people do and the wages and salaries they earn. Urban economists have long recognized that a manufacturing city with its capital-intensive production activites is likely to provide a fairly well-balanced income distribution, with a relatively large proportion of middle-income jobs. Not so for the service-based economy. A study by the staff at Conservation of Human Resources shows that for the nation the services tend to provide disproportionately large numbers of both well-paying and poorly-paying jobs, but relatively few in the middle range.[8] Good jobs are likely to be held by well-trained or experienced professionals, managers, executives, and technicians; poorly-paid jobs by clerical, stenographic, and a wide variety of so-called service-worker personnel. Moreover, lower-level service-sector jobs are to a disproportionate extent "female-labeled" (offering few work opportunities for young males), part-time, and poorly protected by either licensing or other credentialing or by union membership. Finally, there is typically little opportunity at the lower end of the earnings spectrum for upward mobility through promotion and tenure.

Marcia Freedman's and Anna Dutka's recent study of training requirements in the United States includes a special analysis that sheds considerable light on the New York City work force in the mid-1970s.[9] Although earnings experience is not examined, employment is cross-classified by industry and occupation with typical pre- and post-employment training experience specified. The picture for the entire city's work force is not unlike that for services in the United States as a whole. Professional, technical, and clerical jobs requiring preemployment training account for just over one-fourth of all employment; managers and officers, another 13%; high-skilled white and blue-collar jobs over 10%. Semiskilled jobs compose only 13% while low-skill jobs make up 37%. Uncounted, of course, are a large number of menial jobs held by illegal aliens.

Moreover, there is evidence of incipient declines in the demand for office clericals and for lower-level service-worker jobs. Data for the United States show that since 1970 these jobs have failed to grow as rapidly as total employment in the specific industries in which they were represented.[3] Since these occupations have tended to be concentrated in fast-growing sectors, their relatively poor performance has not generally been recognized. Important developments may well be underway, however. In the office, new technology (xerography, computers, word processing) is beginning to make itself felt against a rising tide of "paper work." At the same time, rising wage rates and other costs among the employers of service workers are bringing pressure to reorganize work and to utilize special equipment in order to lower labor inputs. Over the years the service sector has been least suited for mechanization and the standardizing, labor-cutting procedures that have characterized industrialism. Now the picture, it seems, is changing. If this is so, such changes will impact New York City's economy with a greater force than most others, for we are strongly committed to the services.

Are services enough? A second look at manufacturing

Such weaknesses in a service-based economy raise the question: Should we take a second look at manufacturing?

In preparing for this paper I did just that. I asked my assistant to examine employment changes for the most detailed industry classifications in manufacturing during the period 1969–77 and to pull out those in which jobs had increased. He laughed and allowed that I was "looking for a needle in a haystack." I told him I was confident that there would be some "needles" — *everything* doesn't go down.

I was right, but just barely. Out of 143 detailed manufacturing classifications only 9 showed a gain of employment during the eight-year period; only 5, an increase of more than 200 jobs. Among the losers there were job decreases of 314,000; among the gainers, job increases of 7,500.

Now this must be seen in perspective. Most manufacturing is probably not viable in the New York City economy. Where scale is important and production is for the national or international market, the city cannot compete. But where scale is small and the product is designed for the special needs of the local market, the case may very well be different. Costs are less important; specialized know-how and an understanding of the customer's needs are critical. It is hard to make the case that there is no place for a modest-sized but vigorous manufacturing sector within a city of 7.5 million centered in a metropolitan region of over 15 million.

The need is twofold. First, a manufacturing sector is required to help provide middle-income employment for those who do not or cannot move through a long period of formal education or who are unsuited for white-collar work. Second, a vigorous if modest-sized manufacturing sector is important also for the health of the remainder of the economy. If manufacturing continues to erode, we stand in danger of losing our pool of mechanical talent and of entrepreneurship in those activities that involve new applications of technology to the problems of our specialized service base. Both skilled labor and entrepreneurial talent are resources that must be renewed continuously. Once depleted, they are extremely difficult to reestablish.

What we must do, I believe, is to reexamine the question of what kind of manufacturing New York City needs. A major criterion is what industries may best provide for the service economy itself. If the city's service economy is characterized by a high level of specialization, its needs are likely to be best served by specialty producers close at hand. Here the printing and publishing industry as it has evolved in the city may prove to be a useful model, for its linkages with the service economy are sensitive and critical. What strategies should be pursued cannot be specified here, but they would probably include provision for appropriate space, financing, and training of manpower.

A second criterion is closely related: What industries can best assist the service economy in meeting the challenge of adapting to the new computer-cum-communications technology? Word-processing and a host of other computer-based innovations are already being introduced by larger firms. Those close to the field assure me that we have seen but the tip of the iceberg. The true revolution in the application of the new technology to services lies just ahead.

Yet the city plays no leading role in developing this technology. By and large it is an importer, not a producer. It does not have an adequate force either of specialized engineers to customize systems or of skilled mechanics and craftsmen to maintain the sophisticated equipment and assure its efficient and imaginative utilization.

What seems to be called for is a developmental policy that will encourage a vigorous but modest-sized manufacturing sector geared to provide for the specialized needs of the service economy, particularly as they relate to adapting to the major technological advances that are likely to be critical to the competitive strength of the city's economy in the years just ahead.

Notes

1. U.S. Department of Commerce, Bureau of Economic Analysis, *The National Income and Product Account of the United States, 1929-1974: Statistical Tables* (Washington, D.C., 1977).
2. U.S. Department of Commerce, Bureau of Economic Analysis, *Survey of Current Business*, July 1978.
3. Thomas M. Stanback, Jr., Peter J. Bearse, Thierry Noyelle, and Robert Karasek, *Services: A New Look at the U.S. Economy* (Montclair, N.J.: Allanheld, Osmun, 1981), Chapter 5.
4. An SMSA is a Standard Metropolitan Statistical Area, officially designated by the U.S. Department of Commerce and including in a designated urban area certain of its surrounding counties. SMSAs are based primarily on commuting patterns. The New York SMSA includes New York City, Westchester and Putnam counties in New York State, and Bergen County, N.J.
5. Conservation of Human Resources Project, *The Corporate Headquarters Complex in New York City* (New York: Columbia University, 1977).
6. Robert B. Cohen, "The Internationalization of Capital and U.S. Cities." Ph.D. Dissertation (New York: The New School for Social Research, 1979).
7. Matthew Drennan and Georgia Nanopoulous-Stergiou, "The Local Economy and Local Revenues," in Raymond D. Horton and Charles Brecher (eds.), *Setting Municipal Priorities 1980* (Montclair, N.J.: Allanheld, Osmun; New York: Universe, 1979).
8. Thomas M. Stanback, Jr., and Thierry Noyelle, *Metropolitan Labor Markets in Transition: A Study of Seven SMSAs* (New York: Conservation of Human Resources Project, Columbia University, 1981).
9. Marcia Freedman and Anna B. Dutka, *Training Information for Policy Guidance*, Research and Development Monograph 76 (Washington, D.C.: U.S. Department of Labor, Employment and Training Commission, 1980).

5

THE ROLE OF NEW YORK CITY'S FOREIGN EXPORTS IN LOCAL MANUFACTURING

Maurice B. Ballabon

Much may be learned about New York City's economy by examining its foreign economic relations. The city developed at the junction of the nation's seaboard and interior axes of historical development, but it is also roughly midway between Cleveland, Ohio, and Rotterdam in the Netherlands on a mapping of costs of surface movement, as well as at the edge of the North Atlantic trade pond. It may also prove to lie at the continental edge of price inflation waves that move into the American interior.[1]

Nearly fifty years ago, Bertil Ohlin in his book *Interregional and International Trade* observed that international trade was but a special case of interregional trade and that the basis for international trade had to be sought in exchanges between regions. Without detracting from the value of economic-base studies and the development of regional accounting systems, data availability and the theoretical constructs that have appeared since Ricardo's wine and cloth comparative advantage model nevertheless favor the international approach.

Examining the foreign trade connection of New York City poses at least two major obstacles. One is the absence of data on values and volumes of the city's foreign exports and imports, and hence the need for estimating and surmise. The other problem lies in the evidence that whatever the size of the foreign trade sector in manufacturing, it is probably quite small. The only "primary" source indicates that export-related manufacturing employment in 1971 engaged 11,000 workers, or 1.4% of the city's manufacturing employment, and accounted for 2.1% of the estimated value of shipments.[2] (At that time, the share of the city's employment in selected industries affected by competitive imports was 56.1%.) Although export-related employment for 1976 was probably some 15,000 workers, this was less than the loss of manufacturing workers sustained by the city over a period of a few months in, say, 1974. What is to be learned, then, from examining a sector of manufacturing activities so small in size and for which there is no published primary material, even at the two-digit Standard Industrial Classification (SIC) level of aggregation? I hope that this brief paper will show that much can be discovered not only about the structure of New York City's export manufactures, but also about the larger local economy of which it is a small part.

Size of the export sector

The close historical association between the growth of New York City and the expansion of U.S. international commerce has been documented extensively, especially in studies by the Harvard Graduate School of Business that appeared in the early 1960s under the sponsorship of the Regional Plan Association. Yet among the nation's metropolitan areas, in 1976, the New York – New Jersey Standard Metropolitan Statistical Area (SMSA) ranked only seventh in value of export shipments and tenth in export-related employment.[3] Detroit, Los Angeles – Long Beach, Chicago, Houston, Seattle – Everett, and Philadelphia all exceeded the New York – New Jersey SMSA in value of export shipments, and additional metropolitan areas, San Jose, Boston, and Dallas – Fort Worth, exceeded it in export-related employment. Indeed, Detroit, Los Angeles – Long Beach, and Chicago each had more that twice the value of New York's export shipments and about twice the level or better of New York's export-related employment in manufacturing. The New York metropolitan area's share of the nation's value of export shipments was only 1.8%, and of export-related employment, only 1.7%. As might be expected, the relatively low placing of New York among the nation's metropolitan areas reflected in part the decline in manufacturing activities in the metropolis relative to the levels in other centers. Perhaps more surprising were the the low shares of export shipments and employment within New York's metropolitan manufactures. With only 4.3% and 2.6% respectively, these were considerably below the national averages of 7.0% and 6.3%, and below those of the other leading export centers. Nineteen seventy-six was a year of national recovery from the recession of 1974 – 75 and a year of moderate expansion in the economies of the nation's major trading partners. It is tempting, therefore, to view the low export shares of New York's manufacturing as confirmation of the decline in the region's comparative advantage vis-à-vis other parts of the country. Like so many other terms, however, "comparative advantage" in its simple Heckscher-Ohlin connotation conveys little of the complexity of the real world of trade and, as will be developed, requires amplification for an understanding of New York City's problems.

The city's export sector probably included some 15,000 jobs directly related to producing manufactured exports in 1976. (If national averages are used, then an additional 9,000 jobs were required to produce materials and parts that were used in products exported from elsewhere in the United States. This study, however, is concerned with directly related activities only.) The 15,000 jobs were estimated on the basis of the city's share in New York metropolitan employment by two-digit SIC groups. There are a number of data gaps at the three-digit SIC level, but using these more disaggregated components suggests a level of direct export employment of some 12,000 workers. The period 1971 – 76, therefore, may have been one in which there was an increase in export employment in the city, and the share of manufacturing employment engaged in exports rose from 1.4% (11,000 workers) to 2.2% – 3.0%. Changes in the definition of the New York SMSA prevent a

TABLE 1
EXPORTS AND EXPORT-RELATED EMPLOYMENT FOR LEADING STANDARD METROPOLITAN STATISTICAL AREAS, 1976

SMSA	Value of Export Shipments			Export-Related Employment		
	Million dollars	Percentage of all shipments	Rank	Thousands	Percentage of all employment	Rank
Detroit	3,753.0	9.1	1	38.0	7.2	3
Los Angeles-Long Beach	3,437.4	7.5	2	53.6	7.1	1
Chicago	3,341.2	6.6	3	50.6	5.9	2
Houston	2,324.2	10.2	4	23.5	12.6	6
Seattle-Everett	2,299.4	29.6	5	22.0	18.4	8
Philadelphia	1,580.7	5.8	6	26.9	6.2	4
New York-New Jersey	1,524.5	4.3	7	19.7	2.6	10
San Jose	1,495.7	16.7	8	26.8	17.2	5
Dallas-Ft. Worth	1,306.4	9.2	9	21.0	8.1	9
Boston	1,192.3	9.7	10	23.1	9.0	7
United States	83,098.0	7.0	--	1,173.2	6.3	--

direct comparison of export employment for the metropolitan area over two recent years, but according to the *Survey of the Origin of Exports of Manufacturing Establishments in 1972*, the New York SMSA of that year (which included Nassau, Rockland, Suffolk, and Westchester counties) had export employment of 17,100 workers, or 2.3% of the total, compared to the 19,700 workers and 2.6% of the SMSA recorded in the *1976 Survey*.[4] For the state as a whole, the period 1972–76 saw exports increase 90% above 1972 values, three times the growth of output, and employment more than double from 41,000 to 84,000. (National growth rates were higher still.)

Value added by export manufacturing would probably be more indicative of the importance of the export sector than value of shipments or employment. No direct measures of this is available, but applying the percentage shares of three-digit SIC group values of shipments entering export trade to their values added produces an estimate of 4.5% of New York metropolitan value added entering direct exports. This is only slightly more than the 4.3% share of factory shipments.

Export composition

The manufactured exports of metropolitan New York are impressive in their range of commodities rather than in the dominance of any one group. Of a total value of shipments of $1,524 million in 1976, the largest single two-digit group, chemicals and allied products, accounted for $266 million, or 17.5% of the total, followed by miscellaneous manufacturing industries ($238 million, 15.6%) and printing and publishing ($213 million, 14.0%). Other categories accounting for $100 million (6.5%) or more included transportation equipment ($177 million), machinery except electric ($150 million) and electric and electronic equipment ($105 million). Apparel and other textile products, which accounted for 17.0% of metropolitan value added by manufacture and was exceeded only by printing and publishing (26.1% of value added), contributed only 3.2% of export shipments.

By contrast, the Chicago metropolitan area, whose value of export shipments was $3,341 million, exhibited a much greater concentration of export industries. Machinery except electric accounted for $1,260 million, or 37.7% of that center's exports, and electric and electronic equipment an additional $535 million, or 16.0%. In Houston, with export shipments at $2,324 million in 1976, chemicals and allied products ($794 million, 34.2%) and machinery except electric ($760 million, 32.7%) dominated the movement of local exports.

There are no published data available on the volume of New York City's export employment. The estimates for the city, based on the city's share of two-digit metropolitan employment in 1976, are probably fairly close to the mark, especially given the rather large shares of the city in the total employment of the larger export employment categories. Printing and publishing, electric and electronic equipment, chemicals and allied products each employed between 2,000 and 3,000 export workers, while the largest city employer, apparel and other textile products, contributed only some 500 export workers. Two-digit categories, however, tend to aggregate industries with many dissimilarities in production and supply functions and in markets. Three-digit levels are much closer to the homogeneous aggregates

TABLE 2

TOTAL AND EXPORT-RELATED EMPLOYMENT FOR NEW YORK REGION—TWO-DIGIT SIC—1976 (thousands)

SIC		Total Employment			Export-Related Employment	
		SMSA	N.Y.C.	Percentage N.Y.C. of SMSA	SMSA	N.Y.C.
20	Food & kindred products	35.4	33.7	95.2	0.5	0.5
22	Textile mill products	29.5	26.4	89.5	0.1	0.1
23	Apparel, other textile products	171.3	154.3	90.1	0.6	0.5
24	Lumber & wood products	4.9	3.6	73.5	0.1	0.1
25	Furniture & fixtures	11.3	10.8	95.6	0.1	0.1
26	Paper & allied products	21.9	17.6	80.4	0.2	0.1
27	Printing & publishing	114.7	90.1	78.6	3.7	2.9
28	Chemicals, allied products	29.7	27.0	90.9	2.5	2.3
30	Rubber, misc. plastic products	16.5	8.5	51.5	0.2	0.1
31	Leather, leather products	19.1	15.2	79.6	n.a.	n.a.
32	Stone, clay, glass products	8.3	4.8	57.8	0.1	0.1
33	Primary metal industries	12.6	8.3	65.9	0.4	0.3
34	Fabricated metal products	34.6	23.7	68.5	1.1	0.8
35	Machinery, except electric	25.4	16.3	64.2	2.7	1.7
36	Electric, electronic equipment	34.9	30.5	87.4	3.0	2.6
37	Transportation equipment	11.0	6.3	57.3	0.6	0.3
38	Instruments, related products	22.2	13.5	60.8	2.5	1.5
39	Miscellaneous manufacturing industries	47.1	46.3	98.3	1.0	1.0
	Totals	650.4	536.9	82.5	19.4*	15.0*

*Tentative

characteristic of individual industries, while more detailed disaggregation leads to excessive "splintering" of categories and easy cross-overs of establishments from one category to another.[5]

There were 27 three-digit SIC categories in which metropolitan New York's share of export values exceeded its average 1.83% of the nation's exports. Those whose shares exceeded 5% of the nation's exports are recorded in Table 3. They are very much geared to consumer markets, especially nondurables, and only 4 of the 14 industries recorded export shipments in excess of $100 million. The value of the largest category, jewelry, silver, and plated ware, was significantly inflated by the high prices recorded for gold and other precious metals, but in this category, and that of books metropolitan New York accounted for nearly half of the nation's exports. Employment shares were less impressive. Altogether, the 14 leading export specializations of metropolitan New York employed some 6,300 workers about half of whom worked in the city.

A more informative view of important export groups is provided by those metropolitan exports that made the largest contributions to the value of export shipments and employment. About half of the value of export shipments out of metropolitan New York were accounted for by ten three-digit SIC categories. These same groups accounted for 46% of export-related employment in 1976 (Table 4). Jewelry, silver, and plated ware (SIC 391) and books (SIC 273) were followed by soaps, cleaners, toilet goods (SIC 284), and drugs (SIC 283), each with export shipments approaching $100 million or more. The other leading categories, largely specialized equipment and machinery of different types, had export sales in each group of some $30 million–$40 million. As expected, employment levels were quite modest, ranging from 2,100 (SIC 273) to 300 (SIC 391).

Probably as a result of foreign export competition and other factors, some of the larger traditional New York industries, such as the garment trades, are not found among these export leaders. Indeed, a food products industry (miscellaneous foods, kindred products, SIC 209) appears only in fourteenth rank, and an apparel-related group (miscellaneous fabricated textile mill products, SIC 239) in seventeenth rank, with export shipments of $14.0 million and $12.3 million respectively. The region's leading exports include commodities that are among the fastest growing categories in U.S. export trade, such as electronic equipment components, communications equipment, and measurement and control instruments. The rapid growth of activities that place a premium on efficient information is clearly reflected in the expansion of these industries.

Based on the city's share of three-digit SIC-groups employment, there appear to be some 5,600 jobs in the city in export-related work in the ten leading export groups. This indicates that the city export jobs are slightly less concentrated in these groups as a whole than in the smaller export industries. Jewelry exports (SIC 391), and exports of soaps (SIC 284) and communication equipment (SIC 366), are probably almost entirely city-based, although the largest export employer is books (SIC 273), with 1,400 of its metropolitan export employment of 2,100 located in city establishments.

TABLE 3
EXPORT SPECIALIZATIONS OF METROPOLITAN NEW YORK, THREE-DIGIT SIC, 1976

		Value of Export Shipments		Export Employment	
SIC	Industry	Million Dollars	Percentage of U.S.	Thousands	Percentage of U.S.
273	Books	139.7	48.97	2.1	43.75
391	Jewelry, silver & plated ware	208.1	48.34	0.3	10.0
317	Women's handbags & purses	1.5	20.00	n.a.	n.a.
205	Bakery products	2.3	16.19	n.a.	n.a.
238	Misc. apparel & accessories	3.9	14.55	0.1	10.0
234	Women's & children's undergarments	7.9	13.69	0.1	9.1
396	Costume jewelry & notions	7.2	11.59	0.2	8.3
284	Soaps, cleansers, toilet goods	125.7	8.77	0.9	7.89
283	Drugs	93.4	8.14	1.0	7.63
275	Commercial printing	9.4	8.09	0.2	7.69
384	Medical instruments & supplies	40.5	7.87	1.2	9.76
208	Beverages	13.8	7.80	0.1	6.20
327	Concrete, gypsum & plaster products	2.4	7.14	n.a.	n.a.
395	Pens, office & art goods	6.3	5.59	0.1	3.70

TABLE 4

LEADING NEW YORK CITY MANUFACTURING EXPORTS, THREE-DIGIT SIC, 1976

		Value of Export Shipments - SMSA				Export Employment SMSA		NYC
SIC	Industry	Million Dollars	Percentage of Industry Shipments	Rank	Thousands	Percentage of Industry Employment		Thousands
391	Jewelry, silver & plated ware	208.1	21.7	1	0.3	2.5		0.3
273	Books	139.7	7.9	2	2.1	9.9		1.4
284	Soaps, cleaners, toilet goods	125.7	10.9	3	0.9	2.2		0.9
283	Drugs	93.4	10.0	4	1.0	9.9		0.5
384	Medical instruments & supplies	40.5	10.7	5	1.2	17.9		0.5
366	Communication equipment	36.0	14.2	6	0.7	11.9		0.7
349	Misc. fabricated metal products	35.9	9.4	7	0.5	6.0		0.2
355	Special industry machines	30.5	16.7	8	0.6	13.3		0.4
382	Measuring, controlling devices	30.2	17.7	9	0.6	14.6		0.1
367	Electronic components, accessories	27.4	20.3	10	1.1	22.0		0.6

A distinguishing feature of the foreign commodity trade of a modern industrial economy is the large volume of intra-industry exchanges that occur between countries. Many American industries both export and import similar commodities at the same time. The share of intra-industry trade for the United States in 1967 amounted to half of the nation's total trade, and commodities with above-average intra-industry shares included several exported by New York metropolitan and city economies — jewelry and related wares (87% intra-industry trade); printed matter (54%); scientific, medical, optical, measurement, and control instruments (54%); telecommunications apparatus (94%); miscellaneous metal manufacturers (76%).[6] Several factors give rise to this phenomenon of countries both exporting and importing products of the same industries. They include seasonal differences in production schedules, differences in quality and markets, specialization in long production runs of different models, price and exchange-rate changes during a given time period, technological developments and products cycle overlaps, and government intervention, among others.[7] One of these factors — changes in exchange rates — not only affects all traded commodities but can shift products from export to import status (and, of course, the reverse) in a matter of months.

It has been observed that the larger the community the larger is the share of its output allocated to local markets. Using as a rough indicator of nonbasic activities the "minimum complement" approach of Ullman and Dacey,[8] it may be estimated that some 10% of the city's total employment is in local-market manufacturing. With some 16% of employees working in manufacturing for local and nonlocal markets, about 200,000 factory workers are therefore working for non-New Yorkers. The 12,000–15,000 who were export-related workers in 1976 were 6%–8% of this nonlocal factory employment (which could be increased to 10%–13% if indirect exports were included). Undoubtedly, the extensive nature of the local market encourages a very wide range of local manufactures for which outside markets are of secondary importance.

Characteristics of export industries

New York's export industries have been shaped by an environment shared with the industrial activities of the city as a whole. This has been documented elsewhere, and only two or three aspects of this environment are singled out for brief comment. The connections between industrial milieu and foreign-export activities are also complicated by the open nature of the system, with its sensitivity to developments abroad as well as at home affecting the many components of a mature yet changing trading economy.

New York has long been and still is a relatively high fuel-cost region. Unit costs of industrially purchased fuels and electric energy in 1976 for metropolitan New York averaged 40.9% above those for the country as a whole, and each of the 17 two-digit SIC manufacturing groups for which local fuel costs are published paid more than the national average for fuel. The differential was considerably greater when compared with many other manufacturing centers. For this and other reasons, the New York region has few metal industries or other natural-resource-oriented industries, some of which rank high in national export trade. This also has important implications for industrial structure and the substitutability of labor skills and other nonmachine inputs in other activities.

The larger American cities, and especially New York City, have been the traditional centers of invention and innovation. In recent years, however, innovative capabilities have been distributed more widely to other centers, and in a broader context, from the old innovation hearth around the North Atlantic to other parts of the globe. The increasing association of innovation with the R&D work of the larger corporations and of government, and the growth of multinational corporations (MNCs) — American, European, and Japanese especially — have resulted in a reduction of the role of technological exports from New York, and seem likely to displace the United States as innovation leader.

Perhaps one of the most pervasive developments for New York City has been the rise of nonmarket employment. As Bacon and Eltis point out, the city market sector employment fell from 3.13 million in 1960 to 2.66 million in 1976, while nonmarket jobs rose from 408,000 to 532,000.[9] High taxation and high public expenditures may involve a proliferation of administrative expenditures rather than the output of more public goods, and the authors hold that in many ways the economy of New York City resembles that of the United Kingdom rather than the United States. Should this be the case, then there are certain very basic issues that deserve much closer scrutiny. If the city government can neither cut taxes not raise its own expenditures, then economic expansion may require a cut in imports (undesirable) or a growth in exports. As there is no New York City dollar that can be devalued or depreciated, this is not readily achieved. The city has a number of elitist industries whose output is destined for high-income markets and whose growth is associated with rising living standards internationally. Manufacturing, moreover, is by no means the only source of the New York region's exports to the nation as a whole or abroad, and despite different opinions on the efficacy of the nonmanufacturing market-sector growth, tourism and the plethora of other services in the city are major sources of external earnings (and competition for market jobs).

A simplified view of the structure of the New York region's export industries is presented in Table 5, which takes its cue from the relative importance of exports in each of the 19 leading export-share industries in the New York – New Jersey SMSA (all those whose export share in 1976 was above the average of 4.3% of factory shipments). The table shows for each industry exports as a percentage of shipments for the United States, the New York – New Jersey SMSA, and for New York City. Industry labor coefficients, capital intensity, and scale indexes are also included for each of the three areas. The data deserve a far more thorough analysis than given here but tend to support the broad image of the city's manufacturing economy as portrayed in the work of others. Sources for the table are the *Annual Survey of Manufactures, 1975-1976,* and the *1972 Census of Manufactures.*

Exports' share in total shipments

The 19 industries export shares in metropolitan New York shipments range from a high of 21.7% for jewelry (SIC 391) to a low of 5.2% for industrial organic chemicals (SIC 286). They include, as well, in order of descending share: electronic components (SIC 367), measuring and controlling devices (SIC 382), special industry machinery (SIC 355), electrical industry apparatus (SIC 362), communication equipment (SIC 366), soaps, cleaners, and toilet goods (SIC 284), medical instruments and supplies (SIC 384), drugs (SIC 283), miscellaneous chemical products (SIC 289), office and computer machines (SIC 357), miscellaneous fabricated metal products (SIC 349), books (SIC 273), refrigeration and service machinery (SIC 358), cutlery, hand tools and hardware (SIC 342), miscellaneous electrical equipment and supplies (SIC 364), pens, office and art goods (SIC 395), metal-working machinery (SIC 354).

Only in the jewelry, communication equipment, medical instruments, soaps, drugs, miscellaneous fabricated metal products industries, and books was the metropolitan share of exports larger than that for the nation, and, of course, national industries with still larger export shares do not appear on this table. The data for New York City were derived using the estimated share of export *employment* and this results in a different ordering than would otherwise appear, notably the exclusion of jewelry from first place. Electronic components, medical instruments, electrical industry apparatus, measuring and controlling devices, office and computer machines, communication equipment, special industry machinery, jewelry and drugs, each had 10.0% – 21.4% of employment in exports.

Labor coefficients

The values for the individual labor coefficients were obtained by taking the share of payroll expenses to value added in 1976 for the United States and the New York – New Jersey SMSA and from the *1972 Census of Manufactures* for whatever borough data were published for New Yok City. Perhaps the most noteworthy feature is the increase in the labor coefficeint for the individual industries as one goes from the nation to the New York – New Jersey SMSA to the city. This occurs in twelve of the seventeen industries for which city data are available. The reverse situation does not occur, and the exceptions are jewelry, electronic components, miscellaneous fabricated metal products, books, and miscellaneous electrical equipment and supplies. The city labor coefficients are highest in communication equipment (.667), electrical industry apparatus (.600), special industry machinery (.582), metal working machinery (.570), refrigeration and service machinery (.561), and electronic components and accessories, measuring and controlling devices, miscellaneous fabricated metal products, pens, office and art goods, and industrial organic chemicals, each of which has a labor coefficient above .500. Low labor coefficients are found in books (.263) and soaps, cleaners, and toilet goods (.291). City labor coeffcents are typically in the order of 15% to 30% above the national level with the exception of industrial inorganic chemicals where the coefficient approaches twice the national level. Only in the cases of books, miscellaneous electrical equipment, and jewelry are the national labor coefficients larger than the city's.

Capital intensity

As capital investment is typically quite volatile year-to-year, the index of capital

TABLE 5
STRUCTURE OF NEW YORK REGION EXPORT INDUSTRIES, THREE-DIGIT SIC, 1976*

SIC	Percentage of Exports as Total Shipments			Labor Coefficient			Capital Intensity			Scale Index		
	U.S.	NYM	NYC**	US	NYM	NYC	US	NYM	NYC	US	NYM	NYC
391	16.0	21.7	10.0	.485	.455	.461	.041	.058	.021	0.37	0.27	0.26
367	23.3	20.3	21.4	.497	.573	.542	.078	.037	.058	1.85	0.62	0.68
382	24.7	17.7	13.4	.512	.512	.538	.037	.016	.054	1.69	0.43	0.62
355	27.6	16.7	11.1	.513	.512	.582	.040	.040	.025	1.01	0.41	0.36
362	24.3	14.8	14.4	.465	.564	.600	.043	.042	.015	2.13	0.89	0.41
366	8.4	14.2	11.9	.519	.617	.667	.040	.045	.047	4.28	2.25	1.43
284	9.9	10.9	9.2	.167	.180	.291	.032	.025	.038	2.41	1.51	0.63
384	10.7	10.7	16.1	.422	.442	.463	.054	.053	.038	1.01	0.76	0.51
283	8.8	10.0	10.0	.238	.232	n.a.	.051	.042	n.a.	5.69	5.70	n.a.
289	12.4	9.8	8.5	.313	.396	.419	.093	.058	.034	0.85	0.45	0.45
357	20.4	9.7	13.2	.404	.435	n.a.	.054	.018	n.a.	4.93	1.39	n.a.
349	7.2	9.4	6.9	.464	.441	.512	.053	.053	.039	0.82	0.42	0.43
273	5.4	7.9	9.8	.344	.253	.263	.038	.020	.028	1.33	2.09	2.32
358	9.9	7.2	3.7	.413	.611	.561	.035	.030	.039	2.51	0.61	0.82
342	6.1	6.2	5.7	.423	.466	.473	.050	.033	.048	1.71	0.69	0.60
369	12.2	5.8	6.7	.434	.454	.404	.056	.042	.028	1.51	0.81	0.54
395	8.7	5.4	7.1	.408	.439	.509	.055	.052	.017	0.58	0.44	0.34
354	11.4	5.3	6.9	.530	.551	.570	.044	.037	.049	0.51	0.17	0.20
286	9.8	5.2	4.0	.206	.315	.505	.212	.125	.029	7.34	1.25	2.06

*1972 data for Scale Index and most NYC data (see below).
**Total employment basis for NYC, not value of shipments.
NYM—New York-New Jersey SMSA
NYC—New York City

intensity for the nation and the metropolitan area was calculated using the mean of new capital expenditures 1975/76 as a proportion of 1976 value added for each of the nineteen industries. City data are based on the *1972 Census of Manufactures* tabulation of new investment in 1972 and value added that year. There is evidence of greater national capital intensity for a dozen of the 19 industries, when the United States is compared with the metropolitan area and another six instances in which the values are essentially the same. National capital-intensity indexes are approximately two to three times larger than the metropolitan area indexes in office and computer machinery, measuring and controlling devices, electronic components and accessories, books, and industrial organic chemicals. Only in the case of jewelry is the metropolitan index notably higher (by some 40% over the national level).

In eight of the industries, there is a decline in capital intensity going from the nation, to the metropolitan area, and then the city, and these eight do not all have their counterpart in the rising labor coefficients noted in the preceding section. In ten industries, especially industrial organic chemicals, electrical industry apparatus, pens, office and art goods, and miscellaneous chemical products, the city capital-intensity indexes are below, occasionally much below, the national levels, and only in one, measuring and controlling devices, is it appreciably higher.

Scale index

Intended to indicate the scale of operations by the average establishment, this index shows value added per establishment in millions of dollars using the *1972 Census of Manufactures* for all three areas. For 11 of the 17 industries with city data, there is evidence of a decline in the scale of operations going from national through metropolitan to city levels, confirming the general impression that city industries are typically smaller-scale operations (even if they also compete in foreign export markets). Only in the case of books is the order clearly reversed, and this industry is also the only one in which the city scale of operations is larger than the national counterpart. In view of the advantages of scale economies that assume such an important place in the explanation of competitive advantages, it is instructive to note that in a dozen of these industries, the typical city establishment operates at about one-third or less of the scale of its national counterpart as indicated by the simple scale index used (and this is two-thirds of the export sample). Clearly, scale economies are quite modest in these industries, or firms are on the upward portion of the long-run average cost curve, or other factors in trading patterns offset scale economies. It is tempting to consider the substitution of the city's pool of human capital for energy-intensive inanimate capital investments as a being among these ''other factors,'' but the evidence remains to be collected.

Export competitiveness

It has been observed, especially by Peter Gray,[10] that while the internationally traded commodity faces competition (and also assistance) from a number of different sources, most items can be grouped into a small number of classes according to their likely success and volatility in foreign markets. If one applies

Gray's approach to New York City's exports, it would seem that elements of monopoly or clear economies of locational concentration help materially in explaining the prominence of books, jewelry, and various chemical products in the city's exports and in the likely maintenance of overseas markets. Technological advantage, which may require renewing and marketing for long-term stability and growth, appears to be a prominent factor in many of the other industries, particularly special machinery and communications equipment, as well as in drugs and medical instruments. Both types of industries have a high probability of export success. At this date, the city's share of those exports facing highly elastic foreign supply curves (and which are therefore quite sensitive to foreign competition engendered by price changes and/or changes in exchange rates) is much more modest than its overall industrial structure would suggest.

Conclusion

It is traditional in ending a paper of this type to point out the numerous gaps in data, method, and coverage that remain to be filled at some future date. A simple listing of these would require another paper. One obvious aspect that deserves a least passing comment is the effect of the sheer size of local and national markets on the incentive to export. It is possible that potential exporters view foreign markets as environments posing so much greater problems that, with few exceptions, they offer limited enticements to the small industrialist. Exports may then become largely outlets for the disposal of merchandise that would be surplus on the domestic markets, and foreign markets rarely receive the attention given them by the exporters of other countries. If this is the case, then many of the assumptions implicit in this paper and others require careful reassessment.[11]

Notes

1. This spatial dimesion to price inflation is under current investigation by the author.
2. U.S. Department of Labor, Bureau of Labor Statistics, Middle Atlantic Regional Office, *Some Dimensions of the World Trade Impact on the New York Labor Market,* Regional Report 39, July 1974.
3. The New York-New Jersey SMSA includes the five city boroughs, Putnam, Rockland, and Westchester counties in New York State, and Bergen County, N.J.
4. Nassau and Suffolk counties had an estimated export employment of 6,000 in 1971 (see Note 2, *above*), and Rockland and Westchester counties had virtually no export employment then. An assumption of 15,000 employed in the city in 1976 would leave 19,700 minus 15,000, or 4,700 export workers in the SMSA outside the city. Putnam County had only 700 workers in 1977 in all manufacturing. Assuming little change in Rockland and Westchester export employment would leave some 4,500 for Bergen County (about 5% of total employment there). A city employment in exports of 12,000 would leave 7,700 for the non-city SMSA.
5. Herbert G. Grubel and P. J. Lloyd, *Intra-Industry Trade: The Theory and Measurement of International Trade in Differentiated Products* (New York: Wiley, 1975).
6. Ibid., Table 3–1.
7. Despite American imports of less expensive clothing from Hong Kong, for example, there appears to be a Hong Kong market for expensive clothes. On the other hand, the Panamanian clothing market appears to be dominated by cheap imports from the United States.
8. E. L. Ullman and M. F. Dacey, *The Economic Base of American Cities* (Seattle: University of Washington Press, 1969).
9. Robert Bacon and Walter Eltis, *Britain's Economic Problems: Too Few Producers* (New York: St. Martin's, 2d edition, 1978).

10. H. Peter Gray, *International Trade, Investments, and Payments* (Boston: Houghton Mifflin, 1979).

11. See, for example, Claus C. Sinai, "An Investigation of Selected Characteristics of Export-Participating Manufacturing Firms," D.B.A. Dissertation (Seattle: University of Washington, University Microfilms International, 1977).

6

NEW YORK CITY'S FINANCIAL INDUSTRY: JUST HOW CAPTIVE IS IT?

Thomas J. Spitznas

No one today will dispute the fact that whatever leadership New York City has lost over the past several decades, it retains the distinction of being the premier financial center of the United States, ranking along with London as a major international money center. The New York financial community remains viable despite periodic credit crunches, negotiated commissions, interest-rate ceilings, and a general attitude among New Yorkers, reflected by certain of its political representatives, that New York's financial institutions are fair game, second only to Westway. Even the city's flirtation with fiscal disaster in 1975, which was viewed at the time as a major threat to the local financial community, had no perceived impact on financial-sector growth in New York. If anything, the fiscal crisis demonstrated to the world just how effectively New York's private financial sector could respond to the plight of the local public sector.

Granted that when it comes to U.S. finance New York is king of the hill — but will it remain so in the foreseeable future? In my opinion, there is nothing in sight that will cause the rest of the world to change its *perception* of New York as our leading financial community notwithstanding the continued rise of the U.S. regional banks and regional exchanges and the rapidly growing demand for financial services outside the New York area. New York is where the top financial talent wants to be and where major innovations in finance take place, and I see nothing on the horizon to change this. In other words, barring a major unforeseen bank failure or scandal, the image of the New York financial community should remain solid for years to come.

Besides image, however, there is another side to the New York financial community. The financial industry also provides a large job and tax base to New York City and, as I shall argue later on, image and job growth need not necessarily go hand in hand. It is this aspect of the financial community that I would like to focus on.

Historical employment trends

During 1979, the standard industrial sector known as finance, insurance, and real estate (FIRE) employed 428,000 workers on average in New York City.[1] Stated differently, about one out of every six jobs in the New York City area is in the FIRE sector. If present trends continue, local employment in FIRE will surpass local employment in manufacturing before many years. However, it should be pointed out that financial-sector employment will eventually surpass manufacturing employment not because the anticipated employment trend in finance is so strong, but because the near-term prospects for manufacturing are so grim! As Table 1 demonstrates, the trend rate of growth in FIRE employment in New York City during the ten years 1969–79 was negative while the U.S. trend in FIRE employment was strongly positive. Even in the heyday of New York City financial employment — the 1964–69 period, when the go-go attitude on Wall Street fueled an unsustainable growth in local FIRE employment — the city's financial employment growth rate fell short of the national rate (Table 1).

Another perspective on the role of financial employment in New York City is shown in Table 2. Clearly, the New York FIRE sector, at just over 13% of total payroll employment, plays a relatively more important role in the local economy than is true for the United States in general, where FIRE makes up around only 5.5% of total employment. What is also apparent is that the FIRE share has been growing much more rapidly in New York than the FIRE share in the rest of the country. This was true even during the 1970s when U.S. FIRE employment growth clearly outstripped New York City FIRE growth.

Still another perspective is seen in Table 3, which shows the New York City FIRE employment share of U.S. FIRE employment, with the New York total employment share of U.S. total employment shown for comparison. Here we see that the New York City financial industry, as measured by number of employees, has been losing ground to the rest of the country, especially during the 1969–79 period.

TABLE 1
PERCENTAGE CHANGE IN FIRE EMPLOYMENT, N.Y.C. AND U.S.

1959–69	22.8	37.8
1959–64	3.9	14.2
1964–69	18.3	20.6
1969–79	−8.1	41.3
1969–74	−8.7	18.1
1974–79	0.7	19.7

SOURCE: U.S. Department of Labor.

TABLE 2
FIRE SHARE OF TOTAL EMPLOYMENT, N.Y.C. AND U.S.

	N.Y.C.	U.S.
1959	10.77%	4.79%
1964	11.06	4.99
1969	12.26	4.99
1974	12.34	5.30
1979	13.06	5.55
Change: 1959-69	1.49	0.20
1969-79	0.80	0.56

SOURCE: U.S. Department of Labor.

TABLE 3
N.Y.C. FIRE SHARE OF U.S. FIRE EMPLOYMENT

	FIRE[1]	Total[2]
1959	14.87%	6.60%
1964	13.53	6.11
1969	13.27	5.40
1974	10.25	4.40
1979	8.62	3.66
Change 1959-69	-1.60	-1.20
1969-79	-4.65	-1.74

SOURCE: U.S. Department of Labor

1. N.Y.C. FIRE employment as a percentage of U.S. FIRE employment.
2. N.Y.C. total employment as a percentage of U.S. employment.

From nearly 15% of the nation's employment in FIRE, the New York City share dropped to around 8.5% in 1979. Of course, total employment in New York City as a percentage of total U.S. employment also declined, but by a much smaller amount than the decline in New York FIRE as a percentage of U.S. FIRE (Table 3). What all of this means is that as a source of employment, the New York City financial industry can be viewed as growing in relative importance locally, but declining in relative importance nationally.

Breaking out the New York City FIRE sector into its component parts provides some further insight into local employment shifts. We found that employment in the banking and the insurance-agents and brokerage industries grew the fastest during the 1969–79 period, while employment in the security and commodity dealers, insurance carriers, and real estate industries registered the largest decline. Also noteworthy is the twenty-year rise in relative importance of the banking and securities industry — despite a major shakeout in the latter during 1969–74 — and the decline in relative importance of the real estate and insurance-carriers industries. The persistent decline in employment in real estate during the past several years is a good example of how one's perception of an industry's performance — in this case, fairly good — need not be in accord with employment trends in that industry — in this case, quite bad. The declining significance of employment in the insurance-carriers industry also appears to be somewhat at variance with perceptions, especially in view of the relatively rapid growth in the insurance-agents and brokers sector.

Another useful comparison is between FIRE employment growth in New York City and FIRE growth in the New York City suburban area.[2] Table 4 illustrates the rapid growth in FIRE employment in New York's suburbs, growth that continued

TABLE 4
PERCENTAGE CHANGE IN FIRE EMPLOYMENT IN THE N.Y.C. AREA

	N.Y.C. Area*	N.Y.C.	N.Y.C. Area Except N.Y.C.
1959-69	25.9	22.8	38.2
1959-64	6.5	3.9	16.8
1964-69	18.3	18.3	18.3
1969-79	1.1	-8.1	33.7
1969-74	-2.1	-8.7	21.0
1974-79	3.4	0.7	10.6

SOURCE: U.S. Department of Labor

*Includes New York City, Nassau, Suffolk, Westchester and Rockland counties and northeastern New Jersey.

unabated during the 1969–74 period when New York City FIRE employment declined drastically.

The rapid growth in suburban FIRE employment during 1969–74 at the same time that New York City FIRE employment declined implies that jobs in this sector were being shifted from the city to the suburbs. That was the period when banks and insurance companies took advantage of the fact that clerical wage scales in the suburbs were well below New York City scales. Rentals and other operational costs were lower, too, and thus prompted the location of computer and data-processing centers in the suburbs. The fact that during the 1974–79 period, suburban FIRE-employment growth slowed, while New York City FIRE-employment growth picked up may indicate that the shift to the suburbs is largely over.

Future employment trends

Future trends in New York City FIRE employment will depend on four basic forces: (1) the perception of New York City as a financial center, (2) the overall performance of the New York City economy, (3) political, institutional, and technological change, and (4) the cost of doing business in New York City. I have already discussed the perception factor at some length and will add only that I expect the continued favorable image of the New York financial community to draw more and more foreign banks to the city with some positive effect on FIRE employment. I expect the second force, the overall performance of the local economy, to exert a neutral impact on FIRE employment. The structural decline that gripped the New York economy beginning in 1970 is largely behind us, and I anticipate that the decade of the 1980s will be more favorable for the New York City economy than the 1970s. That is not to say that we will return to a 1960s environment. I can only envision a local economy that grows sideways in real terms over the next ten years, which means essentially no increase in real financial demand from consumers and local business sources.

The political, institutional, and technological forces likely to affect FIRE employment are more difficult to foresee. Here I must restrict the bulk of my comments to the two subsectors of finance I know best: banking and, to a lesser extent, insurance. These two sectors combined make up nearly 60% of New York City FIRE employment and, judging from recent past performance, are the two sectors with the most stable trends.

Taking the banking sector first, one must be careful to distinguish commercial banks from savings banks. There are substantial differences between the two, although recently enacted federal legislation will begin to blur the distinction somewhat. Savings-bank lending powers are so much more restricted by type and geography, thus savings-bank employment is more closely tied to the New York City economy — in particular, the residential mortgage market. Because of the unrealistically low state mortgage usury ceiling and the intense local competition for savings, the New York City thrift institutions were especially hard pressed during the recent tight-money period. Of course, the thrifts would like, and will probably get, some expanded lending powers. These measures, together with the removal of usuary ceilings, would provide some help for the local thrift industry, but my own feeling is that a substantially lower rate of inflation and, hence, level of interest rates, is the best cure for what ails the thrifts.

Commercial banks, too, face some of the same tight money problems encountered by savings banks — in particular, narrowing profit margins. However, with their broader lending powers, commercial banks are in a better position to protect their margins during periods of high interest rates. Consequently, I do not look for a major employment shakeout in the commercial banking sector as a result of the persistent U.S. inflation problem. Besides, the current emphasis on supply side economics, which was spawned by the inflation problem, could result in further legislation favorable to bank business lending and deposit gathering. However, the artifically low consumer-usury ceiling in New York will prompt New York banks to transfer some of their consumer-lending operations out of New York State to states with higher usury ceilings. The decision by Citibank to move its entire credit card operation to South Dakota may be just the tip of the iceberg.

In my opinion, the legislative change that could have the most significant impact on local banking employment during the 1980s is the enactment of national banking. It is extremely difficult to foresee whether New York City would be a net gainer or loser if out-of-state banks are permitted to branch in New York and New York banks are permitted to branch in other states. The prestige of a New York City address and the sheer size of the local market are bound to attract a disproportionate number of out-of-state banks to New York City. However, there is a counter trend among New York banks already under way which should be reinforced by national banking legislation, and that is the regionalization of the corporate or national lending function. For years, New York banks have been opening loan-production offices, international fund-gathering, and Edge Act facilities throughout the United States. This regionalization of lending makes sense on several counts: (1) it eliminates the cost of constantly shuttling lending officers between headquarters and the territory; (2) it permits a closer identification of lending personnel with the region; and (3) it allows for a better understanding of the territory by lending personnel. Whatever New York City gains directly from national banking could well be offset by the "put them in the field" movement among New York banks. My feeling, therefore, is that national banking legislation will have a neutral to slightly positive impact on local employment.

The other possible legal change which will have an impact on banking employment, in this case a positive one, is a change in regulations that would permit the establishment of international banking facilities, the so-called "free trade zone," in New York. Estimates of employment gains from a free trade zone in New York City range from 1,500 to 2,000 banking occupations alone. These estimates may be too high, but most agree that establishment of a banking free trade zone, which awaits final approval from the Federal Reserve Board, would go a long way toward enhancing the international image of New York as a financial center.

Technological change will also influence employment trends in banking. Most specialists in this area see a new wave of technology, which could slow the growth in clerical employment in banking. An obvious example is the cash machine which obviates the need for tellers. More important than the number of jobs involved is the fact that this new technology will require substantially different work skills than now possessed by the majority of New York City's clerical work force. Unless the city's public school system is able to reverse the downward trend in the quality of its product, a growing share of the new clerical openings in banking may have to be filled from outside the New York City labor force.

Turning to the insurance industry, the major forces which contributed to the downward trend in insurance employment were: (1) above-average worker productivity (the insurance industry was one of the first to make use of large-scale computers); (2) the dispersal of sales personnel to more lucrative markets; (3) relocation of computer facilites outside New York City; and (4) onerous taxes and regulations. It appears that insurance employment in New York City will continue to decline throughout the 1980s, although not as rapidly as during the past decade. Advances in computer automation will continue to lower demand for clerical personnel, which will only be offset by growth in underwriting, brokerage, and management functions.[3]

Recent relaxation in property-liability insurance regulations in New York State indicates that employment in this phase of the insurance industry is likely to expand in New York City during the 1980s. A good example of this is the legislation passed in 1978 creating a New York insurance "free zone" and a New York City exchange.[4] The insurance exchange, which only recently opened its doors, is expected to provide a sizable number of jobs by the end of the decade.

The final factor that I believe could have an important bearing on FIRE employment in New York City is the cost of doing business locally. For the financial industry, one of the major cost considerations is clerical wages. Several years ago, clerical wage levels in New York's suburbs were significantly below the city's. However, the city's sluggish economic performance throughout most of the 1970s served to hold down wage increases until today the wage cost differential has almost disappeared in Westchester County, N.Y. and in Fairfield County, Conn. With the escalating price of gasoline likely to slow labor force growth in the suburbs, New York City clerical wage rates could begin to fall below suburban rates before too long. However, as I mentioned earlier, changing technology will require different skills which, if not found in the New York worker, will tend to blunt any wage cost advantage that may accrue to the city during the 1980s.

Another major cost factor, which varies from one type of financial institution to another, is the state and local tax burden. Much has been written on this subject already, and I won't go into the details of the financial tax. However, I feel compelled to point out that the combined New York (state and city) tax burden on local commercial banks — nearly 26% — is the highest in the United States. Clearly, this and the state usury ceiling are the two biggest deterrents to bank expansion in New York City.

Summary and conclusion

1. In contrast to the positive image projected by the New York City financial community, the trend growth in the city's FIRE employment during the past decade was negative, while the trend in U.S. FIRE employment was strongly positive.

2. As a percentage of total New York City employment, the New York FIRE sector has been growing rapidly — more so than the growth in U.S. FIRE employment as a percentage of total U.S. employment. However, the New York City FIRE share of U.S. FIRE employment declined sharply over the past ten years, more so than the decline in local total employment relative to U.S. total employment.

3. Employment in the banking and the insurance-agent and brokerage industries grew the fastest during the 1969–79 period, while security and commodity-dealer, insurance-carrier and real estate employment declined the most.

4. New York suburban FIRE employment grew especially rapidly during 1969–74, and some of this growth was undoubtedly at the expense of New York City. The recent slowing of suburban FIRE growth and pick-up in New York City FIRE employment may indicate that the shift of financial-sector employment to the suburbs is largely over.

The image of New York City as the nation's leading financial center should remain intact for many years to come. However, this need not ensure adequate growth in local employment opportunities in finance, especially in the clerical positions. In addition to New York's image as a financial center, future growth in local FIRE employment will depend on the overall performance of the New York City economy; on political, institutional, and technological change; and on the cost of doing business in New York.

The expected overall performance of the New York Cty economy during the coming decade will probably exert a neutral impact on local FIRE employment.

The various political, institutional, and technological forces will exert a number of cross-currents, the net effect of which is difficult to foresee. Obviously, a number of national and state legislative changes are necessary to ensure the continued viability of our financial institutions, especially the thrifts. Some of this legislation appears forthcoming, but until it is well in place and until inflation is wound down to a much lower level, employment in thrift institutions will probably contract in New York City.

When enacted, national banking legislation will likely have a neutral to slightly positive impact on local employment — the decentralization effort among New York City banks, which is already under way, will act as at least a partial offset to the prospective inflow of out-of-state banks. However, establishment of a banking and an insurance "free trade zone," plus an insurance exchange in New York, will add a sizable number of local jobs by the end of the decade.

The impact of new technology, especially in the banking sector, may exert some negative impact on the overall level of clerical employment. However, the major impact of technology will be to change the composition of demand, which if not recognized quickly by those responsible for curriculum planning in New York City public schools, could result in a significant number of lost job opportunities for New Yorkers.

So just how captive is New York City's financial industry? There seems little doubt that major financial functions are here to stay and will probably grow somewhat in absolute importance. But it is not at all clear that the more labor-intensive support functions will grow in tandem. The technological revolution that is now taking place in the office sector will probably lead to declining job opportunities in most FIRE clerical functions, as well as produce major changes in the skill requirements for such jobs. Therefore, it is difficult to foresee an upward trend in employment in the New York City FIRE sector, and my guess is that by the end of the current decade, employment in this sector will be slightly below today's level.

Notes

1. This is the revised U.S. Department of Labor payroll estimate adjusted to the 1979 benchmark date. The FIRE category is made up of the subcategories: banking, security and commodity brokers, insurance carriers, insurance agents and brokers, real estate and combinations with insurance, etc., and credit agencies other than banks, building, and other investment companies.
2. In this case, the suburban area is defined as Nassau, Suffolk, Westchester, and Rockland counties in New York State and northeastern New Jersey.
3. See Janet S. Young, "New York's Insurance Industry: Perspective and Prospects," *Federal Reserve Bank of New York Quarterly Review,* Spring 1979, pp. 9– 19.
4. The "free zone" legislation authorizes certain qualifying insurance companies to write large-premium contracts that are exempt from state rate and policy filing requirements. The insurance exchange provides a marketplace for reinsuring large commerical risks, similar to Lloyd's of London.

7

THE COMMERCIAL PRINTING INDUSTRY: IS IT STILL MADE IN NEW YORK?

Emanuel Tobier and Mark A. Willis

It is not news that manufacturing in New York City has fallen almost uninterruptedly since 1950 (or that it may well decline still further in the future). But, until fairly recently, one particular line of blue-collar work, commercial printing, seemed relatively immune from this decline. Through the 1960s, this industry showed remarkable stability in terms of its local level of activity. The main reason for this seemed to be the symbiotic relationship with the city's growing white-collar sector which required that printers be located nearby.

In the first half of the 1970s, however, the bottom fell out of New York's commercial printing business. Employment dropped by almost one third; and though it stabilized toward the end of the decade, it is unlikely that such employment will soon return to anything resembling its earlier levels. An examination of the technological, market, and other forces that have been influencing the kinds of locational decisions made by printers shed much light on the changes in the so-called agglomeration (or external) economies, which have always been important in the development of New York City's economy. It also provides some insight into the general outlook for blue-collar work in New York.

The Census defines the commercial printing industry as those establishments that are primarily engaged in printing by letterpress, lithographic process, screen printing, engraving, and gravure. In New York City 92% of all employment in commercial printing involves letterpress and lithography (also called offset printing). A similar pattern prevails at the national level.

Commercial printing statistics, however, can be somewhat misleading since they do not include the many printers who work in establishments that are classified as part of other industrial categories. For example, shops that specialize in printing newspapers and periodicals for others are included within the commercial printing industry, but those that specialize in printing books for other are excluded, as are newspapers that do their own printing (which happens to be that industry's overwhelming practice). Moreover, many businesses now have in-house printing operations and handle much of what had previously shown up, statistically, as commercial printing work.

Market ties

A key characteristic of printing is that customer service is an important part of the product. One reason for this is that much of the work is done under very tight time constraints. For example, copy for lawyers' brief, financial offerings, concert programs, advertising campaigns, and the like often tends not to be prepared until right before the final printed product must be ready. Customer demands must often be met in a matter of hours. The commercial printer has to be practically around the corner from his customers to compete for this kind of work. For firms serving more than neighborhood businesses, these same pressures favor a central location.

Further reinforcing the need to locate near customers is the fact that printing is not generally an operation in which the producer makes a standard item and stockpiles it. Almost every printed product is a unique item, tailored to the detailed specifications of the individual customer. The printer frequently functions as the designer of the final product and the consultant on methods and materials. Therefore, unless the printing runs are long or the layout of the job has been standardized, it is important for the printer and customer to be close to each other to facilitate the required and nearly continual contact.

Analysis of the role of market ties becomes more complicated when, as is often the case in printing, the customer for the job is not the final user. For example, advertising firms may order and oversee the printing, but they actually serve only as brokers for their clients who often distribute the products widely across the country. A similar distinction can be made within the publishing industry between the companies that contract for the printing and the readers who ultimately "use" the newspapers, books, and periodicals. In these cases, if there is no large advantage for the printer to be near the customer, then it may locate near the user, at points with good transportation facilities, for example, so that the product can be shipped easily and at minimum cost.

Of course, if the customer and the user are in the same location, then it does not matter which of these two forces predominates. Newspapers, for example, are locally oriented both in their news-gathering and editing operations and in their distribution. Thus even if the printing could be physically separated from the editorial offices, it would have to remain in the vicinity to be near the readers. The exact location or locations would depend, of course, on the cost of transmitting the copy to the printing plants, cost variations within the local area of running a printing operation, and relative access to the distribution network.

However, in publishing, the customer and the user are usually located in different places. And since contact with the customer is not a major problem, it has little effect on the location of printing process. Thus, in this sector of the industry, printing plants are often located where labor and shipping costs of the books and periodicals can be minimized. For example, the several printing plants that turn out, in press runs of hundreds of thousands, Book-of-the-Month Club selections have little need to locate close to the editorial offices in midtown Manhattan. The company distrubutes its product nationally, and the cost of the printing process alone comprises a significant portion of the overall costs. Thus, while much of the editorial end of the book and magazine business is concentrated in New York City

— still the world's preeminent media capital — the printing end is decidedly not. In contrasting the situation in this industry with that for newspapers, it should be noted that production workers comprise 60% of the city's newspaper employment compared to only 7% of the city's periodicals employment.

As for the commercial printing industry, different parts of it lie at various places along this spectrum from consumer to user orientation. Changes over time in the relative importance of these different submarkets and in their positions along this spectrum have had a major impact on the commercial printing industry in New York City.

Employment trends in the Sixties

Table 1 records the long-term employment trends that characterized the commercial printing industry between 1959 and 1970 both nationally and within the New York metropolitan region. As shown here, printing employment in the United States increased by 23% during this period, from 285,500 to 350,500. For the region as a whole, however, the absolute level of printing employment showed little change, but because there was little growth, the region's share of the nation's printing employment fell from 16% to 13%, reflecting the fact that the region's population and economic base were growing less rapidly than the rest of the country. As migration and differential rates of economic and population growth caused a redistribution of markets in this country, some of the printing industry apparently followed along.

Despite its smaller share, the region still demonstrated an above-average attraction for the nation's commercial printing industry. As of 1970, the region's 13% share of the nation's commercial printing employment compared favorably with its 7.7% of the nation's population and 8% of all nonagricultural employment. At the time, the conventional (and undoubtedly correct) explanation given for the indus-

TABLE 1
TRENDS IN COMMERCIAL PRINTING EMPLOYMENT, 1959-77 (in thousands)

New York Region	1959	1965	1970	1975	1977
New York City	31.9	31.1	30.1	20.9	21.2
Manhattan	n.a.	24.2	23.6	16.8	16.2
Rest of city	n.a.	6.9	6.5	4.1	5.0
Rest of NY region	14.5	16.3	16.8	16.3	17.7
Totals	46.4	47.4	46.9	37.2	38.9
U.S.	285.5	309.6	350.5	350.0	358.0

SOURCE: County Business Patterns.

try's continuing degree of relative concentration within the region was the need for these printers to remain physically close to certain significant markets or, more accurately, to the originators and conceptualizers of printed material who themselves continued to be located within the region and, more particularly, within Manhattan's Central Business District (CBD).

Furthermore, as of 1970, over 50% of the region's printing employment was located within Manhattan (most of it in the area south of 61st Street), compared to 30% of the region's overall employment. Between 1959 and 1970 there was relatively little internal redistribution of commercial printing employment within the region away from Manhattan. The percentage had fallen slightly, during this period, despite the more rapid growth of population and employment outside of the city. While printing employment in the rest of the New York metropolitan region barely grew from 14,500 to 16,800, printing employment in New York City sagged only slightly from 31,900 to 30,100.

One reason for this stable pattern is that an increasing proportion of the printing work being done within the city — and notably within Manhattan — was in response to the demands generated by the city's growing white-collar sector and particularly by the elite portion of that group which continued to locate inside the CBD.

Another reason is that New York City printing firms could not suburbanize like many of their customers because of their small size and high degree of specialization. They found it necessary to stick close to each other in order to share some essential product or service — so called "external economies" — that the individual firm could not economically purchase or provide on its own. The outsider could provide services economically because it catered to many firms, each needing only a small fraction of its capacity.

In the case of the commercial printing firms in New York City, the utilization of external economies manifested itself in the small army of neighboring printing trade firms that offer typesetting, engraving and plate printing, photo engraving, and electro and stereotyping services. Therefore, it is not surprising that the ratio of printing trade employees in New York City was (and for that matter remains) much higher in relation to employment in the commercial printing sector than elsewhere in the country (or in the New York region) indicating the environment rich in related specialist firms that New York City, and particularly Manhattan, presented to the commercial printing sector. By locating in Manhattan, the typical commercial printer placed himself in a position from which he could gain easy access and be accessible to labor, suppliers, and other firms that engage in printing lines complementing his own. So strong were these needs — together with the basic requirement of being close to their customers — that a high proportion of the firms involved were apparently willing to pay higher rents, taxes, and other costs in order to be in Manhattan.

Declining in the Seventies

Between 1970 and 1975, however, the commercial printing industry in the New

York region declined at a very rapid rate. Employment fell from 46,900 to 37,200. As the nation's employment in this industry stabilized, the region's share declined sharply, falling to only about 10% by 1975. Although this was still above its share of the nation's total population or of its share of total nonagricultural employment, it was still a considerable drop.

Most of this decline, moreover, was concentrated in New York City. Indeed, the city's commercial printing employment fell from 30,100 to 20,900 while printing employment in the rest of the region slipped only slightly from 16,800 to 16,300. In Manhattan alone, printing employment fell from 23,600 to 16,800. The rate of decline in New York City's printing employment was faster than in the city's overall manufacturing employment, a strange fate for an industry that superficially seemed so closely tied to the city's white-collar sector. This sector, while experiencing its own troubles still showed a good deal of resilience.

Since 1975, however, there has been a modest revival of the printing industry within both the New York region and the central city, as reflected in its employment totals. Still, because the national printing employment total has grown at an even faster rate, the region's and the city's shares have continued to drop; it is now below 10% and 5% respectively.

But the optimism this recent improvement engenders should be tempered. It may be that what is happening is the spillover effect of of the rapid growth of printing employment nationwide. As demand has expanded, printing plants elsewhere may have begun to strain against their capacity limits. How permanent these gains in commercial printing in New York City will be depends on its competitive position. To gain a sense of what the future holds, it is necessary to separate out the forces that caused the debacle of the early 1970s.

Technological change

Although the dispersion of its customers would have produced some contraction in the ranks of New York's commercial printers, it was the cumulative effects of technological advances made over the previous decade that brought the fall. The printing industry in this country has been revolutionized; the traditional pattern of operation and locational have been changed. This has weakened the ties that bound a large proportion of the printing industry to locations within New York City (and even the region as a whole) and accelerated the exodus.

To understand the forces of decline in New York's printing industry, it is necessary to examine some of the more important technological innovations. The major advancements have been in lithographic printing, which has now replaced letterpress as the dominant printing method. The share of employment by offset printers has increased nationally from 30% in 1959 to 51% by 1979. In fact, over this period letterpress employment fell by over 10% nationally, despite the significant growth in overall employment within the commercial printing industry. Similar trends have affected the composition of commercial printing employment within the New York region and in New York City.

The basic reason for this switch reflects the fundamental characteristics of the offset printing process which favors its use over letterpress. Offset printing does not require the casting of heavy lead slugs of type from molten lead. Instead of printing the image by inking a raised surface, the offset process reproduces the image with thin metal plates which are sensitized by exposure through photographic negatives and which maintain the image through a delicate balance of ink and water. The plates are easy to handle and can be bent around a cylinder on the press to print image after image in a continuous motion. So superior has the offset process become, in the course of striking improvements in its technology in the last decade or so, that little new letterpress equipment continues to be made. Existing letterpress machinery is often kept going only through cannibalization of older equipment for spare parts.

When offset technology first came into vogue after World War II, it offered little advantage over letterpress in terms of equipment size for comparable output. The larger versions of these offset presses could print a number of colors on one pass-through, but they were very large and heavy, and thus not well-suited for the average Manhattan loft. But newer lines of offset equipment are more lightweight and flexible, and so are much easier to accommodate within the typical New York loft structure. However, in addition to being smaller, they have become immeasurably more productive. Printing firms have therefore been able to increase their output greatly without increasing either their employment or need for production space. But, with greater productivity, the firms with a fair amount of medium to long run jobs needs to stock large paper inventories, taking up a much larger area compared to press space than was the case in the past. Therefore, although the average number number of employees per firm has barely increased over the last few decades, the space required for the average firm has grown. Only firms involved in short-run work, for which press preparation consumes a significant part of the day, have paper-handling and storage requirements similar to those of the printers in the past. For printers now processing large volumes of paper, ease of access had become an ever more important factor in the selection of a location.

The technical advances in offset equipment have also made it possible to achieve a higher quality of work with a less skilled work force. Nowadays, almost anyone can learn how to run a small one-color press fairly quickly and still produce acceptable results. Even making the plates for the presses has been greatly simplified by the introduction of machines that make a plate from camera-ready copy in one step. Larger presses, and, in particular, web presses with multiple printing heads, can now be operated with fewer and less skilled personnel than would have been the case just a few years ago. The need for longer apprenticeships has passed, and so the pool of suitable labor has been significantly enlarged.

Offset has also made it progressively easier to replicate at the press stage exactly what the customer wants and has approved at the proof stage. The extent of personal contact required between printer and customer has been reduced because proofs can be easily made and sent through the mails. Since the same negative is used to make both the proof and the printing plate, the room for error in going from one stage to the next has also been reduced substantially. Furthermore, improvements in the standarization of inks and of available control systems have greatly enhanced the pressman's ability to achieve the effects sought by the customer. With less need for consultation, there is less need for physical proximity. And, in those cases in which a separate firm handles all the work through the proof stage, the customer may not even have to see the printer or supervise the press run in order to feel confident that the final product will closely match the proof.

Going it alone

The proliferation of in-house printing departments in large corporations has also broken the need for close proximity between printers and their customers. With the simplification of the printing process and the development of highly productive but relatively small and quiet printing presses, it has become much simpler to set up and operate a printing shop. Many companies with large printing needs can easily justify the investment. These in-house plants are often able to handle a large amount of the work previously sent out. Achievement of acceptable quality is not difficult for one-color work on standard-sized paper, and most of these plants can do short-to medium-run jobs at costs comparable to or cheaper than those of commercial printers. Furthermore, even without the cost savings, companies gain by having their own printing capability because it allows them to set their own priorities for rush jobs and maintain confidentiality when desired. Therefore, to some extent, the loss in printing employment, as recorded in the official statistics over the past few years, has been more apparent than real as many New York-based headquarters offices have begun to satisfy part of their printing requirements internally.

With more companies doing their own rush and short-run work, the proximity of the commercial printer becomes a less important factor in the competition for customers. Except when the in-house plant is filled to capacity, the bulk of work sent out to commercial printers is likely to consist mainly of longer runs and complicated work that can be done more cheaply on specialized presses. For these types of jobs, the cost of a few trips back and forth between printer and customer can be quite minor compared to the overall costs of the work.

The changing technology has also reduced the need for printers to group around other firms providing specialized services to the industry. For example, with offset printing, there is no need to be concerned about transporting heavy trays to type from the typesetter to the printer. Moreover, the lower cost, smaller size, and compatibility of the new technology with an office environment have made it possible for many more printers (and even their customers) to have their own phototypesetting machines. And these machines require much lower skill to operate than the old linotype machines.

The same trends have affected the procurement of other printing services which, because of recent innovations, printers are now more often able to perform economically for themselves. In such cases there is no need for printers to locate near each other to share outside services. In fact, the technological advances have made it possible to set type in one, say downtown, location and print elsewhere, in the suburbs or even in some other city, for example, with little risk of error.

As the importance of agglomeration has faded, the advantages of locating printing operation outside the CBD have increased. Although printers traditionally thrived in the city's multi-level loft buildings, the internalization of printing services and the vast increases in the paper consumed per hour by printing presses have made this industry more like other manufacturing operations, functioning best when organized on one level. It has also become more important to have easy access for the trailer loads of paper regularly consumed even by medium-size operations. Multilevel lofts available downtown just don't fill the bill.

The outlook

The future of the commercial printing industry in New York City depends on four factors: the extent to which the industry has adjusted to previous changes in technology and in the location of customer; the impact of innovation on the overall demand for the services of commercial printers; the future growth of New York City; and any relative changes in the costs of printing operations in New York City or other regional locations.

There is some evidence to suggest that the adjustment to changes in technology and customer location is essentially over. After falling off sharply in the early 1970s, commercial printing employment in New York City has stabilized. This fact, combined with the fall in New York's share of national printing employment to a level more closely approximating its share of total business activity, suggests that the printing still done in the region is closely tied to local markets and so is unlikely to be lost in the future to printers outside the region. On the other hand, more firms might expand their own in-house operations.

Moreover, those product markets in which New York City printers still retain a disproportionate share nationally are the ones that are particularly concentrated here. Two important examples are the financial-legal and advertising markets. Nationally, approximately one-quarter of the sales of commercial printing firms are derived from these two sources of demand (with advertising printing being approximately five times as important as a source of revenue). For the New York metropolitan region, the comparable figure is in the 40%-45% range with the relative importance of the two markets being about the same as they are nationally. A reasonable estimate for the Manhattan CBD is over 75%, with financial and legal printing accounting for a higher share than nationally or regionally and advertising printing accounting for a considerably smaller share.

The possibility that major innovations will decrease the size of the overall market for commercial printers does exist, but is slight. Although tremendous advances have been made in the electronic transfer of information, it does not appear that these forms of communication will replace the printed page. In fact, the information explosion resulting from more extensive use of computers has undoubtedly increased the amount of printed material produced each year.

The third major factor that could affect the size of the printing industry in New York would be a further dispersal of its customers across the country. Although New York's share of national output may continue to fall in all sectors, it seems unlikely that there will be periods in which local employment falls as precipitously in a relatively short period as it did between 1969 and 1975. Some sectors may even resume moderate upward growth as the city's overall competitive position improves. In particular, there is no reason to think that New York's role as a major financial, legal, and advertising center will be lost. Many of those large corporations that move their headquarters operations out have retained close ties with New York's business services sector.

Relative operating costs

Perhaps the most important determinant of the future of commercial printing in the New York area will be any changes in the relative cost of operating in the city, in the suburbs, and elsewhere in the country. Those firms left in the region remain mainly because they need to be here in order to provide the level of service their customers require. There do not appear to be any changes on the horizon that will loosen these ties significantly enough for other cost considerations to become paramount. However, there are forces that could affect the choice between a suburban and city location.

A major disadvantage to printing firms in New York City is the relatively high level of taxation relative to that in other parts of the region and nation. In addition to state taxes, the city imposes a 9% income tax on corporations, a 4% tax on unincorporated businesses, and a tax on commercial rents in addition to a property tax. Although the payments due under these taxes are deductible from taxable income for federal tax purposes and so cost a firm much less than the nominal tax rates would suggest (e.g., for a corporation paying at the maximum federal rate, the net cost equals only 54% of the amount paid to the local jurisdiction), these costs come off the top. Therefore, only if printers can earn higher profits before taxes by virtue of a New York City location, will they stop looking to move outside the city as their leases expire and they need more room to expand.

Recently, the relative tax disadvantages of a New York location have decreased. The city and state have reduced taxes from their fiscal-crisis highs. In contrast, New Jersey, which has previously benefited disproportionately from the suburbanization of printing plants, has raised its corporation tax from 7.5% to 9%. Furthermore, businesses in New York City are now eligible for a number of additional and expanded tax incentives. For example, the state now provides investment tax credits for new equipment. However, because of constraints imposed by the creation of Municipal Assistance Corporation, the city was not able to tamper directly with the sales tax and so only provides for the applicable sales taxes to be taken as a credit income tax. Even though they eventually get the money back, New York City companies are still at some disadvantage since they must raise additional capital to cover the cost of the sales tax, which still continues to be imposed at the time the investments are made.

One area of particular concern has been the continued conversion of loft space from manufacturing to residential use. The actual impact of this phenomenon, though, is hard to determine. While the supply of loft space in general and for manufacturing use in particular has clearly decreased, the demand for it has also fallen. Recent trends in rents do suggest that this market is now tightening. However, the amount of rent may not be a critical factor in the choice of a site. As noted earlier, there are many other factors (e.g., access and plant layout) that have drawn printers out of the city. As for those firms still left in the city, the advantages of proximity to customers and of space appropriate for small businesses may allow many of them to continue to compete successfully for the loft space that remains.

Regardless of demand, the amount of space available to manufacturing operations such as commercial printers in the CBD has been declining. This is part of the overall decline in CBD loft space; between 1959 and 1977, according to the city's Real Property Assessment Department, the number of Manhattan's loft buildings fell from 6,272 to 4,186, a 33% decline, mostly in its downtown area, with no comparable replacement construction. Much of this demolition has taken place in Lower Manhattan. In addition, there was a substantial conversion of loft space from manufacturing to nonmanufacturing purposes with virtually no movement in the other direction. Both of these processes are expected to continue.

The adequacy of existing space revolves around two considerations — one related to the movements of goods into and out of the building, the other to the characteristic of the space itself. Any shortcomings of existing space in both of these respects depends on any further developments within the industry that increase the average size of printing operations in terms of output (but not necessarily in terms of employment or number of presses). To handle this potential problem, some improvements may be necessary within the loft districts regarding egress and ingress, and the off-street loading facilities of existing buildings would need to be upgraded considerably, as would elevator capacity. The suitability of the space itself relates to such questions as the size of the individual floors, ceiling heights, and floor load capacities.

Since the weight and size of printing equipment is, if anything, falling, the main problem in the CBD will be the continued rarity of buildings with large areas per floor, e.g., those with lot coverage of 10,000 square feet or more.

On the other hand, small-scale printing firms — those employing fewer than 20 workers — can get by comfortably with 5,000 square feet or less per floor. These smaller firms may in fact find it easier to contract for the space they need in the city (although perhaps not in the CBD) than in the suburbs, since suburban industrial parks generally require tenants to take larger spaces. This advantage may bode well for the outer boroughs, since smaller firms are likely to prevail as the predominant force in the industry. In 1977, 82% of all printing firms both in the nation and in the New York region had fewer than 20 employees. Another 11% had between 20 and 99 workers and only 8% employed in excess of 100 employees.

The competitiveness of the city's outer boroughs as locations for printing operations may actually be improving. Wages and prices are now rising less rapidly in New York than in the rest of the nation, and the city is becoming much more aggressive in keeping manufacturing operations in the city. It may no longer be necessary for growing firms to move out in order to compete. Indeed, the number of large firms in the outer boroughs has increased.

In conclusion, the big losses in employment in the commercial printing industry in New York City and in the region are probably over, and the industry may even resume moderate growth in line with the local economy. It is unlikely, however, that printing will ever again become a leading growth sector. Nevertheless, printing will continue to be a significant employer of blue-collar workers and so provide an important source of upward mobility for the unskilled, who can easily qualify for entry-level jobs. The New York printing industry, particularly if the in-house operations are included — as they should be — is sure to remain a significant sector in the local economy and the largest single concentration of printing services in the nation for many years to come.

8

NEW YORK CITY'S COMPETITIVE POSITION: A REVIEW OF SELECTED MANUFACTURING AND SERVICE INDUSTRIES

Pearl Kamer and Dennis Young

Between 1970 and 1977, New York City lost approximately 270,000 manufacturing jobs or about 30% of its 1970 manufacturing base. Employment losses affected virtually all industries, with 18 of the 20 major two-digit groupings posting employment losses of 20% or more during that period. The city's dominant manufacturing industries — apparel and printing and publishing — contracted by almost 100,000 jobs, thereby accounting for approximately one-third of the city's manufacturing losses. Statistics such as these raise serious questions as to the city's competitiveness for production-oriented manufacturing jobs and cast doubt upon the contention that industrial development is a viable economic strategy for New York City.

A number of recent studies have stressed the need to bolster New York's manufacturing base and to retain production jobs within the city. The Temporary Commission on City Finances, while recognizing that the transition from a manufacturing-oriented to a service-oriented economy is both inevitable and desirable, suggested that "an attempt must be made to retain . . . the city's manufacturing base [in order to] halt job losses, reduce attendant budgetary pressures, and provide employment and mobility opportunities to members of the resident labor force who cannot find employment opportunities in other areas of the city's economy."[1] The Port Authority of New York and New Jersey concluded that "the persistent severe loss in manufacturing in the Port District is at least partially responsible for the erosion of other sectors of the regional economy."[2] The Port Authority is committed to a program designed to retain industrial jobs and to expand the region's industrial base by creating a combination of physical, environmental, cost, and institutional advantages for incoming manufacturing firms. This program will entail a public investment of $500 million, which is expected to attract another $500 milliom in private investment, to support an additional 30,000 jobs within the region, and to generate an annual payroll of more than $300 million.

The success of this program hinges to a large extent on the city's current competitive position for production-oriented manufacturing jobs. This paper deals with this question. It also examines the recent growth of service jobs in New York and discusses service-industry employment as an alternative to industrial jobs.

New York's manufacturing sector: how competitive is it?

The impact of national growth patterns

Manufacturing activity in New York City has been constrained both by the concentration of employment in declining national market industries and by the general shift of manufacturing jobs from the northeastern and north central states to the West and South. In 1977, seven industries — food, textiles, apparel, printing and publishing, electrical equipment, fabricated metals, and miscellaneous manufacturing — accounted for two-thirds of New York City manufacturing jobs. Between 1970 and 1977, the city sustained substantial employment losses in each of them. Apparel, textiles, food, and electronic equipment, which accounted for 40% of New York City's manufacturing base in 1977, declined nationally as well.

The city's manufacturing woes have been compounded by the pronounced shift of manufacturing jobs from the northeastern and north central states to the West and South. Between 1970 and 1977, the Northeast lost almost 800,000 manufact-

TABLE 1

NATIONAL GROWTH PATTERNS IN N.Y.C. DOMINANT MANUFACTURING INDUSTRIES, 1970-77
(thousands of jobs)

SIC	Industry Description	N.Y.C. Employment 1977	Net Change 1970-77 N.Y.C.	Net Change 1970-77 U.S.	Percentage Change 1970-77 N.Y.C.	Percentage Change 1970-77 U.S.
20	Food & kindred prod.	25.8	- 23.9	- 97.4	-52	- 6
22	Textile mill prod.	24.2	- 7.4	- 64.6	-77	- 7
23	Apparel, other textiles	159.9	- 70.4	- 80.1	-31	- 6
27	Printing & publishing	99.3	- 27.7	+ 45.5	-22	+ 4
34	Fabricated metals	24.3	- 11.9	+163.1	-33	+12
36	Electric & electronic equipment	25.4	- 17.9	-170.3	-41	- 9
39	Misc. manufacturing industry	43.3	- 17.7	+ 18.2	-29	+ 4
	Totals	594.5	-269.3	-122.7	-31	*

SOURCE: County Business Patterns, New York, U.S. Summary, 1970, 1977.

*Less than 1%.

TABLE 2

INTERREGIONAL EMPLOYMENT SHIFTS IN N.Y.C. DOMINANT
MANUFACTURING INDUSTRIES, 1970-77
(thousands of jobs)

		Net Change in Employment, 1970-77				
SIC	INDUSTRY DESCRIPTION	Northeast	North Central	South	West	United States
20	Food & kindred prod.	- 71.7	- 39.4	+ 0.6	+ 13.2	- 97.4
22	Textile mill prod.	- 51.1	- 5.8	- 15.4	+ 7.7	- 64.6
23	Apparel, other textiles	-155.6	- 11.2	+ 48.0	+ 38.7	- 80.1
27	Printing & publishing	- 19.6	- 1.4	+ 41.5	+ 25.0	+ 45.5
34	Fabricated metals	- 17.8	+ 71.2	+ 66.8	+ 42.9	+163.1
36	Electric & electronic equipment	-165.4	- 73.3	+ 62.4	+ 6.0	-170.3
39	Misc. manufacturing ind.	- 13.6	+ 1.1	+ 14.5	+ 16.2	+ 18.2
	Totals	-780.5	-170.1	+531.1	+296.7	-122.7

SOURCE: County Business Patterns, Selected States, 1970, 1977.

uring jobs and the north central states lost 170,000 such jobs. This was offset, to some extent, by an increase of 500,000 manufacturing jobs in the South and 300,000 manufacturing jobs in the West. The northeastern states sustained large employment losses in each of New York City's dominant two-digit manufacturing industries.

New York's competitive position for manufacturing

A number of theories have been advanced to explain the shift of manufacturing jobs away from the Northeast. Wilbur Thompson attributes manufacturing losses in the Northeast to the fact that northern cities are not innovating fast enough to replace jobs in mature manufacturing industries which have decentralized to smaller metropolitan areas and to nonurban places.[3] Sternlieb and Hughes underscore the constraints imposed by rising energy costs. "The sharp rise in the cost of energy is likely to encourage further movement of jobs and households from aging areas which already experience high costs of living to energy rich states such as Colorado, Texas, and Wyoming."[4] *Empire State Report* summarized the problems of the Northeast as follows: "Climatic conditions, high energy and transportation costs, a lack of indigenous raw materials and political and economic decisions to move industries and military bases to other parts of the country have all served to stall the economic growth of the Northeast."[5]

Two factors which are frequently cited in explaining the shift of manufacturing production jobs away from older cities such as New York are low labor-force productivity and high wages. This section attempts to assess the validity of that argument. It analyzes labor-force productivity, wage costs, and industry profitability for New York's dominant manufacturing industries using data from the *1977 Census of Manufactures*. Productivity is defined as value added per production worker man-hour. Wage costs are defined as production worker wages per production worker man-hour. Industry profitability is defined as value added in manufacturing per dollar of wages. The latter is used as the yardstick for measuring New York's competitive position for given industries vis-à-vis that of other states, counties, and metropolitan areas.

The methodology is similar to that used by Stevens and Trainer, who correlated manufacturing profitability with subsequent moves by Boston manufactures.[6] The authors measured manufacturing profitability in terms of "value added minus payrolls" (VAMP) per worker. The coefficient of value added per dollar of wages, as used in this study, is limited by the fact that it ignores interarea variations in other costs of production such as taxes and transportation costs. The present methodology also does not consider the competitive threat from overseas manufacturing locations, a pertinent fact for the garment trades, among others. Nevertheless, labor costs are generally the largest cost element in production-oriented manufacturing. Therefore, value added per dollar of wages should accurately measure New York's relative competitiveness for production jobs in selected manufacturing industries.

Productivity vs. wage costs, all manufacturing industries. In 1977, value added per production worker man-hour averaged $20.76 in New York City.[7] This was below the average level of productivity in most other large manufacturing SMSAs including the newer Sunbelt SMSAs.[8] However, wages per production worker man-hour averaged $4.71 in New York City, lower than average manufacturing wages in 30 of the 32 metropolitan areas studied. Given these relatively low wage levels, New York City's coefficient of value added per dollar of wages, $4.41, compared favorably with that of the other metropolitan areas studied. These results are shown in Table 3.

Productivity vs. wage costs, selected three-digit manufacturing industries. In order to standardize for interarea differences in industry mix, wage costs, labor force productivity, and industry profitability were computed for 15 of New York City's dominant three-digit manufacturing industries. These include industries in the apparel trades, printing and publishing, paper, and miscellaneous manufacturing industries. Collectively, these industries accounted for 250,000 New York City manufacturing jobs in 1977 or for about 43% of all manufacturing jobs in the city. The industries selected and their national and regional growth patterns are shown in Table 4.

1. *Apparel and related industries.* Five industries — knitting mills, men's and boys' furnishings, women's and misses' outerwear, women's and children's undergarments, and children's outerwear — were selected to represent apparel and related industries in New York City. In 1977, these industries accounted for almost 125,000 New York City jobs. The largest, women's and misses' outerwear, alone accounted for 72,000 jobs. Each of these industries declined nationally between 1970 and 1977. During that period, New York City lost approximately 52,000 jobs in these industries.

TABLE 3

LABOR FORCE PRODUCTIVITY AND WAGES, ALL MANUFACTURING INDUSTRIES, 1977, N.Y.C VS. SELECTED SMSAs, BY REGION

	Value Added*	Wages*	Value Added/ Wages	New Capital Spending per Production Worker
New York City	$20.76	$4.71	$4.41	$ 1,524
Selected SMSAs				
Northeast	23.91	6.09	3.93	2,771
New York-New Jersey	21.31	4.93	4.32	1,844
Boston	24.03	5.60	4.29	2,605
Newark	27.34	5.85	4.67	3,400
Philadelphia	23.93	6.21	3.85	2,714
Pittsburgh	21.61	7.73	2.80	2,612
Providence	15.24	4.65	3.28	1,746
Allentown	19.34	6.05	3.20	2,303
Buffalo	23.00	7.61	3.02	4,585
Nassau-Suffolk	19.92	5.19	3.84	1,744
Rochester	43.39	7.15	6.07	4,157
North Central	24.56	6.95	3.53	3,286
Chicago	24.45	6.27	3.90	2,568
St. Louis	25.76	6.88	3.74	3,488
Detroit	23.59	8.15	2.89	4,635
Minneapolis-St. Paul	24.57	6.30	3.90	2,820
Cleveland	22.71	7.06	3.22	3,108
Milwaukee	23.91	7.02	3.41	2,803
Cincinatti	28.54	6.51	4.38	1,595
Indianapolis	23.90	7.19	3.32	4,092
Kansas City	26.47	6.63	3.99	4,220
Dayton	21.65	7.45	2.91	3,535
South	25.18	5.91	4.26	5,956
Dallas-Ft. Worth	23.04	5.35	4.31	2,977
Houston	36.05	6.33	5.70	20,945
Atlanta	24.27	5.78	4.20	2,917
Louisville	30.06	6.79	4.43	2,629
Baltimore	24.67	6.80	3.63	3,657
Greenville-Spartanburg	12.96	4.42	2.93	2,612
West	27.40	6.25	4.38	3,785
Los Angeles-Long Beach	23.13	5.63	4.11	2,188
Anaheim	23.53	5.64	4.17	2,816
San Francisco-Oakland	29.97	6.91	4.34	3,239
San Jose	35.70	6.30	5.67	5,940
Denver-Boulder	24.78	6.07	4.08	4,485
Seattle-Everett	27.27	6.93	3.94	4,043

SOURCE: Authors' computations based on data from 1977 Census of Manufactures.

*Refers to value added and wages per production worker man-hour; New York City figures are weighted averages.

TABLE 4

NATIONAL, REGIONAL, AND LOCAL GROWTH PATTERNS, SELECTED N.Y.C. MANUFACTURING INDUSTRIES
(thousands of jobs)

SIC	Industry Description	N.Y.C. Jobs 1977	Net Employment Change, 1970-77 N.Y.C.	N.Y.State	U.S.
225	Knitting mills	17.6	- 3.1	- 3.0	-19.6
232	Men's, boys' furnishings	13.4	- 2.9	- 4.4	- 8.7
233	Women's, misses' outerwear	72.1	-31.5	-37.6	-18.2
234	Women's, children's undergarments	10.6	- 8.9	-10.4	-23.0
236	Children's outerwear	8.9	- 5.6	- 6.5	-11.9
264	Misc. converted paper products	9.5	+ 0.6	- 5.2	+ 5.1
265	Paperboard containers & boxes	6.3	- 3.4	- 5.4	-19.8
271	Newspapers	15.8	+ 0.2	- 4.6	+ 9.9
272	Periodicals	25.3	- 2.9	+ 4.1	+ 3.5
273	Books	18.7	- 0.9	- 2.4	+ 5.4
275	Commercial printing	21.2	- 8.9	-11.2	+22.7
279	Printing trades services	6.6	- 2.7	- 2.1	+ 2.2
391	Jewelry, silverware	12.7	+ 0.3	+ 0.2	+ 6.6
394	Toys & sporting goods	7.6	- 3.9	- 4.0	- 1.1
396	Costume jewelry, notions	7.8	- 5.3	- 6,2	- 1.1

SOURCE: Authors' computations based on data shown in County Business Patterns.

Surprisingly, high wages and low labor-force productivity did not loom large as causes of New York City's recent job losses in the apparel trades. The dominant cause appeared to be that these were declining national market industries for which the United States, as a nation, was no longer competitive. For example, value added per dollar of wages in SIC 233, women's and misses' outerwear, averaged $3.72. This exceeded value added in the adjacent New Jersey SMSAs and in Sunbelt states like Georgia, Florida, and Texas. New York City also enjoyed a favorable competitive position vis-à-vis other geographic areas in terms of the other garment industries studied. In New York City, value added per dollar of wages averaged $3.86 in men's and boys' furnishings, $4.16 in women's and children's undergarments, and $3.25 in children's outerwear. With few exceptions, these exceeded comparable value-added figures for adjacent metropolitan areas and counties and for competing states. Only in SIC 225, knitting mills, was New York City at a competitive disadvantage relative to southern states like Virginia, North Carolina, and South Carolina.

New York City's competitive edge in the garment trades stems from the fact that its labor costs were competitive with those in other areas and that its labor productivity exceeded that of other areas. For example, New York City wages averaged $3.77 per man-hour in women's and misses' outerwear, somewhat above the $2.95 per man-hour paid in the state of Georgia. However, value added per man-hour in New York City averaged $14.03 as compared with only $8.10 in Georgia. The findings clearly demonstrate that for the garment trades, low wages and low worker productivity tended to go hand-in-hand, much to the detriment of some southern states.

2. *The printing trades industries.* Five industries — newspapers, periodicals, books, commercial printing, and printing trades services — were selected to represent the printing and publishing industries in New York City. Collectively these industries accounted for 90,000 New York City manufacturing jobs in 1977. Each of these industries expanded nationally between 1970 and 1977. Virtually all of them contracted in New York City during this period, resulting in a loss of some 15,000 jobs.

Automation coupled with the general dispersion of people and jobs away from New York City were probably more significant than labor factors in explaining the city's recent job losses in these industries. In SICs 2721, periodicals, and 273, books, value added per dollar of wages in New York City was significantly above value added per dollar of wages in virtually all other areas studied. In book publishing, for example, value added per dollar of wages averaged $42.81 in New York City, $20.68 in Illinois, $8.15 in Massachusetts, and $5.88 in Bergen County, N.J. Wages per man-hour for this industry in New York City, $5.72, were roughly comparable to those in Illinois, $5.15; Massachusetts, $5.57; and Bergen County, $5.64. However, worker productivity, as measured by value added per man-hour, averaged $244.89 in New York City, as against only $106.53 in Illinois, $45.38 in Massachusetts, and $33.14 in Bergen County.

New York City was also competitive with other areas studied in SIC 275, commercial printing, and SIC 279, printing trades services. Only in SIC 2711, newspapers, were high wage costs and low labor-force productivity factors in recent New York City job losses. For example, value added per dollar wages in New York City, $2.97, was well below value added in the adjacent New Brunswick SMSA, $14.10. It was also well below value added in states like Florida, $8.08; New Jersey, $6.78; Texas, $6.59; and California, $5.85. In this industry, New York City wage costs, $12.37 per man-hour, were well above wages in the other areas studied, and worker productivity, $36.71 per man-hour, was the lowest of the fifteen areas studied.

3. *Paper and allied products.* Two industries — miscellaneous converted paper products and paperboard containers and boxes — were selected to represent paper and allied products in New York City. In 1977, these industries accounted for approximately 16,000 New York City jobs, a relatively small number when compared with apparel and printing and publishing. Between 1970 and 1977, the converted paper products industry gained jobs nationally and in New York City; employment in paperboard containers and boxes declined nationally and in New York City.

In 1977, New York City was not competitive for miscellaneous converted paper products. Value added per dollar of wages in this industry averaged only $3.11. As a result, New York City ranked third lowest of some 17 states and areas studied. New York's wages per man-hour, $5.09, were competitive with those of other areas. However, value added per man-hour in New York City, $15.82, was less than half that of Pennsylvania, $33.18; Wisconsin, $33.53; and adjacent New Brunswick, N.J., $33.34.

New York's competitive position for paperboard containers and boxes was also relatively weak. Value added per dollar of wages averaged only $2.71 as compared with $3.22 in Michigan, $3.19 in Texas, and $2.90 in Bergen County, N.J. Both wages costs and worker productivity in New York City were lower than in any of the other areas studied.

4. *Miscellaneous manufacturing industries.* Three industries — jewelry and silverware, toys and sporting goods, and costume jewelry and notions — were selected to represent the miscellaneous manufacturing industries in which New York City specializes. In 1977, these industries accounted for a total of 28,000 jobs. All but jewelry and silverware declined nationally between 1970 and 1977. This was true in New York City as well.

In 1977, New York City was relatively competitive for production jobs in jewelry and silverware but less competitive for jobs in toys and sporting goods and in costume jewelry. In jewelry and silverware, value added per dollar of wages averaged $4.56, higher than that of adjacent counties and most adjacent states. New York City wages, $4.97 per man-hour, were competitive with wages in other areas studied; value added per man-hour, $22.67, was the highest of any of the areas studied.

By contrast, value added per dollar of wages in toys and sporting goods averaged $4.11 in New York City. This was higher than value added in the adjacent Jersey City SMSA, $2.60, and above value added in nearby Nassau County, $4.00. However, it was significantly below value added per dollar of wages in states like California, $5.59; New Jersey, $4.92; Minnesota, $4.70; and Massachusetts, $4.63, where the industry is also well represented.

New York was no longer highly competive for costume jewelry and notions, according to the *1977 Census of Manufactures.* In this industry, value added per dollar of wages averaged $3.16 in New York City, $4.23 in Massachusetts, $3.76 in California, and $3.60 in Rhode Island and Georgia, states in which much of the industry is located.

New York City's potential for production-oriented manufacturing: how real is it?

There is some reason for optimism concerning New York City's competitive position for manufacturing production jobs. The fact that in 1977 wages per production-worker man-hour were lower in New York City than in 30 of the 32 metropolitan areas studied represents a departure from historical trends. Apparently, manufacturing wages in New York City have been slow to rise because of the disastrous slide in manufacturing jobs which started in the late 1960s. High unemployment in New York's manufacturing sector appears to have dampened wage increases to such an extent that the city ratio of value added per dollar of wages, $4.41, now compares favorably with that of other medium-to-large metropolitan areas. This, in turn, may signify that New York City has reached the "tipping point" at which it again will become attractive for certain types of production-oriented manufacturing jobs.

Another positive factor is that in industries where wage costs are high, such as printing and publishing, worker productivity is also disproportionately high, thereby offsetting any disadvantage in terms of wage costs. The unusually high productivity of workers in printing and publishing has undoubtedly contributed to the resurgence of this industry in New York City since 1977.

The results nevertheless indicate that New York City continues to face obstacles to production-oriented manufacturing. In some low-wage industries, notably paperboard containers and boxes, worker productivity was comparably low, thereby nullifying any competitive edge conferred by low wages. Such low productivity may reflect inadequate investment in manufacturing capital plant within the city. In 1977, for example, new capital spending averaged $1,524 per production worker in New York City, well below capital spending in most other SMSAs studied, including those located in the Northeast.

Low manufacturing wages are also a mixed blessing. To the extent that low worker productivity and low wages are interrelated, New York City's blue-collar labor force may remain at the bottom of the economic ladder, unable to break the cycle of poverty for themselves and their families.

Most economists agree that New York City cannot afford to "write off" manufacturing production jobs. Most economists also agree that subsidizing inefficient industries is a policy blunder. A *New York Times* article by John Hekman may offer a solution to this dilemma.[9] The author contends that regions don't grow old. Instead it is the products they manufacture that eventually become obsolete. If this argument is valid, the solution to industrial outmigration may be to replace mature industries with new and growing industries. In today's economy, these include such high-technology fields as aerospace, electronics, computers, and instruments. This strategy has worked in New England and could easily work in New York with its array of technical and research facilities. However, the transition would not be painless, especially for those blue-collar workers who lack the skills to adapt to high-technology manufacturing.

New York's Services Sector: Hope for the Future?

As the manufacturing sectors of the New York City economy have declined, and as the service-producing sectors of the national economy have grown relative to goods production, it is natural to inquire if service industries might help compensate for New York City's losses in manufacturing jobs and economic product. Here we review employment and productivity patterns and trends for selected service industries that contribute to New York City's economy.

Changes in employment

Table 5 displays the 1970–77 patterns of change in employment for the services sector as a whole, and for major New York City two-digit service sectors (those that employed over 30,000 in the city in 1977). New York City's growth or decline in these industries is compared to that of the New York–New Jersey Standard Consolidated Area (SCA), New York State, and the country as a whole, in order to discern how changes in the city's service employment are related to the wider

TABLE 5
EMPLOYMENT CHANGES: MAJOR N.Y.C. SERVICE INDUSTRIES

SIC	Industry	N.Y.C. 1977 Employment	N.Y.C.	Net Changes 1970-77 SCA (Region)	N.Y. State	U.S.
72	Personal services	32,630	-19,638 (-38%)	- 27,118 (-29%)	- 24,418 (-26%)	- 101,406 (-10%)
73	Business services	193,043	-19,002 (- 9%)	+ 8,675 (+ 3%)	+ 7,613 (+ 3%)	+ 675,751 (+41%)
80	Health services	178,215	+27,803 (+18%)	+ 56,377 (+21%)	+ 98,468 (+33%)	+1,436,731 (+50%)
81	Legal services	37,004	+ 7,007 (+23%)	+ 13,405 (+33%)	+ 12,914 (+31%)	+ 155,017 (+65%)
	All selected service industries	769,588	-24,170 (- 3%)	+105,887 (+ 9%)	+121,365 (+ 9%)	+3,598,526 (34%)

SOURCE: County Business Patterns, 1970 and 1977.

economies in which the city is embedded.

It may be observed that the service sector as a whole declined by 3% in the city, grew by 9% in the metropolitan area and state, and increased nationally by 34% over the 1970–77 period. This largely reflects the global patterns of shifting population and goods production from the Northeast to other parts of the nation. The decline in New York City's service sector, for example, approximately paralleled its population decline.[10] (From 1970 to 1976 New York City's population declined by 5.69% while that of the metropolitan region, as defined by the Regional Plan Association, declined for the first time in history, by 0.01%.)

The patterns of change are different among individual service sectors, however. For example, personal services (SIC 72) and business services (SIC 73) both declined in New York City from 1970 to 1977. However, personal services followed a national and regional pattern of decline, while business services declined in a period when national employment in this part of the economy was growing substantially and regional and statewide employment was stable.

The decline in personal services was more severe for New York City than for the region or state and considerably more severe than for the nation as a whole. Within SIC 72, three-digit classification 729 (a miscellaneous category which includes Turkish baths, reducing salons, clothes rental, coin-operated machines, checkroom concessions, custom dressmaking, and income tax preparation) was the only bright spot, growing by 1,987 jobs (64%) in New York City compared to increases of 120% for the metropolitan (SCA) area, 141% for New York State, and 260% for the U.S. as a whole.

Within the category of business services there were two growing three-digit sectors contained within a general pattern of decline. Personnel supply services (SIC 736, which includes employment and placement agencies) has been a source of steady growth in New York City since 1959. From 1970 to 1977, it grew by 21,152 jobs, or 386%, compared to 491% for the (SCA) region, 516% for the state, and 716% for the U.S. as a whole. Sector 733 (mailing, reproduction, steno) was the only other business service to show positive growth in New York City — 1,672 jobs, or 17% in the 1970–77 period. This compares with growths of 12%, 11%, and 48% for the metropolitan region, state, and nation, respectively.

Both health services (SIC 80) and legal services (SIC 81) exhibited substantial growth in New York City over the 1970–77 period, but less rapid than that of the region, state, or nation. Within the health industry, three-digit sector 801 (physicians' offices) was the fastest growing, increasing by 3,462 jobs (28%) from 1970 to 1977. This compared to an increase of 113% for the region, 50% for the state, and 61% for the U.S. as a whole.

In general, the major service sectors in New York City present a rather sobering picture. In sectors where service employment is growing in the city it is doing so at rates less impressive than that of the nation, state, or metropolitan area. Employment is actually declining in business services despite stability or growth elsewhere. In personal services the decline in employment is more severe than it is regionally and statewide, and much more severe than it is nationally.

For the purpose of discerning whether smaller service sectors can potentially replace jobs lost from New York City's more well-established manufacturing and

TABLE 6

EMPLOYMENT CHANGES: SMALLER N.Y.C. SERVICE SECTORS WHICH ARE GROWING NATIONALLY

SIC	Industry	N.Y.C. 1977 Employment	Net Changes 1970-77 N.Y.C.	U.S.
75	Auto repairs services, and garages	17,094	- 2,661 (-13%)	+ 93,227 (+24%)
76	Misc. repair services	9,441	- 1,234 (-12%)	+ 51,524 (+25%)
79	Amusement and recreation	21,943	- 2,333 (-10%)	+154,570 (+36%)
701	Hotels and motels	21,728	-13,796 (-39%)	+209,208 (+32%)
891	Engineering, architect, and surveying services	18,700	- 256 (- 1%)	+108,694 (+42%)
072	Dental labs.	2,567	- 84 (- 3%)	+ 10,774 (+45%)

SOURCE: County Business Patterns, 1970 and 1977.

service industries, Table 6 presents employment data on six service sectors selected because they experienced major growth nationally over the 1970–77 period. Despite the fact that these sectors grew from 25% to 45% in the U.S. as a whole, every one of them declined in New York City, from 1% to 39%.

Labor productivity and wages

Since labor is the major cost component of service industries, New York City's comparative advantages and disadvantages can usefully be examined by comparing the cost of labor to the productivity of labor across jurisdictions. For services, gross receipts are used as the measure of output. It must be recognized, however, that components of cost other than labor may be significant for particular service industries, and that these cost components may also vary among geographic jurisdictions. Hence, in the discussion that follows, our comparisons of labor costs, and revenues generated per labor unit, must be taken only as approximate indications of productivity and profitability.

Table 7 demonstrates that New York City and its immediate environs constitute both a high-cost and high-productivity locale for services production, with New York City slightly outpacing the rest of the SMSA on both counts. The New York-New Jersey SMSA exhibits both the highest labor costs and the highest level of output per employee of SMSAs examined. These effects result from both higher levels of output and labor costs within component industries and differences in the mix of service industries across metropolitan areas.

The last two columns of Table 7 indicate the net effect of the two New York City SMSA factors — high cost and high output. On the basis of receipts generated per dollar of payroll, the New York City SMSA may be seen as rather average, ranking fifteenth among the 30 SMSAs examined. In terms of receipts, less payroll

TABLE 7

LABOR FORCE PRODUCTIVITY VS. WAGES IN SERVICE INDUSTRIES, 1977, N.Y.C. VS. SELECTED SMSAs BY REGION
(thousands of dollars)

	Receipts per Employee	Payroll per Employee	Receipts per Payroll	Receipts less Payroll per Employee
New York City	32.50	12.45	2.83	22.75
Selected SMSAs by Region				
Northeast				
New York-New Jersey	34.20	12.05	2.84	22.15
Boston	27.31	10.10	2.70	17.22
Newark	25.91	9.71	2.67	16.21
Philadelphia	24.33	8.86	2.75	15.47
Pittsburgh	29.99	10.08	2.98	19.91
Providence	22.02	7.57	2.91	14.44
Allentown	21.49	7.14	3.01	14.35
Buffalo	22.04	7.81	2.82	14.24
Nassau-Suffolk	29.11	9.50	3.06	19.61
Rochester	25.59	8.52	3.00	17.07
North Central				
Chicago	29.07	10.48	2.77	18.59
St. Louis	25.69	8.72	2.95	16.96
Detroit	28.81	10.31	2.79	18.50
Minn.-St. Paul	23.30	8.64	2.70	14.66
Cleveland	25.07	9.15	2.74	15.93
Milwaukee	21.43	8.18	2.62	13.25
Cincinnati	25.05	8.37	2.99	16.68
Indianapolis	23.67	8.07	2.93	15.59
Kansas City	25.78	9.31	2.77	16.47
Dayton	22.50	8.19	2.75	14.30
South				
Atlanta	25.63	8.83	2.90	16.80
Louisville	20.50	6.98	2.94	13.52
Baltimore	21.33	7.97	2.68	13.36
Greenville-Spartanburg	23.30	8.43	2.76	14.87
West				
L.A.-Long Beach	31.08	11.11	2.80	19.97
S.F.-Oakland	30.04	10.35	2.95	20.12
Anaheim	27.60	9.27	2.98	18.33
San Jose	29.48	11.23	2.62	18.26
Denver-Boulder	24.84	8.72	2.85	16.12
Seattle-Everett	28.01	9.55	2.93	18.46

SOURCE: 1977 Census of Selected Service Industries.

TABLE 8

RECEIPTS PER EMPLOYEE, 1977
(thousands of dollars)

SIC	Industry	N.Y.C.	Region SMSA	SCSA	N.Y. State	U.S.
72	Personal services	19.07	18.94	18.65	18.32	16.80
721	Laundry	19.31	19.23	19.24	18.90	17.52
722	Photo studios	31.82	34.40	32.64	31.66	28.25
723	Beauty shops	12.84	12.57	12.35	12.19	11.74
724	Barber shops	11.61	12.23	12.76	12.50	15.62
725	Shoe repair	17.57	17.99	18.61	18.57	20.93
726	Funeral service	52.06	50.97	49.14	47.28	36.92
729	Miscellaneous	14.97	15.17	14.63	13.52	12.12
73	Business service	28.27	27.99	26.08	26.11	21.76
731	Advertising	45.48	45.15	43.78	43.57	37.74
734	Service to dwellings	12.52	12.66	11.56	12.20	9.88
81	Legal services	54.22	53.19	49.75	49.11	43.74
	Selected services (all)	35.20	34.20	31.96	31.58	25.91

SOURCE: 1977 Census of Selected Service Industries, based on data for "establishments with payroll."

TABLE 9

PAYROLL PER EMPLOYEE, 1977
(thousands of dollars)

SIC		N.Y.C.	Region SMSA	SCSA	N.Y. State	U.S.
72	Personal services	6.95	6.81	6.62	6.52	6.02
721	Laundry	7.14	7.07	7.03	6.90	6.34
722	Photo studios	7.92	8.17	8.13	7.82	7.22
723	Beauty shops	6.91	6.11	5.83	5.89	5.65
724	Barber shops	5.69	5.72	5.68	5.71	6.56
725	Shoe repair	5.78	5.89	6.00	5.75	5.53
726	Funeral service	11.95	11.61	11.19	10.82	8.89
729	Miscellaneous	5.48	5.29	4.88	4.58	3.88
73	Business service	12.38	11.99	11.11	11.23	9.08
731	Advertising	21.05	20.82	20.05	20.03	16.17
734	Service to dwellings	8.41	8.40	7.42	7.85	5.29
81	Legal services	16.50	16.08	15.10	14.41	13.31
	Selected services (all)	12.45	12.05	11.23	10.91	8.85

SOURCE: 1977 Census of Selected Service Industries.

TABLE 10

RECEIPTS PER PAYROLL, 1977
(thousands of dollars)

		N.Y.C.	Region SMSA	SCSA	N.Y. State	U.S.
72	Personal services	2.75	2.78	2.82	2.81	2.79
721	Laundry	2.71	2.72	2.74	2.74	2.77
722	Photo studios	4.02	4.21	4.02	4.05	3.91
723	Beauty shops	1.86	2.06	2.12	2.07	2.08
724	Barber shops	2.04	2.14	2.25	2.19	2.38
725	Shoe repair	3.04	3.05	3.10	3.23	3.79
726	Funeral service	4.36	4.39	4.39	4.37	4.15
729	Miscellaneous	2.73	2.87	3.00	2.95	3.13
73	Business service	2.28	2.33	2.35	2.32	2.40
731	Advertising	2.16	2.17	2.18	2.18	2.33
734	Service to dwellings	1.49	1.51	1.56	1.55	1.87
81	Legal services	3.29	3.31	3.30	3.41	3.29
	Selected services (all)	2.83	2.84	2.85	2.90	2.93

SOURCE: 1977 Census of Selected Service Industries based on data for "establishments with payroll."

TABLE 11

RECEIPTS LESS PAYROLL PER EMPLOYEE
(thousands of dollars)

		N.Y.C.	Region SMSA	SCSA	N.Y. State	U.S.
72	Personal services	12.12	12.13	12.03	11.79	10.79
721	Laundry	12.17	12.15	12.21	12.00	11.19
722	Photo studios	23.91	26.23	24.52	23.84	21.02
723	Beauty shops	5.93	6.45	6.52	6.30	6.08
724	Barber shops	5.91	6.51	7.08	6.79	9.06
725	Shoe repairs	11.79	12.09	12.60	12.82	15.40
726	Funeral service	40.11	39.36	37.95	36.47	28.02
729	Miscellaneous	9.50	9.88	9.74	8.94	8.25
73	Business service	15.88	16.00	14.96	14.88	12.69
731	Advertising	24.43	24.33	23.72	23.54	21.57
734	Service to dwellings	4.11	4.25	4.13	4.35	4.58
81	Legal services	37.72	37.12	34.66	34.71	30.43
	Selected services (all)	22.75	22.15	20.73	20.67	17.07

SOURCE: 1977 Census of Selected Service Industries, based on data for "establishments with payroll."

per employee, an indicator of profitability (per worker), the New York SMSA fares considerably better, however. Indeed, it ranks first among SMSAs examined. However, this must be considered against the likelihood that other costs as well as labor costs are higher in this area, thus cutting into New York's apparent profitability advantage. Furthermore, this measure inherently favors high-wage areas like New York.[11]

Further insights may be gained by examining the foregoing indicators for individual industries. In Tables 8 through 11, labor cost and productivity are presented in detail for New York City, for the metropolitan region defined narrowly by the New York-New Jersey SMSA and widely by the New York-New Jersey-Connecticut Standard Consolidated Statistical Area (SCSA), for New York State (NYS), and for the U.S. as a whole, for those major New York City two- and three-digit service industries available from the 1977 Census of Selected Service Industries.*

Table 8 displays the comparisons on receipts per employee. Generally, it may be observed that New York City is more productive by this measure than the surrounding jurisdictions and that receipts per employee decline markedly as one moves within industries from the city to the region to the state to the nation. Exceptions to this rule are barbershops (724) and shoe repair (725), which behave in the reverse manner, and photo studios (722) where the metro region outpaces the city.

Table 9 displays the figures on labor costs (payroll per employee) by industry. Again there is a rather marked, steady decline as one moves from New York City to the region, state, and nation. New York City is thus a high-labor-cost as well as high-labor-productivity area for most of the examined service industries. Exceptions again include SIC 724 and 725, as well as 722, which exhibit irregular patterns.

Table 10 indicates the net effects of New York City's relatively high labor costs and productivity, in terms of receipts generated per dollar of payroll. Generally speaking, the labor-costs effect tends to dominate the productivity effect, leaving New York City less productive per dollar spent on payroll than its surrounding jurisdictions. Exceptions to this rule are photo studios (722) and funeral service's (726), where the city keeps pace with the region and state, which in turn outpace the nation. For legal services (81), the various jurisdictions appear to break relatively even with one another.

As with our comparisons of SMSAs (Table 7), the picture changes substantially if we compare net receipts (receipts less payroll) per employee. By this measure New York City fares rather well, generating net receipts generally on par with the metropolitan region, and greater than the state or nation. (However, these results must again be viewed against the caveat stated earlier, that differentials in other cost components are likely to erode the apparent advantages.) Exceptions to the general pattern include beauty shops (723) and barbershops (724), where New

---

*Note that figures examined for the New York-New Jersey Standard Consolidated Area (SCA), which excludes Connecticut, approximate those of the SCSA fairly closely. Note also that the health/sector (SIC 80) data was not yet available when this paper was compiled.

York City compares unfavorably with all of the surrounding jurisdictions; shoe repair, where there is a marked increase in productivity as one progresses from city to region, to state, to nation; and services to dwellings (734, cleaning, exterminating, maintenance, etc.), which follow the latter pattern to a less substantial extent.

Overview

In summary, the picture for service industries in New York City is not particularly encouraging. With the exception of the health and legal sectors, major New York City service sectors are declining, and in no case is employment growth keeping pace with growth rates in surrounding jurisdictions. Neither is there any indication that smaller service industries which are growing nationally have taken root in New York City. Indeed, quite the reverse seems to be true — i.e., such industries are also declining in the city. Examinations of labor-cost and productivity indices show that while New York City service employees are generally more productive as revenue generators compared to those elsewhere, their wage costs generally keep pace with those productivity advantages. As a result, New York City exhibits no clear competitive edge in its major service industries. Indeed, the reverse seems true for the most part.

New York City appears to be roughly competitive in certain specialized areas such as legal services and probably health services, which potentially might provide sources of economic growth relatively independent of the rest of the economy. Business and personal services are probably tied more closely to the declines that have occurred in population and in other sectors of the local economy, and seem to offer no promising alternatives for economic development.

Notes

Owing to lack of space, tables computed by the authors based on data from the *1977 Census of Manufactures,* showing wage costs vs. labor productivity, 1977, for New York City vs. selected areas, for the apparel and related industries, for printing and publishing, for paper and allied products, and for miscellaneous manufacturing industries, have been omitted from this article, but copies may be obtained by writing to Pearl Kamer, Chief Economist, Long Island Regional Planning Board, and Adjunct Professor, W. Averell Harriman College for Urban and Policy Sciences, State University of New York at Stony Brook, or to Dennis Young, Director of Research of the College.

1. Ninth Interim Report of the Temporary Commission on City Finances, *The Effects of Taxation on Manufacturing in New York City* (New York, ecember 1976), p.1.
2. The Port Authority of New York and New Jersey, *Industrial Revitalization in the New York-New Jersey Region* (New York, May 1978), p.4.
3. Wilbur Thompson, "Economic Processes and Employment Problems in Declining Metropolitan Areas," in George Sternlieb and James W. Hughes (eds.), *Post-Industrial America: Metropolitan Decline and Inter-Regional Job Shifts* (New Brunswick, N.J.: Rutgers University Center for Urban Policy Research, 1975), pp. 187-96.
4. Sternlieb and Hughes (eds.), *Post-Industrial America:* p. 199.
5. "The Future of the Northeast," *Empire State Report,* Vol. 2, No. 9 (October–November 1976), p. 353.

6. Benjamin H. Stevens and Glynnis A. Trainer, *A New Approach to the Prediction of Regional Industrial Growth and a Preliminary Test for the Boston SMSA* (Philadelphia: Regional Science Research Institute, 1976).

7. This represents a weighted average, the weights being manufacturing employment in each borough.

8. The SMSAs with which New York City was compared each contained at least 100,000 manufacturing jobs in 1977.

9. John S. Hekman, "Regions Don't Grow Old, Products Do," *The New York Times*, November 4, 1979.

10. The decline in New York City services might have been more severe if not for social services (SIC 83) which employed 45,198 in 1977 but was not tabulated in the 1970 census.

11. For example, consider cities A and B with the same ratio of receipts per payroll:

City A: Receipts = $1,000
Employees = 10
Payroll = $500
Receipts per payroll = 2
(Receipts minus payroll) per Employee = 50

City B: Receipts = $1,200
Employees = 10
Payroll = $600
Receipts per payroll = 2
(Receipts minus payroll) per Employee = 60

9

URBAN INDUSTRIAL PARKS
VERSUS THE EXODUS OF MANUFACTURING

Edwin P. Reubens

After the fiscal crisis of New York City exploded in 1974, and an incredulous world watched for long months as the great city teetered on the verge of bankruptcy, it became generally accepted that a declining local economy was the basic cause — however much aggravated by social and political factors. The economic decline was traced back at least as far as the late 1950s, and its accelerating slide was tracked in shrinking production, employment, and incomes, an exodus of business firms and of middle-class residents, and a consequently shriveling tax-base, along with a growing proportion of dependent population, expanding public services, and augmented public employment with soaring wages and fringe benefits.

In this explanatory pattern, the decline of manufacturing in New York City was singled out for particular emphasis — partly because its decline (as measured by firms, fields, and employment) was so clear and striking, and partly because the causes could be so easily attributed: high local costs of operation in many features, as well as deteriorating environment, official red tape, the superior attractions of other locations, among others. Still another reason for focusing on the manufacturing trend was that its social effects were so directly devastating — notably in reducing the job opportunities for young unskilled males — with all the consequences for undermining family life, frustrating hopes and dignity, tending toward social disorder and overt violence.

It seemed obvious that local governmental policy must seek to halt and reverse this industrial decline. While little could be done to reduce the attractions of other locations (although the political drive to reallocate federal grants and revenue-sharing has helped along that line), much could be attempted in raising labor training, in ameliorating the character of urban life, and especially in reducing the costs and improving the conditions for processing operations in New York. For the latter costs and conditions, the principal instrument was to be the creation of industrial parks, along with some advances in transportation, refuse collection, and crime control.

The emphasis on industrial parks seems, in turn, to derive from a certain conception of the causes of high costs and other obstacles to manufacturing in the city, and also from a certain emulation of the industrial promotion devices used so successfully in many southern localities. Most crucially, it was supposed that industrial firms were leaving New York City mainly because of lack of land and buildings suitable to modern one-story technology, and secure against theft and vandalism. Accordingly it seemed wise for the municipal government to create areas of available land and buildings, separated from the decaying old areas, and supplied with all necessary utilities, including security, and offered at competitive prices or rentals (if not actually subsidized to undercut the competition). This definition distinguishes an industrial park from the similar-sounding device of an "enterprise zone" — since the latter device is anti-interventionist in method, and is probably more applicable to services than to manufacturing.[1]

In retrospect, it is remarkable how widely the doctrine of industrial parks became conventional wisdom, without any in-depth analysis of the causal model that is implied; and without considering whether an alleged necessary condition would be sufficient to produce the desired changes; and without any close follow-up on the initial experiments along this line, including any benefit/cost measurement of the returns to the city economy from its outlays on industrial parks. Likewise the belief in this approach has prevailed without serious attention to the severe problems of manufacturing in the whole national pattern: problems ranging from the trauma of the U.S. auto industry, steel makers, television assembly, watches and cameras, textiles, and indeed the garment industry (the latter being the prime staple of the New York City manufacturing sector); through the slow growth of all manufacturing employment (even in booming manufacturing sectors abroad as in France, Germany, and Japan) and its declining share in the total of U.S. employment; down to the regional shift of manufacturing away from the older locations in the Northeast and North Central cities to the Sunbelt cities of the South, Southwest, and West, or to foreign locations.

Indeed, to this day, many boosters of New York turn instinctively to the promotion of industrial parks and seize upon each new turn of events to bolster the claim that manufacturing can be revived in New York and that industrial parks are the way to do it.[2] This appears to have been the position of the Port Authority of New York and New Jersey, in a report issued in May 1978 which recites New York's alleged physical advantages without mentioning wage matters, unions, and other labor problems.[3] Similarly, officials of the city's Public Development Corporation (PDC) as late as mid-1980 pledged their faith in a local industrial renaissance.[4] An extreme expresssion of such faith is the effort by State Senator Galiber and some New York officials to bring to the South Bronx some Japanese automobile manufacturing. Perhaps the broadest, most specific promise was outlined early in 1980 by Leonard Yaseen, the former chairman of Fantus Corp. (which specializes in finding industrial locations) in an article entitled "Advice for New York."[5]

Yet these optimistic views are not unopposed. Just two weeks after Mr. Yaseen's article appeared, a forecast by Chase Econometrics Inc. projected for the New York area by 1990 a net loss of about 130,000 jobs, or over 4%, half of them in manufacturing, whereas the service sector was given reasonably good prospects for growth.[6] Similarly, at about the same time as the PDC was accentuating the industrial positive, an economist for the Regional Plan Association pointed out the continuing decline of business investment in the region.[7] Likewise, the Twentieth Century Fund's Task Force on the Future of New York City declared, in a report released in 1979, its opposition to large-scale industrial parks on the ground that "experience with them in other areas has shown that they fail to yield enough jobs in return for the substantial amounts invested in them.''[8]

Opinions versus realities

Among these diverse views, Mr. Yaseen's claims are the most explicitly based on alleged recent developments as well as on a widely used model of industrial trends; his arguments recur in the more recent statement by PDC officials and therefore are worth some scrutiny in a larger perspective. As Mr. Yaseen now sees it — and contrary to his view in 1975 — New York at present offers strong positive advantages for manufacturing firms. The soaring price of gasoline and diesel oil is making auto and truck transportation so expensive, he thinks, that many manufacturing firms to want to locate closer to their large New York City market; this location would minimize direct trucking costs as well as the travel expenses of their employees which would otherwise have to be covered by raising wages. Almost as important, Mr. Yaseen now perceives labor costs to be no obstacle to locating in New York, because (average) hourly wages in the city are reported to be lower than in a number of nearby cities and towns. He finds the only important obstacle now to be the lack of a coherent and efficient city program for industrial parks.

To begin with the factor that Mr. Yaseen stresses, transport costs, he must assume that it is greatly affected by the oil price jump, and in turn is an important element in total costs of manufacturing and in the total cost of living of workers. The former assumption has some substance, of course — at least to the extent of perhaps a 25% rise in transport rates when gasoline and oil prices rise 100%. But the second assumption finds little justification in the operating cost schedules of most industries, where trucking and other direct transport amount to a small percentage of total processing costs. Even in those industries where transport costs bulk particularly large, they will hardly reach an amount "exceeding raw material costs," as Mr. Yaseen claims, since the latter commonly amount to about half the total cost of the manufacturing operation. As for the workers who commute by private car, even if we accept Mr. Yaseen's estimate that by the end of 1980 the average commuting driver would be spending a minimum of $1,700 a year for gasoline alone (a figure implying either a severe new boost in oil and gasoline prices, or a very far commute, or a very inefficient car, or no weekends or holidays off from work), still the incremental effect is only a doubling of his former expenditure on gasoline, which is an increment of $850 per year, calling for additional after-tax wages of about $17 per week (an additional $0.42 per hour). This is an appreciable amount, but not overwhelming. Indeed, if car pools are formed, say by no more then every two workers, the above figures would be cut in half, down to quite minor magnitudes. Finally, manufacturing firms are more sensitive to the inter-city differentials in energy costs; and New York City's cost is about 25% above the national average.[9]

The second important feature, which Mr. Yaseen stresses as favorable to manufacturing in New York City, is a reported inter-city differential in labor costs, claiming that average hourly earnings as well as unit labor costs are actually lower in New York City than in most of the competing nearby areas or more distant locations. This position is so divergent from common impressions and the "conventional wisdom" that it calls for some analysis. To begin with, Mr. Yaseen's measure of a dollars-and-cents wage differential is an average for each region. It therefore represents the industrial and occupational mix of manufacturing jobs in each region; and for New York City it reflects the well-known predominance of rather low-skilled and low-paying jobs (garment sewing, metal-stamping, toy-making, plastics-molding, and the like), together with the absence of high-paying jobs like steel-making, auto-assembly, aircraft, shipbuilding, and the like). In addition, when the aggregate index is broken down into detailed occupational comparisons — as can be done for a few occupations, using BLS data[10] — a complex pattern is found; my own finding is that New York City shows comparatively moderate wage rates for highly skilled work (e.g., in various specialities in the printing trades and other craft work) along with relatively high wage rates for low-skilled work in manufacturing activities — the very ones reporting competitive disadvantages in New York City! A further element is the role of fringe benefits which are relatively high in New York City and must be added to the basic hourly pay rate. Taking a temporal perspective,[11] we may note that during the past few years New York City earnings have lagged appreciably behind other regions and the whole U.S., reflecting in part in the high rates of unemployment in the city, and the very decline of the manufacturing employment in question, as well as the lag of living costs behind other cities and behind the rate of inflation — but the prospects now are for wage rates to catch up, as the city's tendency to high cost of living cannot be avoided forever.

Beyond all these considerations on relative wages in New York City, we must recognize that labor in the city presents to manufacturers some other acute problems. As will be detailed from employers' survey responses, the availability of workers, their regularity and stability, their trainability, their willingness to cooperate, are crucial matters in this city. The negative judgments on some of these features give overall measures of real productivity and unit labor costs that often put New York City in a less than attractive rank.

The foregoing considerations on labor costs and on transportation costs bring us to a more comprehensive view of all the input elements that enter into a manufacturer's locational decision. This is a large and complex picture which I cannot fill in here in detail, but instead I will cite some actual experience and some attitudinal surveys.

Recent studies

A study by Weinstein and Firestine, published in 1978,[12] on actual locational decisions, and their correlation with various factors supposed to enter into those decisions, shows that the most important factors include the supply and productivity of labor, wage levels, and access to raw materials, markets, and means of transportation. Meanwhile, tax incentives — which are widely used by state and local governments to attract industry, especially in the South — show no significant correlation with actual industrial locations (i.e., many southern states probably lose the tax revenues from relocations that would have occurred anyway!).

Similar listings of the relevant factors operating across New York State, but putting more emphasis on high taxes than do Weinstein and Firestine, are found in Foltman's 1975 study. A long list of New York City's disadvantages, on top of New York State's disadvantages, is given in Foltman and McClelland (1977).[13]

In June 1980 a panel of scholars, convened in Washington by the President's Commission for a National Agenda for the Eighties, generally affirmed that migration out of the cities would continue from the 1970s into the 1980s. The forces making for the dispersal of economic activities — both industry and services — as well as tending toward the decentralization of population, were expected to prevail over the influence of scarce and expensive energy which in itself tends to favor reconcentration in urban locations.[14]

Businessmen's attitudes

If we look away from aggregative experience, and instead at businessmen's attitudes and evaluations, we can draw upon a revealing survey done in 1979 in the New York City area by Louis Harris and Associates, questioning almost 700 of the small and medium-sized firms that are the main locus of our concern.[15] For our purposes, one of the significant questions was: "At the present time, is your firm considering relocating to another facility?" Answers in the affirmative were given by 25% of the respondents for all types of business in the whole metropolitan area, the respondents in New York City alone indicating 26%. Of those considering relocating, two-thirds were thinking of new locations outside New York City (but most of these would go no farther than the surrounding counties). The poll found — somewhat surprisingly but probably reflecting the costs of moving plant and equipment — that only 20% of manufacturing firms were considering relocating but 80% of them would go outside New York City. Of course the key question for our present purposes would concern manufacturing firms now located in New York City; unfortunately, the Harris tabulations do not show this cross-classification, but their available data — proportionately adjusted — suggest that as many as 40% of New York City manufacturers were "considering" a new location, in most cases outside the five boroughs.

The next significant question in this survey inquired as to the motivations of the potential movers: "Which two or three of the following reasons would be the most important for your firm expanding or relocating outside the New York area?" Setting aside the "social, personal, and environmental reasons" — which were mentioned by only 14% of the respondents — the business reasons given by all the respondents in the New York metropolitan area, for all businesses and for manufacturing separately, are listed (in percentages of the total number of

TABLE 1
MOTIVATIONS OF POTENTIAL MOVERS
(in percentages)*

	All Businesses	Manufacturing
Lower taxes	35	39
Lower general costs	34	32
Lower land building costs	21	20
Better cheaper labor	20	35
Better access to markets	18	13
Better treatment by government	11	18
Less crime	10	15
Better transportation	10	20
Better attraction for management	9	10
Lower energy costs	4	10
Better access to raw materials	3	2

*Based on 3,175 total responses from all businesses and 782 total responses from manufacturing firms.

---

responses) in Table 1. This tabulation, stated in descending order for "All Businesses" shows the rank importance to business firms in New York (metropolitan area) of the tax burden, general costs, property costs, and labor costs. For manufacturing alone, the tax burden is still the most important consideration, but labor cost is second, closely followed by general costs, which is then followed by property costs tied with transportation problems. Other problems which are prominent for manufacturing in the New York area, but are less important for other businesses in the city, are the roles of government bureaucracy, crimes against persons and property, and high electricity rates. In short, the New York area confronts the manufacturing firm with a host of difficulties and costs, many of which can be substantiated by inter-city comparisions, but all of which are perceived as problems and deterrents in New York City for a large proportion of manufacturing firms.

It would be desirable to have the foregoing reasons broken down for New York City firms in manufacturing alone. This breakdown is not directly available from the survey organization, but their listing of the "business reasons" given by New York City firms (in all industries) for considering a relocation is nearly identical with the reasons given by all-area firms. It may therefore be suspected that the motivation of New York City manufacturers is fairly close to the pattern for all-area manufacturers, namely the outstanding importance of taxes, labor costs, and other costs, but closely followed and with even greater emphasis by transportation problems, governmental regulations, crime against persons and property, and the level of electricity charges. It is also worth noting that while the supply, quality, and cost of labor are important considerations — ranked second in importance by New York area manufacturers — the matter of unionization "does not appear to make executives any more likely to have considered relocation," according to the Harris *Survey* (p. 23).

A survey of industrial parks in New York City

Our discussion of industrial parks — including both private and public parks — begins with a detailed examination of the Brooklyn Navy Yard operation; and continues with a less-detailed survey of the Flatlands operation, the Zerega Avenue and Lyons operations, the North East Marine Terminal, and College Point Industrial Park, and then considers two other parks wholly or mostly in the planning stage, namely Bathgate and Staten Island.

1. The Brooklyn Navy Yard was purchased for a little over $22 million by the city in 1966 from the federal government, which had terminated its operations of naval shipbuilding and ship repair in that facility. In 1969 it was turned over to a private, nonprofit corporation, the Commerce, Labor, Industry Corporation of Kings, known as CLICK, to be operated as an industrial park. The rental agreement calls for CLICK to pay the city $200,000 a year, which represents about a 1% annual direct return to the city on its initial outlay, and additional amounts based on operating profits.

The Yard comprises 4 million square feet of area, with 33 buildings, 5 piers, 6 drydocks, and a coal-fired power plant, plus railway trackage, trucking bays, and other transportation facilities.[16] Space is leased to private firms, particularly those whose employment policy favors workers of minority origin and disadvantaged background. Rents in 1975 were $1.25 – $1.60 per square foot per year. After considerable vicissitudes, the Yard by early 1979 had attained full occupancy, with 37 firms conducting diversified operations ranging from shipbuilding, through the manufacture of a sugar substitute, to the distribution of paper supplies; shipbuilding and repairing was by far the largest activity there, carried on by the Seatrain Shipbuilding Corp. and the Coastal Drydock and Repair Corp.

During the first half of 1979, the total employment in the Yard was 6,000 workers, of whom 3,000 worked for Seatrain and 1,000 worked for Coastal. Most of the firms had between 7 and 100 employees; 85% of the workers were blacks and Puerto Ricans.

In May 1979, Seatrain discontinued the construction of new vessels there, citing its inability to compete with foreign shipbuilders, whom it declared to be "subsidized," and blaming the federal government for rejecting a cargo-preference bill that would have raised the percentage of oil imports required to be carried in U.S.-flag tankers from the present 3% to between 4.5% and 9%.[17] Consequently, Seatrain's work force shrank from 3,000 to a mere 200, so that the total employment in the Yard now stands at about 3,000.

Almost all the other firms in the Yard appear to be prospering and successful, but the whole operation is subject to certain conditions and factors that restrict volume in the Yard and limit its contribution to the city, according to a questionnaire survey which the present writer conducted in the spring of 1980 among these firms.

Perhaps the most significant finding is that most of the nonshipbuilding firms had moved to the Yard from some previous location elsewhere in New York City. The only exceptions are a few new firms which conceivably could have located anywhere, and chose the Yard; also a few other firms which have expanded their operations in the Yard by absorbing some outside companies. The implication for the majority of cases is that the Brooklyn Navy Yard may be helping to retain some manufacturing firms in New York City but is attracting only a few from outside.

One of the limiting conditions on total employment in the Yard is the fact that a large portion of the jobs are work on contract with the U.S. Department of Defense (chiefly ship-repair work by Coastal Drydock for the U.S. Navy). These contracts are dependent on the fluctuations of the Defense budget and negotiations with alternative contractors. The dependency parallels the Seatrain case which was contingent upon federal intervention in a competitive market, with the effect of raising costs and prices to the consumers.

The next major problem in the Yard is the high cost of electric power, which is an important input factor there and in other industrial parks in the city. Until 1972, the Yard generated its own power in a coal-fired plant on the grounds; but this was shut down because of its new environmental-protection laws, rising coal prices, and financial difficulties in CLICK. Electric power is now obtained from Consolidated Edison (Con Ed), whose rates are generally agreed to be very high, far out of line with the rates in competing locations elsewhere (rates in nearby New Jersey are two-thirds of Con Ed rates). Con Ed alleges that its high rates are largely due to its heavy burden of local taxes, claiming that local government seeks to raise necessary revenues by heavily taxing a regulated utility which can only pass along these exactions in the form of higher user charges, and that this is a deceptive device which in effect pretends to relieve the ordinary taxpayers at the expense of cutting industrial activities and jobs. An alternative power source that has been under considerable discussion would be a garbage-to-electricity plant, which for an investment of between $185 million and $267 million would provide low-cost power as well as dispose of much of the city's garbage and yield a number of valuable by-products; but the pioneer plants of this type in other places are still plagued by severe problems.[18]

Problems also arise in some features of the Yard which are usually claimed as its strength and appeal. Maintenance of the facilities has been badly neglected. Transportation capability, one of the Yard's foundation features, is nevertheless the subject of several complaints by resident firms. It appears that long-distance transport — by sea and by air and by inter-city trucking or railroads — is satisfactory and indeed outstanding; the trouble is in intra-city transport, where clogged roads, potholes, and waiting time are handicaps of a familiar but nonetheless acute kind. Similarly, the security provisions, which the Yard management describes with pride, are apparently unsatisfactory to some firms, which complain that the actual screening process discourages legitimate visitors more than undesirables. Furthermore, the supply, quality, and cost of labor are the subject of numerous complaints of varying kinds: Some report a shortage of desired skills; others seem to feel that wage costs are too high here compared to other locations. Several firms complained about local capital supply and interest rates. Nearly all firms protested the burden of taxation — city and state as well as federal — and denounced the complexities of dealing with the local bureaucracy.

Curiously the rent charged by the Yard — in 1980 mostly below $2 per square foot, and supposedly its principal attraction — was judged by six out of ten respondents to be merely "market rate"; three out of ten conceded the rent to be lower than at other locations, but one called it "a little too high." Evidently the services were as low as the rents!

Overall, the tone of the replies to this questionnaire among the responding firms indicated that most of the Navy Yard firms are surviving, and some are prospering, but few are enjoying the experience. Several had complaints against the management of the Yard.

Subsequent to that questionnaire survey, New York City officials in July 1980 released findings of an audit of the Yard's management, indicating "fraud, mismanagement, and waste" which minimized stated profits and thereby deprived the city of incremental revenue due under the rental agreement. A month later, CLICK's Board of Directors dismissed the corporation's president and its chief executive officer.[19]

2. Flatlands, located in south Brooklyn, is a private industrial park managed by Rentar Development Corporation.[20] The area of 100 acres is fully occupied by twelve firms employing 6,000 persons. Rents currently are reported as ranging from $2 to $3 per square foot. All the firms have been there for five years or more, and — most significantly — all of them came from other locations within New York City. Indeed, one manager of Flatlands declared it is an illusion to suppose that industrial parks can attract manufacturing firms from outside the city.

3. The Zerega Avenue Industrial Park, located in the Bronx, is another private operation, managed by Westchester Creek Corp, since 1970.[21] In 1975 it contained four firms, representing 15% occupancy; in 1980 there were three firms, engaged in diversified manufacturing; and representing 50% occupancy. Capacity to attract more firms is limited by the relatively high rental rates, ranging from $3 to $3.50 per square foot in 1980.

4. Adjacent to the Zerega Avenue site is the James J. Lyons Industrial Park, owned by the City of New York and managed by the city's Public Development Corporation (PDC). Of eight firms in this park that were studied in 1981, only two were engaged in manufacturing there, four were warehouses engaged in distribution in the New York area, one was a terminal for a private bus company, and the eighth was a cosmetics research center that was planning to move soon to New Jersey. None of these firms had come to the park from outside New York. Space in this park was also occupied by a truck depot of the city's Department of Sanitation.

5. The North East Marine Terminal is a public facility, located in Brooklyn and operated by the city's Department of Ports and Terminals.[22] Its 240 acres were 30% occupied in 1975, but were reported to be 90% occupied in 1980, including ten firms engaged in diversified manufacturing ranging from leather tanning to food processing.

6. The College Point Industrial Park, managed by PDC, is located in Queens, on Flushing Bay near the Flushing Airport.[23] It was originally proposed in the 1960s, at a planned land cost of $7 million, but to date it has absorbed $33 million. Of a

total area of 550 acres, some 51 acres are occupied by 13 firms plus two more about to start up; total employment in all 15 firms will be just over 2,000 persons. These were essentially New York City firms that made a move into that park. The slow progress of occupancy there is particularly constrained by the tendency to flooding from rains — the area is a kind of "natural inland sea" — for which proper drainage costs would run at $70 – 80 million.

7. The Bathgate Industrial Park, located in the Bronx alongside Crotona Park, is a project now being planned by the PDC as a small-scale or "vest-pocket" industrial park. On a total site of 55 acres, the PDC is proposing to construct buildings of approximately 100,000-square-foot size, and of single-story type, on 21.5 acres of land, enlisting federal funds and private-sector participation, with a view to renting space to small manufacturing firms and generating about 1,500 jobs. The site is on the Cross Bronx Expressway, and has easy access to major city streets and highways. The potential clientele, according to the PDC's Plan for Bathgate, "is assumed to be that of the small and medium size industry presently located in the city, but in search of new efficient space in one-story structures that are well located and provide convenient amenities";[24] in other words, few firms are expected to come from outside the city. One of the main problems for Bathgate in attracting any firms is competitive costs: The Meadowlands area in nearby New Jersey offers modern manufacturing space at $2.85 per square foot (including local taxes), while utility rates there are about two-thirds of Con Ed rates in New York City. The PDC estimates that "new construction at present financing rates cannot be brought in to achieve rental levels much under $3.75 – $4 per square foot," and therefore cannot be competitive "unless a major subsidy is provided." Such subsidization raises serious questions as to the optimal use of municipal funds.

8. While the College Point Park shows the slow growth of occupancy and the heavy infrastructural costs in a new and heretofore unused location; and while the Bathgate Park shows the necessity of major subsidies to be competitive where new one-story buildings are to be constructed in an already developed area, the record of the Staten Island Park combines many of the drawbacks of both the College Point Park and the Bathgate project. The Staten Island project dates back to at least 1972, when the PDC completed a plan (called "Phase II") for a large industrial park on a 775-acre site. It was not until 1976 that the West Shore Expressway was completed so as to provide the site with direct access to the neighboring Staten Island Expressway, the Goethals and Verrazano bridges, and the New Jersey Turnpike. Meanwhile, the problems of severe local flooding from rains has not been resolved, and will be very expensive to cure. The total construction costs — which, curiously, are listed in the official *Environmental Impact Statement* as "short-term construction benefits" — are projected over the next twenty years at over $503 million for "partial development" and at over $600 million for "full development"; and this is without any allowance for inflation, cost overruns, and design changes. These huge outlays will at best create some additional jobs for New York City residents (over and above "no public action") amounting to 1,460 and 2,600 for the two stages of development respectively, over twenty years.[25] Indeed, that environmental statement does not face up to the twin problem of: (a) the probable need to subsidize the rents if the leases are to be competitive with

nearby sites, and (b) the calculation of a benefit/cost ratio to learn whether the city and its residents will ever get a positive real return on their investment in this project — let alone whether this project offers the highest available benefit/cost ratio for the use of the city's scarce funds.

Three more promising special potentials

Turning from dreams of great industrial parks to more modest and more appropriate special potentials, there are at least three lines of promising action.

"Vest-pocket industrial parks" would offer industrial space in already-developed small areas of the city, especially in areas becoming vacant by the abandonment of housing, and acquired by the city through *in-rem* proceedings. Such areas already have the necessary sewers, water supply, power lines and telephone lines, police and fire services, as well as mass transit and highway access. In some cases, existing buildings can be used or adapted. In short, the infrastructure — which is so costly to build nowadays, and especially in unused areas that have been left unused usually for a good reason — already is in place in vest-pocket areas, or can be made usable by relatively small marginal expenditures and quick timing. As outlined by former Deputy Mayor Peter Solomon in 1979 the city's plan would be "to use federal money to build simple 100,000-square-foot buildings that could be divided and rented to small manufacturing companies."[26] The hope is that such facilities, available at close-in locations and at low rentals, will be sufficiently attractive to small businesses, to overcome the various obstacles to manufacturing in the city. The same hope underlies the Twentieth Century Fund's Task Force endorsement of the vest-pocket concept.[27]

A second positive approach involves the "high technology industrial research park." Here the emphasis falls on research and development conducted on the frontiers of technology, by highly qualified technical personnel together with skilled operatives to do laboratory set-ups, trial runs in manufacture, testing in house and in the field, etc.; for manual work, some unskilled local residents would be employed. In contrast to ordinary manufacturing firms, which move large volumes of materials and products, and utilize mostly unskilled or semiskilled labor, the high-technology shops are primarily skill-intensive or equipment-intensive, and turn over their discoveries for mass production elsewhere. Such shops would draw upon the city's large stocks of specialists in the universities and in commercial enterprises, and the city's capacity to train many more if the demand is forthcoming. Such parks would provide common facilities — computer, duplication, library — and stimulating association of personnel. As the space requirements are not extensive, this approach might fit in well with the vest-pocket park concept. It would also fit in well with the efforts now being made for the revitalization of Harlem, South Bronx, and Bedford-Stuyvesant. In Harlem, the City College is working with the Harlem Urban Development Corp. (a subsidiary of the state's Urban Development Corp.) in evolving a plan along practical and non-Utopian lines, for such a high-technology park in the 125th Street area.[28]

Related to that Harlem project is the third special potential to be reported here. This is a proposal for product processing in a free-trade zone to be established in

Harlem — possibly in some affiliation with the existing zone in the Brooklyn Navy Yard — in order to promote trade and processing via Harlem links to certain foreign countries, notably in Africa, the Caribbean, and Latin America. A special linkage with Nigeria has already been established via City College initiatives. Existing legal provisions and commercial practices furnish the opportunity for technology-transfer and cost-saving operations, since a free-trade zone avoids some tariff and quota restrictions that still prevail in U.S. trade regulation, even after introduction of the GSP system of tariff concessions.[29] Materials and components may be brought into such a zone free of duties, quotas, or extensive documentation, and may be processed in the zone either for duty-free exportation to third countries or for importation into the U.S. market by paying duty only on the foreign components. If entrepreneurs can find profitable opportunities along these lines, the facilities can be provided by collaboration of the City College, the Harlem Urban Development Corp., the Uptown Chamber of Commerce, the existing Zone No. 1 in Brooklyn, and the endorsement of the Foreign Trade Zones Board in Washington.[30]

Industrial parks and the unemployment problem

There remains the severe and ominous problem of inadequate jobs in manufacturing to absorb the large numbers and staggering proportions of unemployed young men in New York and similar cities. Three lines of relevant programs may be considered:
   1. Some of the unemployed youths may be adaptable for jobs in the expanding commercial and personal services. By means of outreach efforts, reorientation sessions, and specific training programs, some of the unemployed youths may be brought into the present growth sectors of the metropolis. The potential for these young people lies not only in newly generated jobs, but also in the replacement of undocumented alien workers — provided that native-born youths are willing to enter and perform in the kinds of low-level jobs that currently employ many of the illegals.[31]

Further development of the services not only provides employment for residents but also provides the city with a certain degree of resistance to national recessions, as was demonstrated in the downturn of 1979 – 80.[32]

   2. Manufacturing jobs may be retained and expanded in the city if we are willing to make the large required subsidization. Provision of industrial park space is only one device along this line. Complementary or alternative devices include tax allowances, loan guarantees, municipal purchasing contracts, differential rates charged by public utilities, improvement of local transport, abatement of environmental controls, and intensified control of theft and vandalism.[33] Among these, the deregulatory actions taken as a group comprise much of the concept of the Enterprise Zone which is an alternative to the industrial park, but may have still less attraction for manufacturing firms.

The main problem for the city is to assess the feasibility of promoting manufacturing along all the necessary lines that collectively may add up to sufficient conditions for "reindustrialization." Then the city must evaluate the desirability of supporting the factory form of employment, as against all the other uses for its limited funds, and all the other interests at stake.

3. It would not be adequate just to retain the present jobs in manufacturing, in view of the many thousands of local youths and adults who are unemployed at present. Yet the prospects for attracting new firms from outside, to add large volumes of manufacturing jobs, are not very promising, as indicated in the preceding pages. Eventually the city, the state, and the federal government may be obliged to undertake relocation programs: encouraging and assisting urban residents, youths in particular, to migrate to other locations where their numbers will be better adjusted to the local support capacities. Such programs — which were advocated by President Carter, along with retraining of workers, as part of his Economic Revitalization program issued in August 1980 — would tend to complement the autonomous exodus of the middle classes during the past two decades and bring about a better balance of population groups in older cities such as New York.

To be sure, a net process of contraction of population is not exhilarating — even though some particular service sectors do show a boom spirit. And the net process may cost the city some elective seats and some federal transfer funds. Yet as an alternative to deepening unemployment, alienation, and social stress, orderly contraction may be a preferable course.

Notes

Research for this paper was aided by Arthur Borut and other officials of the Office of Economic Development of the City of New York, but they are not responsible for its interpretations. Graduate student M. Klitat also assisted.

1. An Enterprise Zone — a device originated in Britain toward the end of the 1970s, promoted in the U.S. by The Heritage Foundation and by Representative Jack Kemp (Republican of Buffalo, N.Y.), and specifically adopted by John Anderson in his 1980 presidential platform — seeks to attract private business firms to redevelop a depressed area by reducing governmental controls, restrictions, and taxes in the designated zone. Thus it is opposed to the governmental outlays and programming that are inherent in public industrial parks. Furthermore, the Enterprise Zone is not aimed exclusively or even primarily at manufacturing enterprises, and seems more likely to appeal to service firms by way of deregulations that may be sufficient incentives for such firms, since they are not very vulnerable to the material damages that deter industrial firms. On the subject generally, see Stuart M. Butler, *Enterprise Zones* (New York: Universe, 1981). On the net doubtful employment benefits of an Enterprise Zone in a depressed area, see Hugh Price, "Rep. Kemp's Zone Offense," *The New York Times*, October 15, 1980. On the limitations of the tax-cutting feature, see E. P. Reubens, "The Pitfalls of an Taxpayers' Revolt," letter, *The New York Times*, June 14, 1978.

2. Many other old northern cities and their states officals share the faith in an urban industrial renaissance, although not always by way of urban industrial parks. For example, Massachusetts officials unveiled a program, utilizing state and federal funds, aimed at drawing specifically foreign manufacturing firms to that state's cities showing high unemployment rates (*Berkshire Eagle*, August 20, 1980).

3. Port Authority of New York and New Jersey, *Industrial Revitalization in the New York – New Jersey Region*, May 1978, p. 9, and a still larger proposal in May 1981.

4. See article by Amy J. Neches and Philip E. Aarons. in *New York Affairs*, Vol. 6, No. 2, June 1980.

5. Leonard C. Yaseen, "Advice for New York," *The New York Times*, February 18, 1980, Op-Ed page.

6. See "Computer Study Predicts Job Loss," *The New York Times*, March 28, 1980.

7. A study by Regina Belz Armstrong for the Regional Plan Associates, reported in *The New York Times*, June 1, 1980, p. 38.

8. Twentieth Century Fund, Task Force on the Future of New York City, *Report*, 1979,

p. 17. For an early critique of schemes to revive manufacturing in inner cities, see E. P. Reubens, "Economic Strategies for the Ghetto," *City Almanac*, Vol. 4, No. 6 (April 1970).

9. Source cited in Note 6, *above*.

10. U.S. Bureau of Labor Statistics, *Industry Wage Surveys*, reporting on selected production occupations in selected cities, at various dates in the 1970s.

11. Based on BLS data reported in *The New York Times*, February 23, 1980, pp. 1 and 9, and August 23, 1980, pp. 1 and 9.

12. B. L. Weinstein and R. E. Firestine, *Regional Growth and Decline in the U.S.* (New York: Praeger, 1978).

13. See F. F. Foltman and P. D. McClelland, *New York State's Economic Crisis* (Ithaca, N.Y.: Cornell University, School of Industrial and Labor Relations, 1977), Chapters 1 and 8, especially pp. 4–7.

14. See "Experts Do Not Expect Energy Problems to Halt Population Shift Away from Cities," *The New York Times*, June 9, 1980.

15. Louis Harris and Associates, Inc. *Looking Toward the 1980's*, a survey for the Chemical Bank of New York (New York, November 1979).

16. Data from press releases of CLICK, plus sources cited in Note 21.

17. *The New York Times*, May 9, 1979, p. 1.

18. Ibid., August 19, 1980, pp. 1 and B9.

19. Ibid., July 7 and August 8, 1980; also "Great Expectations for Brooklyn Navy Yard Yield to Reality," October 13, 1980.

20. An effort was made to distribute among the Flatlands firms the same questionnaire as was circulated in the Brooklyn Navy Yard. However, the managers of Flatlands, while repeatedly pledging cooperation, failed to distribute the forms and blocked direct approaches to the tenant firms. Reported data obtained from the managers and from sources cited in Notes 21-23, *below*.

21. Data from *Site Selection Handbook* (Atlanta: Conway Publications), Vol. 20, No. 4 (November 1975); and New York City; Office of Economic Development, Mr. Arthur Borut.

22. Data from *Site Selection Handbook*, cit. sup.; and New York City, Department of Ports and Terminals, Mr. E. Zielman.

23. *Site Selection Handbook*, cit, sup,; also former Deputy Mayor Peter Solomon, "City Planning Sites for Small Industry," *The New York Times*, April 6, 1979; also Public Development Corp. press release, "College Point Industrial Park Development Projects," dated October 22, 1979, and other PDC press releases.

24. New York City, Public Development Corp., *Bathgate Plan Project Report*, Spring 1980, pp. 36–37.

25. Public Development Corp., *Environmental Impact Statement* for Staten Island Industrial Park, October 1979, pp. 4–8.

26. Statement by Peter Solomon; see Note 23, *above*.

27. *Report* of the Task Force on the Future of New York City (see Note 8, *above*), p. 18.

28. See memorandum by E. P. Reubens, "A High-Technology Industrial Park in the City College/Harlem Area," City College of New York, Office of Vice-President for Community Relations, November 30, 1979.

29. GSP — for Generalized System of Preference — provides certain reductions of tariff on manufactured products that originate in less developed countries (LDCs). These reductions are limited as to type and as to volume or value of the imports, and extend only to approved LDCs — e.g., members of OPEC are not eligible.

30. See memorandum by E. P. Reubens, "Feasibility and Impact Study of Free Trade Zone in the Harlem I.T.C.," City College of New York, Office of Vice-President for Community Relations, March 18, 1980.

31. On the problems of substitution between native and alien workers, see E.P. Reubens, "Aliens, Jobs and Immigration Policy," *The Public Interest*, Spring 1976; and E.P. Reubens, *Temporary Admission of Foreign Workers*, Special Report 34 of National Commission for Employment Policy (Washington, D.C.: USGPO, 1979), pp. 29–35.

32. "City Economy Found Resisting Recession," *The New York Times*, August 23, 1980, citing a study by Karen Gerard, Chase Manhattan Bank; also "Tax Receipts in City Reveal Surprising Gain," August 26, 1980.

33. In August 1981, Con Ed proposed to offer a 25% discount on power rates to new or expanding business firms in economically depressed areas *(The New York Times,* August 9, 1981). The Kemp-Garcia bill for Enterprise Zones proposes general streamlining of official regulations for such firms.

10

A REGIONAL ECONOMIC DEVELOPMENT STRATEGY

Marilyn Rubin and Ilene Wagner

Perhaps nowhere in the United States today is the intraregional competition for jobs more intense than in the New York metropolitan area. And perhaps nowhere else in the nation is this competition more detrimental to the economic growth and development of all jurisdictions within the region. Though not a new phenomenon, the economic rivalry between New York City and its neighbors prior to the late 1960s was, in hindsight, relatively mild. But the national recessions in 1969–70 and 1973–75 fueled this rivalry as localities began competing for increasingly scarce jobs.

New York City was especially hard hit by the economic downturns, losing more than 600,000 jobs between 1969 and 1976. Jobs leaving the city, however, did not all flock to the Sunbelt, as the popular media would have us believe. Many were lost as businesses contracted operations or closed down completely. And most of those that did leave tended to relocate within a relatively circumscribed area. Two-thirds of the Fortune 500 companies that moved from New York City between 1965 and 1975 relocated to nearby suburbs;[1] three out of every four manufacturing jobs that left New York City from 1961 through 1976 migrated to New Jersey, Connecticut, and other parts of New York State.[2]

But although the bulk of the jobs leaving New York City since 1961 have remained in the tri-state area, with the passage of time a growing number have indeed left the region altogether. To illustrate, from 1961 through 1964, 15% of all reported manufacturing moves from New York City were to area outside the tri-state region; from 1970 through 1976, the proportion had increased to 36.3%.[3] Jobs from other jurisdictions within the New York area also are leaving the region in increasing number for other parts of the nation. For example, from 1970 through 1976, almost half of all reported manufacturing job moves from Nassau and Suffolk counties were to southern and western states. This compared to no reported manufacturing job moves at all out of the region from Nassau and Suffolk from 1961 through 1964.[4] Because the regional job movement is no longer only a loss for New York City and a gain for the rest of the area, the idea of a regional strategy to stem the outflow of jobs has gained widespread support.

For decades, academics and urban planners have advocated regional cooperation in transportation and housing. Of late, they have been joined by public and private sector officials in calling for a regional economic development strategy. In 1979 alone, several organizations sponsored conferences around this theme. To illustrate, in June 1979 the Port Authority of New York and New Jersey sponsored the Congress for Regional Recovery to present to the region's leaders findings of its Committee on the Future. A report of the committee's Regional and Economic Development Task Force states:

> Many of the challenges facing the New York – New Jersey Region in the next decade transcend local and state jurisdictions and require that there be cohesive response at the regional level. . . .
> A regional economic development strategy . . . suggests the need to moderate the intensity of intraregional competition. While political and taxation jurisdictions remain a reality, the region does not benefit from the pirating of business and industry from one community to the next.[5]

In October 1979, as a follow-up to the Port Authority conference, the Tri-State Regional Planning Commission sponsored "a conference to obtain advice from public-and private-sector leaders on the commission's role in regional economic development." Among those present, there was little dissension on the overriding goal of regional cooperation. There was less agreement on just what regional economic development actually means and a feeling that "it's easier said than done." Indeed, in his opening remarks at the conference, Frank Johnson, executive director of the commission, posed a question that, until answered, will remain a formidable obstacle to the formulation of any regional economic development strategy: "How does the metropolitan Planning Organization decide on the strategic steps for promoting economic recovery in areas of our region suffering from severe economic distress, but simultaneously sustain economic growth where it stands on a strong foot?"[6]

The formulation of a regional strategy is thus impeded not only by the obvious political constraints but also by the less obvious constraints resulting from differences in industrial growth and structure especially between distressed and healthy areas. Whereas employment in the entire New York – New Jersey Standard Consolidated Area (SCA) decreased from 6.7 million jobs in 1969 to 6.5 million in 1978, the SCA without New York City actually experienced an increase of 389,300 jobs during this period. A case can thus be made for focusing on the primary area that lost jobs — New York City — in a regional strategy aimed at job generation and/or retention, but such an approach is not likely to gain popular support outside of the city.

The purpose of this paper is to highlight differences in growth structure in New York City and in the rest of the SCA that make regional problem-solving in economic development such a difficult task and to identify possible areas where a regional approach is possible.

For analytical purposes and based upon data availability, the New York – New Jersey SCA has been used to define the region, which has been divided into two parts: New York City and the remainder of the SCA. No attempt has been made to separate the remainder of the region into its urban and suburban components.

The regional economy: an overview

In 1960 there were 5.7 million jobs in the New York– New Jersey SCA of which 62% were in New York City. In 1969 there were 6.7 million jobs in the SCA of which 57% were in New York City. By 1978, New York City employment represented only 49% of the SCA's 6.5 million jobs.

It should be noted that while New York City's share of total SCA employment was declining, the absolute number of jobs in the rest of the SCA was increasing.

Not only was there a change in the relative distribution of jobs inside and outside the city but so too there were structural changes in their economic bases. Manufacturing employment in New York City represented 26.8% of total employment in 1960 and the service sector 17.2%. In 1969 manufacturing was 21.7% and services 20.5% of total employment in the city. By 1979, manufacturing had declined to 16.6% and services had risen to 25.3%.

In the rest of the SCA, manufacturing accounted for 37.4% of total employment in 1960 and services represented 13.5%; in 1969 manufacturing was 32.4% and services 16.0%. By 1978 manufacturing had declined to 25.4% but remained relatively more important than the service sector, which has increased to 19.2%.

The changing relationship between manufacturing and service-sector employment in the SCA between 1969 and 1978 was more closely akin to the national pattern than to that of New York City. It is interesting to note that employment growth rates in the non-New York City portion of the SCA through the 1970s were also more similar to those in the national economy than to those in the New York City economy, which continued to decline throughout most of the decade.

The decline in city employment occurred in most sectors of the economy, with manufacturing accounting for almost half of the total job loss. In the rest of the SCA, manufacturing was the only major economic sector that declined during the 1969–78 period. It would thus seem logical that a top regional economic development priority would be to bolster the region's faltering manufacturing sector. But formulating a regional strategy directed at even one sector of the economy such as manufacturing is difficult because of the differences in the growth and structure of manufacturing inside and outside of the city.

Manufacturing in the New York region: growth and structure in New York City and the rest of the SCA

Growth

In 1969 there were 1,765,900 manufacturing jobs in the SCA; New York City accounted for 48% of these jobs. By 1978, total manufacturing jobs in the SCA had declined to 1,371,600 an New York City's share had declined to 38%.

The relative and absolute decline in New York City's position resulted from an increase in business closings and contractions, a decrease in expansions and openings of new firms, and the migration of jobs to the surrounding areas and, to a somewhat lesser degree, to other parts of the nation. Meanwhile, the relative and

TABLE 1
EMPLOYMENT IN NEW YORK CITY BY SECTOR, PERCENTAGE OF TOTAL EMPLOYMENT

	1960	1969	1978
Total number of jobs all industries (in thousands)	3,538.4	3,797.7	3,223.7
Private industries	88.5	85.6	84.0
Mining	0.1	0.1	*
Manufacturing	26.8	21.7	16.6
Contract. construction	3.5	2.8	2.0
Transp. & public utilities	9.0	8.5	8.0
Trade	21.0	19.7	19.2
Finance, insurance, and real estate	10.9	12.3	12.9
Services	17.2	20.5	25.3
Government	11.5	14.4	15.9

TABLE 2
EMPLOYMENT IN SCA (MINUS N.Y.C.), BY SECTOR, PERCENTAGE OF TOTAL EMPLOYMENT

	1960	1969	1978
Total number of jobs all industries (in thousands)	2,176.1	2,903.2	3,292.5
Private industries	87.5	85.6	82.8
Mining	*	0.1	*
Manufacturing	37.4	32.4	25.4
Contract. construction	5.3	4.7	3.5
Transp. & public utilities	7.2	6.5	6.3
Trade	19.6	21.4	23.2
Finance, insurance, and real estate	4.5	4.5	5.2
Services	13.5	16.0	19.2
Government	12.4	14.3	17.3

SOURCES: U.S. Department of Labor; New York State Department of Labor.

*Less than .05% of total employment.

absolute ascendancy of the SCA's position resulted from business expansions, births of new firms, and the inmigration of jobs primarily from New York City.

In fact, there was a definite effort on the part of neighboring states to assist New York firms in the relocation of their facilities. Of the eleven out-of-state firms given assistance by the New Jersey Economic Development Authority in 1976, eight were from New York. Interestingly, all eight firms moved to the most urbanized counties in New Jersey which are part of the New York City Standard Consolidation area. Thus, on balance, much of New York City's loss was the rest-of-region's gain.

Structure

In 1978 more than two out of every three manufacturing jobs in New York City were in nondurables and 45% of all of the city's manufacturing jobs were in apparel and printing.

TABLE 3

MANUFACTURING EMPLOYMENT IN N.Y.C., SELECTED YEARS, 1950-78
PERCENTAGE OF TOTAL MANUFACTURING

	1978	1969	1960	1950
Total Number of Manufacturing Jobs (in thousands)	534.8	625.8	964.8	1,038.9
Durables	30.1	31.4	32.1	29.2
Lumber	0.7	0.7	0.6	0.7
Furniture & fixtures	2.0	2.1	1.9	2.2
Stone	0.9	1.0	1.2	1.2
Prime metal	1.3	1.6	1.4	1.4
Fabricated metal	4.3	4.5	3.7	3.1
Machinery except elec.	3.1	3.5	3.7	3.1
Electric	6.0	6.0	6.4	5.1
Transportation equip.	1.2	1.0	1.2	1.4
Instruments	2.2	2.7	2.6	2.5
Miscellaneous	8.5	8.3	7.9	7.8
Nondurables	69.9	68.5	67.9	70.1
Food	6.0	7.4	8.6	9.5
Tobacco	0.5	0.4	0.3	0.4
Textiles	4.4	4.2	3.8	3.7
Apparel	28.4	27.1	28.2	32.4
Paper	3.4	3.1	3.2	2.7
Printing	17.0	15.2	13.4	11.5
Chemicals	5.0	5.1	4.8	4.1
Petroleum	0.7	1.0	1.0	0.8
Rubber & plastics	1.6	1.5	1.1	1.3
Leather	2.8	3.6	3.3	3.6

SOURCES: U.S. Department of Labor; New York State Department of Labor.

In the rest of the SCA, there is no single industry that is equal in magnitude to the city's apparel industry. Chemicals, the largest single employer, represents 15% of all manufacturing, a proportion about equal to the printing industry in New York City.

Given the above differences in growth and structure it should be obvious why it is so difficult to formulate a regional strategy aimed at the most important manufacturing industries. Which industries should be targeted in the overall regional strategy? Should retention of the city's apparel industry be the number-one priority of a regional economic development priority? Or should the number-one priority be attracting the chemical industry which is of relatively minor

TABLE 4

MANUFACTURING EMPLOYMENT SCA (MINUS N.Y.C.), SELECTED YEARS, 1950-78
PERCENTAGE OF TOTAL MANUFACTURING

	1978	1969	1960	1950
Total Number of Manufacturing Jobs (in thousands)	836.8	941.1	814.4	694.0
Durables	51.7	55.9	57.5	50.0
Lumber	0.7	0.5	0.6	0.7
Furniture & fixtures	1.4	1.4	1.4	1.2
Stone	1.9	2.1	2.1	2.1
Prime metal	2.9	4.0	4.9	4.7
Fabricated metal	7.6	7.3	6.5	*
Machinery except electric	9.7	9.9	7.7	6.4
Electric	12.4	14.0	14.4	12.2
Transportation equip.	5.8	7.8	8.9	7.6
Instruments	5.8	5.6	6.3	4.1
Miscellaneous	3.2	3.6	3.7	4.9
Nondurables	48.3	44.0	42.5	50.1
Food	5.9	6.1	7.0	7.2
Tobacco	*	*	*	0.4
Textiles	7.1	8.0	8.8	11.7
Apparel	4.2	3.5	3.5	3.0
Paper	4.2	3.5	3.5	3.0
Printing	7.4	5.6	5.0	3.9
Chemicals	14.9	11.8	9.6	9.7
Petroleum	1.0	*	1.0	1.7
Rubber & plastics	3.9	3.9	2.9	2.8
Leather	0.9	1.0	1.2	1.6

SOURCES: U.S. Department of Labor; New York State Department of Labor.

*Less than .05% of total employment.

importance to the city but the largest manufacturing industry in the non-New York City portion of the SCA?

The targeting question applies to other sectors of the economy as well. In 1978 the finance, insurance, and real estate industries (FIRE) in New York City accounted for 13% of total employment compared to only 5% in the rest of the SCA. Thus, retaining firms in these industries is much more critical to New York City's economic development efforts than to those of the rest of the region.

Toward a regional economic development strategy

The Port Authority recently instituted an industrial park program to retain and attract manufacturing jobs into the region. After many months in the formative stages, the program represents one element of a yet-to-emerge comprehensive economic development strategy for the region.

In the Port Authority's Committee on the Future Report, a number of other strategies were presented: commercial revitalization, waterfront development, and the development of an effective regional marketing strategy.

It is difficult to argue with these overall recommendations; in fact, they do indeed form the basis for a comprehensive strategy. However, there is no indication in the report of how to reach the regional consensus necessary for strategy implementation. According to the report, an effective regional marketing strategy would include a promotional campaign to "engender" a regional identity. The strategy would stress the region's assets and would be directed at "identified target industries." But, the wide variation in the industrial growth and structure inside and outside the city makes it quite difficult, if not impossible, to target specific industries.

If industries are to be targeted, rather than looking at the industries themselves it might be more appropriate to examine the backward and forward linkages of the major industries in the region in an input-output type of framework. Such an analysis would identify common markets and resources utilized by all industries in the region, regardless of location, and would point out those industries and resources that are of major importance to the region as a whole. For example, energy used by all industries throughout the region is more expensive than in any other part of the country. A strategy for municipalities to share information on the design and operation of alternative energy sources would contribute to the region's economic viability. As Peter J. Solomon, former New York City deputy mayor for economic policy and development, has stated:

> Several municipalities have begun to experiment with resource recovery plants, and many others are considering this solution to the problems of generating power and disposing of garbage. The lessons we learn can speed the installation and efficient operation of those plants all over the region and subsequently reduce our dependence on foreign oil.[7]

Although it is beyond the scope of this paper to discuss other possible areas for regional cooperation, it is evident that there are many constraints to overcome and diverse interests to satisfy before a truly regional economic development strategy can be put in place.

Notes

1. The Conservation of Human Resources Project, *The Corporate Headquarters Complex in New York City* (New York: Columbia University, 1977), p. 40.

2. Marilyn Rubin, Ilene Wagner, and Pearl Kamer, "Industrial Migration: A Case Study of Destination by City-Suburban Origin Within the New York Metropolitan Area," *Journal of the American Real Estate and Urban Economics Association,* Winter 1978/79.

3. Ibid. This analysis was based on more than 90,000 manufacturing job moves from New York City and Nassau and Suffolk counties between 1961 and 1976. The sample is based solely on moves reported to the New York State Department of Commerce.

4. Ibid.

5. The Port Authority of New York and New Jersey, *Regional and Economic Development Strategies for the 1980's* (New York, 1979), pp. 33–34.

6. Frank Johnson, remarks from a speech given October 24, 1979 (New York: Agenda for Regional Economic Development, 1979).

7. Peter J. Solomon, remarks from a speech given October 24, 1979 (New York: Agenda for Regional Economic Development, 1979).

11

NEW YORK CITY AFTER THE 1970s: A CASE FOR GUARDED OPTIMISM

William J. Lawrence

New Yorkers had considerable cause for deep concern during the spring of 1980. For nearly five years of crisis-oriented headlines, matched by what may ultimately be recognized as the most innovative and exhaustive measures ever devised to monitor and reestablish a rational public financial mechanism for a local government, New York City was laid out flat, almost belly up. Many analysts and pundits were waiting for the last nudge that would expose the city and possibly the entire region to the executioner's final blow.

This attitude followed nearly a decade of hemmorhaging in the city's labor markets. On the demand side more than 690,000 jobs had left the central city. On the supply side more than 736,000 people had left for other parts of the region and country. With them went a large portion of the city's tax base. Corporate headquarters seemed to disappear overnight, the streets got dirtier, crime rates increased, the parks became unlivable. Housing markets in both the city and its suburbs seemed to fall apart, transportation in and out of the city became a daily drudgery, and the whole Northeast seemed to be moving to the Sunbelt.

Nevertheless, the city was not witnessing the dramatic decline in jobs that characterized the early part of the 1970s. Although it continued to lose both durable and nondurable manufacturing employment, the rate at which this loss was occurring changed considerably. In fact, there was a slight net increase of 1.2% for 1979, and total employment for the city had increased from 2.7 million in December 1975 to 2.8 million in December 1979, or approximately 3.4% (compared to a 15% rate of growth for the nation for the same period).

One has only to look around the city and the region and see that the economy was incredibly more robust in 1980 than it was in 1975. Every indicator pointed to the fact that, even with the national recession anticipated, New York would fare relatively better than it did in 1974–75 — the worst postwar downturn our nation has had. Business failures were down over the last cycle. New York City had 1,051 failures in 1974. For the first nine months of 1979, business failures were only 282 compared to 329 for the same period in 1978. Clearly this trend could be viewed as a positive sign. Hotel occupancy rates continued to be strong at almost 85%. A large amount of contract construction was taking place with a net increase of 6,700 jobs, or over 10% for 1979. If one combined these facts with the policy of the preceeding four years of no increases in corporate and personal income taxes for the city, it was difficult to see where the deep recession anticipated by some would come from.

Another excellent indicator was the growth in retail sales. Increasing slightly under 16.0% in 1979 for the city, retail sales significantly outstripped those of the rest of the nation at 10.4% for the same period. At first, some of us attributed this phenomenon to the gas lines in the suburbs and elsewhere in the United States. "Of course people come to New York to shop," we said. "They don't have to worry about driving their cars here." The gas lines stopped. Yet retail sales continued to climb.

Still looking for a reason, we then attributed the increase to the tourist trade — approximately 17.5 million tourists visited New York in 1979. Certainly this could account for the improvement, but when the autumn came and the height of the tourist season was past, retail sales were still up. Let's face it: New York City is one of the major shopping centers of this nation, and well it should be. Three hundred eighty-one thousand persons are employed in retail businesses in New York — no small reason for the growing business momentum. One disappointing factor was that, despite the dramatic increase in retail sales, retail employment increased only 0.4% in 1979 compared to 3.2% for the nation. This could have been an example of labor hoarding; however, I have no empirical evidence to substantiate this hypothesis.

Finally, the New York region was in a more competitive position vis-à-vis the rest of the country than it had been for the past decade. Wage rates were increasing more slowly than in the rest of the nation. Our local inflation rate had been consistently below the national averages for more than 18 months. To the extent that the CPI accurately reflects local inflation, we could rejoice in the 10.6% average increase in 1979 compared to the national increase in prices of over 13.3%. The March 1979-to-March 1980 rate of inflation for New York was 12.0% compared to 14.7% for the nation over the same period. The figures showed further that the total inflationary pressures continued to be less for New York than for the nation.

National increases in energy costs were steadily converging on local costs in 1980, as the rest of the nation moved toward world energy prices, where the New York region had been for almost a decade. The last two quarters, however, revealed relatively greater increases in energy costs for the city than for the rest of the nation. New York's total energy costs from February 1979 to March 1980 increased by 46%. To summarize, the New York region had already made major adjustments to its economy, adjustments other regions throughout the nation might yet have to undergo. The net effect was that the cost of doing business in New York and the region was becoming more and more competitive with each passing year, and the outlook could be viewed somewhat more optimistically.

The city typically contracted more deeply and quickly than the nation and recovered more slowly and less dramatically. On balance, the city may be viewed as having reversed that trend for the 1980 recession; key indicators held up through

1979; and I felt that this momentum would continue for at least two or three more quarters, the period of the expected national downturn.

In the immediate future, retail sales and contract construction should continue to grow, although at reduced rates. Hotel occupancy rates may decline somewhat, but this will be a result mainly of the increase in new hotels. Manufacturing employment will decline by about 3.0%, or about 16,000 jobs, and the extent of this will be directly linked to the severity of the national downturn. A critical statistic to watch is the local unemployment rate, which continues to be higher than the national rate. Herein lies one of New York's most formidable problems to which I shall return later.

The future of New York City in the longer run

The tide is turning in favor of the city. During the last three decades there was a mass exodus out of the city, but more recently we have witnessed a reduction in this outflow of families. We know the initial reasons for the exodus: rising prices and falling employment opportunities, high rents, rising crime rates, poor school systems, lack of open space for recreation, etc. *I now foresee a reversal in the declining population.*

The time is ripe for a move back to the city, perhaps not a mass migration, but a perceptible increase both in very young households and in possible older households — people in their early fifties who are not ready for retirement, no longer have children at home, and do not wish to continue supporting three- and four-bedroom homes. In addition, because of the growing trend toward smaller families, the marginal cost of living in an urban environment is not as great as it was. For a family with three children, it was often the additional cost of housing and private schools that made urban living impossible and drove the family to the suburbs, but now, with the one- or at most two-child family more likely the norm, the time is fast approaching when living in the city may actually be less expensive. Why?

Energy will certainly be one of the most critical problems of the 1980s; we don't need sophisticated forecasting techniques to detect that. Even a two- or three-person family in the suburbs must have at least one car, usually two. With the skyrocketing cost of gasoline, New York's crowded and aged public transportation system suddenly looks much more attractive to a family that must send its breadwinners to work and its children to school. The family car (or cars), once an integral part of the American dream, is rapidly becoming a pain in the American neck.

The cost of heating a suburban home also will be a major factor in the coming decade. And energy is only one of the many maintenance expenses connected with suburban homeowning. A suburban house on a quarter-acre of land is incredibly energy- and cost-inefficient relative to its urban counterpart. A suburban house is not merely a home; it is a lawn, storm windows, driveway, roof, siding, shingles, and on and on. At the rate at which such maintenance expenses can be expected to increase, the cost of maintaining a family in a split-level home may well outstrip that of apartment dwelling, despite the escalating rents and prices of co-ops and condominiums in the central city.

In the 1980s, both urban and suburban middle-income families may have to send their children to private schools. Certainly, this is increasingly the case today as more and more suburban public school systems experience the same difficulties with rising costs and declining quality of instruction that the city systems have experienced for years. After all, private school enrollment for suburban households steadily increased during the latter 1970s.

To be realistic, however, although there are problems for both the city and its suburbs, the city's ills are much harder to cure. For example, it is easier to turn around schools in the suburbs than it is in the city. A suburban-oriented legislature is far more likely to appropriate additional funds for school systems outside of New York City than for city schools, especially in light of declining enrollments. It is also true that the city's school problems have been around for years, and nothing, not even substantial expenditures, seems to have helped them. Still, the city's schools must be trimmed down and made more responsive to the educational needs of middle-income families. It can be done, and I believe that the Koch administration is dedicated to that goal.

I must stress, and stress again, however, that *all of this is worth nothing if those who make policy for the city do not act decisively and act now.*

Parks. Free open space is a critical area. New York's parks must become safe, attractive, and inviting for the families who will otherwise move to the suburbs to seek land for recreation and breathing space. It is hard to impress policy-makers with the importance of this, but parks are more than a potential safety hazard or a marketplace for illegal drug traffic; they are a tremendous plus if treated properly, and they must receive greater budgetary priority than they do now if we wish to bring the tax base back to the central city.

Streets. Sanitation is an unwieldy and apparently unsolvable area, but it must be addressed. A recently instituted experiment should give us some insight into one possible solution. The commissioner of sanitation is going to test the efficiency of private cartage for two or three of the city's 59 community districts. Other cities have found a significant decrease in cost per ton with a shift to private firms. Will increasing private cartage make our streets cleaner? I do not know if this is the best solution; I just feel that one must be found and very soon.

Safety on the streets is, of course, key. This is not easy to turn around, especially in view of the disappointing fact that New York's violent crime rate increased in 1979 after two years of decline. Murders increased 15%; robberies were up 11.5%. St. Louis, Atlanta, Houston, and Miami all exceed New York in the increasing rate of homicides, and crime rates on a per capita basis are also on the rise in the suburbs. Crime is not an inner-city exclusive; it is endemic to our frenetic, disoriented 20th-century society.

Are these insoluble problems? I think not. I cannot stress enough how optimistic I am about the ultimate future of New York and its environs — providing that the right policy steps are taken. New York is one of the best cities in the world in which to live. If you think, for example, that it is expensive to live in New York, try Tokyo, Paris, London, or watch San Diego, Denver, Portland, Chicago, Detroit, Boston, Washington, or Miami in the coming years.

There will be some tough policy decisions to make in the 1980s, and we cannot leave them all up to government. Cities and towns are comprised of *people*; and people have to have pride in where they live and work, but also in their streets and parks. We as individuals have the ultimate responsibility for a safe, clean, livable society.

Jobs. The city's continuing loss of jobs in durable and nondurable manufacturing has slowed down somewhat, but it is still very much in evidence, and there are no solid signs of reversal. This is a particularly worrisome problem because of the occupations involved. The industries that will show increases — retail trade, banking, communications, and business services — cannot absorb the bulk of those unskilled or semiskilled workers unemployed as a result of the decline in manufacturing employment.

Several solutions have been suggested, none panaceas, but we must review them and institute the most promising. One solution is the proposition supported by Peter Goldmark of the Port Authority and Peter Solomon, former deputy mayor of New York City for economic policy and development, for the building of industrial parks to lure manufacturing back to New York City. Although I am less certain about this particular project, I certainly believe it should be tried. The cost of creating such parks is relatively low, and the advantage, if successful, is that manufacturing represents hard, stable business. Once a factory has located here, it will tend to be much less mobile than, say, a company headquarters or any other industry that simply rents office space. Also — and this is a big plus — every industrial park successfully established here will mean jobs for people in our region who might not otherwise find employment.

But while we are attempting to lure manufacturing jobs back to the city, we must remain realistic about who can and who cannot be expected to do business in New York. We must evaluate industries that can function in a vertically oriented urban environment, where horizontal space is at a premium. There are some industries — business services, communications, and other high-technology industries — for which we are ideally suited and some we simply should not waste time and money trying to attract. No high-density urban area like ours can compete for industries that require horizontal space. That's why we lost much of the garment industry — and it is fruitless to suppose we will get it back. Here is an excellent opportunity for the city to work closely with the surrounding suburbs. Let's keep the industry within the region and seek the opportunities and policy options to encourage this. We must learn to think and plan on a regional basis.

One source of the kind of jobs we need should be the construction industry. I have already mentioned that contract construction has undergone a renaissance in the last three years. But what about badly needed residential construction?

Housing. The apartment shortage in the city is reaching crisis proportions — if it hasn't already reached them. Because of an energy crisis that makes locating in the city desirable, because there has been very little new residential construction for several years, because New York is daily attracting business people from abroad who need living space, and for countless other reasons, housing, especially low- and middle-income housing is at an unbelievable premium. Here is an ideal situation for the construction industry: First, there is a heavy demand relative to the existing stock of housing; second, unemployment in the city is uncomfortably above the national average; finally, the current high interest rates notwithstanding, the financial institutions to support this construction are right here in New York. Our decision-makers must find a way to pull these three components together, stimulate residential construction, and create low- and middle-income housing.

This would be an ideal way to create needed economic activity for New York. John Maynard Keynes recommended during a period of much greater economic stress that some people be hired to dig holes and others to fill them up. It seems to me that residential construction would be a lot less drastic and a more practical remedy, with the same salutary results. It will require imaginative and creating thinking on the part of all involved, public and private sectors, management and labor. It's been done before and can be done again.

Fourteen thousand permits for residential units were issued in 1979, a 21% increase over the previous year, and 1979 witnessed a 44% increase in units completed over 1978 levels. These figures are very encouraging. But we still need much more housing. Furthermore, without the J-51 tax-incentive program these unit completions would have been less than half what they were. The city itself manages over 24,000 properties; it is the largest single landlord in the city and probably not the most efficient one.

Human Capital. But while we are developing industries, we must also develop people.

One of the primary requirements for the 1980s is that we place a much higher priority on vocational and technical education. *We must find the key to making this area of education an honorable pursuit* or we will never solve our manpower and employment problems or attract new business to the area. After all, even if New York is increasingly becoming a white-collar service-oriented city, how can workers in the service communications, banking, or financial industries function without people who can fix their cars, typewriters, and television sets — never mind their computer terminals. In an energy-scarce world, we can no longer afford to throw away our shoes and our watches simply because a sufficient number of trained repairmen and repairwomen do not exist. We need a drastic turnaround in our educational philosophy. The present philosophy, which still puts a premium on a liberal arts education in a classic university or high school setting, is needed, but it cannot be the sole emphasis of our educational resources. More and more holders of bachelor's degrees in liberal arts subjects find, after months of fruitless job hunting, that these degrees are useless. Paradoxically, they often take refuge in graduate school to get a more advanced degree only to witness the same frustration again.

But I am not speaking primarily about developing vocational education for those who are over educated and underemployed. I am speaking of courses for those who cannot, and do not, function in a classic academic environment, high school as well as college. Not long ago, *The New York Times* reported that our high school dropout rate had reached 50%. No wonder youth-related crime rates are rising as fast as youth unemployment. We must address this problem, forcibly and at once. As our society rapidly moves toward a more cybernetic lifestyle that seeks to automate more and more functions out of our daily lives, we will have to rely more heavily on technically trained individuals to perform these functions. Traditional education will not prepare these people. They will need specialized skills that will lead to meaningful employment. Perhaps some of the approximately 40 school buildings throughout the city that are designated to be closed could be converted for this training.

Conclusions and recommendations

New York has all the resources and potential to meet the challenges of the 1980s. It is ironic that because New York City is the center of one of the great industries of this century — communications, and more specifically, television — our local news is automatically national news. Every fire, subway incident, water-main break, and robbery in New York is flashed from coast to coast, although a similar incident that occurred in Des Moines or Baltimore would probably never make it out of the state. But even this disadvantage can be used to our advantage, if we are creative. A shining example is the "I Love New York" campaign, probably one of the most demonstrably successful advertising efforts in the history of the state.

New York is one of the richest consumer markets in the world. Within a 50-mile diameter, more than 13 million people live, work, and shop. New York State ranks first in the nation in commercial bank assets, second in value added in manufacturing. Furthermore, New York is a truly international city. In the recent past and continuing into the present, there has been a major influx of foreign banking into the city. Given current trends, this should continue, bringing additional people and purchasing power with it.

Also, according to a recent paper by Peter Goldmark, over one million *legal immigrants* settled in the New York metropolitan region during the past decade. People come here because they see boundless opportunity here. We, too, must see this opportunity and take advantage of it. We must recognize that public expenditures have to be reduced, and this means a reduction in public services. Our natural resources, including the existing and potential labor force, must be effectively utilized — and this means good vocational education that will meet the needs of a contemporary and changing labor market.

Finally, the region must pull toether. There is no reason why a solid, effective confederation of regionally oriented organizations cannot be established to investigate as a unit the advantages and disadvantages of each subarea throughout the region. The Port Authority of New York and New Jersey, the Regional Plan Association, Citizens' Union, the Chamber of Commerce, and hundreds of other business and "good government" associations from this area should be forged into a cohesive, united force working for the good of the entire region. I submit that a confederated regional approach would serve to unite these various groups and make them even more effective. Such a confederation should function first in an analytical capacity, studying each unique area carefully within the confines of available markets and the limits of existing policies and resources in order to compile an inventory of what each has to offer. This inventory should be comprised of a careful listing of what the city and each of its suburbs offers in economic development potential and how each of these assets can best be used to our joint advantage. Rather than concentrate on the old city-suburb tension, the confederation should coordinate and consolidate the goals of the entire metropolitan region. New Yorkers are often criticized for thinking of themselves first on national issues. I do not think we really do this, but maybe we should.

But the confederation must not stop here. In addition to establishing an analytical capacity, it must then be able to mobilize a lobbying power at the national level. The New York region must develop a better organized lobby in Washington and Albany, comprised of leaders in the business, academic, and general community.

The overall theme for our recovery and renewed growth must stress the quality of life. We must focus on those factors that are vital to a return of the tax base to the urban center. We must (1) exploit the advantages we have in light of the expected long-term expectations of our economy, (2) enhance to the extent possible those factors that are within our control to adjust, (3) recognize inherent weaknesses that we might not be able to do anything to alter, and (4) coordinate our efforts with the surrounding metropolitan region to exploit our joint strengths and minimize our joint weaknesses. Here are specific suggestions that would move us closer to these objectives.

1. *Capitalize on the energy crisis.* Use our greater density to effect the natural economies of scale an urban center can achieve, despite the relatively higher costs of energy in the metropolitan area. The changing structure of the family unit and the relatively higher energy cost of an urban living through greater energy utilization and demand will benefit the urban center.

2. *Focus on technical education.* Recognizing the skills most likely to be demanded of our local labor force, we should seek to establish technical-vocational-oriented education services to meet that demand, bring our expanding population of youth back into the mainstream economy and provide retraining for those older workers who have been displaced either through technological change or the changing pattern of our employment opportunities that gradually took place throughout the last two decades. This educational program must be designed to recognize the nonacademic nature of its potential student body while being mindful of the need to function in the world we live in. Perhaps some of the 40 schools that are planned to be closed could be utilized for this purpose through a joint private-public sector project before these vacant buildings become contributors to the blight of our urban neighborhoods.

3. *Housing.* The recognized and critical shortage of adequate low- and middle-income housing, unacceptably high unemployment rates, and the existence of sophisticated financial institutions should be coordinated to solve the housing shortage in New York. The public sector must move to get city-aimed properties back on the tax roles. We cannot expect to attract the tax base back to the city if we do not have any place for them to live. We must also look beyond Manhattan for new housing units through a concentrated redevelopment of Brooklyn and the Bronx.

4. *Streets and parks.* These are vital to a thriving urban center. Private cartage

experiments must be given every chance to be tested. Fines and penalties should be levied against violators of existing litter laws. Tax incentives should be granted to owners of store fronts and buildings that wash, sweep, and generally maintain their sidewalks and surrounding public places. Park use should be more carefully administered to prevent further erosion of our clean, green spaces.

5. *Balanced budget.* It is critical that we move quickly toward a balanced budget for the city government. The financial and fiscal reasons for this strategy are well documented. We must show to an overly critical world that fiscal prudence and effective planning for the future are the rule in New York City. I believe that ultimately history will show that New York City was only the first of many urban centers hit with fiscal stress. We may not even prove to be the hardest hit. Other urban centers are yet to undergo the problems New York has witnessed. We will be viewed by analysts as a leader in creating the fiscal measures — albeit under duress — needed to stave off bankruptcy. These measures will be adopted by other local governments as they attempt to deal with their own fiscal problems.

6. *Balanced growth.* New York City should use the relatively flat long-term growth to continue a prudent strategy for effective planning. If a more rapid long-term growth forecast were anticipated we would be more prone to repeating the mistakes of the 1960s when financial stringency was not a consideration. Instead, due to a limited growth in the public revenue base, we will be forced to be prudent and cautious with our strategies in the 1980s. This more modest growth should be reflected in a relatively more modest demand for public services. Re-entry into private money markets must be accompanied with a specific purpose, with goal-oriented objectives and performance criteria that measure both the costs and benefits to be realized.

7. *Infrastructure.* Our long-run strategy must include a careful analysis of infrastructure needs. This provision has also been documented by the Port Authority in its report on the future. We cannot wait until a disaster occurs before the public- and private-sector planners are compelled to move on this problem. The very nature of the buildings, bridges, and tunnels involved can insure that any serious breakdown is bound to be extremely costly in both lives and the loss of services to the city.

8. *Confederation of local analytical and quasi-public research institutions.* New York City contains a number of groups and organizations dedicated to analyzing a vast array of issues of concern to the city and the region. A federation of these groups would provide a tremendous capacity to provide a united front to policy- and decision-makers. Whether confronting Albany or Washington in need of funds and program support, establishing long-run goals for the city and region, seeking solutions to critical issues or simply organizing, in a systematic way, an inventory of the resources, capabilities, and limitations of each segment of the region, the federation could be a highly efficient instrument to best utilize our local analytical talent and collective knowledge and information. The member institutions of the federation should collaborate as a unit but maintain their separate identities and organizational structure.

We who love New York and are devoted to its advancement must adopt a new attitude toward economic development, a more competitive attitude with respect to the rest of the country. We must use our productive labor force, our gateway to international markets, our unique cultural and artistic resources, our industrial strengths, and the spirit that built this great city and region to aggressively seek new markets and promote new industries. We can do it and we must do it. We certainly have the talent to do it. We have a great city; we have a great region. I believe we have the resources to make even the New York metropolitan area greater in the years ahead.

12

STRATEGIES FOR NEW YORK CITY ECONOMIC DEVELOPMENT

Irving Leveson

Between the hyperbole and love-it-or-leave-it attitude of some New Yorkers and the gloom-and-doom predictions of others lies a stark reality — the reality of a city struggling to build on enormous strengths to overcome seemingly endless challenges. The city has been swept up in a tide of powerful forces, many national and global in nature, and finds itself remaining especially vulnerable to some, while at the same time well positioned to take advantage of others. Amid these circumstances is the recognition that some of the city's own actions of the past years, however well-intentioned, have reduced its competitiveness and vitality and jeopardized its ability to respond to new conditions. Today there are hopeful signs that the city will achieve a position from which it can better guide its destiny, and will aim to compete more effectively, even when that is not the easy course for the moment. But it will have to overcome major problems, and the adjustment will take many years.

For decades, those who would seek to direct the city's economy from board rooms and council chambers have devised broad strategies to orchestrate the innumerable decisions that are constantly being made. With the climate changing rapidly and growing increasingly complex, it is no longer possible to find a single strategy or course that can mobilize the vast energies and resources the city has at its disposal. The search for a more sophisticated set of strategies in this new climate requires a rethinking of possible directions and approaches for shaping the future and a realistic assessment of the pressures and realities that must be faced.

Any serious discussion of strategies for economic development must fully recognize how much has been promised and tried and how uneven has been the experience with efforts to formulate and utilize strategic thinking. Suggestions that any bold new strategy will solve our problems deserve to be treated with great skepticism. To parody a phrase, in statistical parlance,"We are all Baysians now." Nevertheless, we should continue to recognize that deliberate strategies encouraging movement in an announced direction can lead to reinforcing actions in scattered parts of a large and complex system, and the synergistic effects of these actions can greatly magnify beneficial results of public and private actions. Before we look at strategic directions we will consider forces influencing U.S. cities and the nation and some changes in the economic landscape of New York.

Forces influencing urban and regional development

The dramatic changes that have taken place in the size and structure of the economy of New York City reflect powerful forces operating on a national scale. The huge demand for single-family homes in the high birth rate years of the 1950s was associated with explosive suburbanization. The suburbs reached farther and farther out, spawning their own suburbs, and generating populations increasingly independent of the cities from which they originated. In the early post-World War II years, city-wide population declines were evident in a few cases such as Philadelphia. But the more general pattern was one of a handful of declining neighborhoods. By the latter half of the 1960s, and through the 1970s, declining central-city populations became commonplace. At the same time, population growth became rapid in sparsely populated areas even far removed from major population centers. And the shift to the Sunbelt continued unabated.

Underneath many of these changes is the search for lifestyle. Migration patterns appear increasingly to reflect concerns with where people live, rather than where jobs are located. Patterns of migration throughout the century have greatly narrowed differences in incomes among regions and cities, and in the last decade clearly contributed to the narrowing of price differences as well. At the same time, the economies of previously less well-developed areas have matured, rounding out their industrial structures as regional hubs increasingly took on functions previously handled only in national centers. When one looks at the nine census geographic divisions, the most rapid growth in employment in the fastest-growing areas between 1940 and 1970 came not in manufacturing but in finance. With income, price, and industrial structure increasingly similar among geographic areas, the migration that occurs reflects responses to lifestyle concerns more than ever.

The continued movement to lower density is the result of ongoing adaptation to new technologies as well as to climate, labor costs, and other factors. As Harrison and Kain noted, the development of cities can be viewed in terms of a layering process in which the density of the added layers reflects the technologies available at the time they were constructed, so that older cities, like Boston, are much more densely populated than newer cities, like Los Angeles.[1] The urban structure of America has far more adjustment to make simply to respond to the opportunities created by the existence of the automobile and truck, the telephone, and air travel. Modern transportation and communications systems, ranging from electronic mail to interactive cable TV, will only enhance the ability of the population to live in dispersed arrangements in search of lifestyle goals.

High costs of energy create pressures for smaller housing units and reduce the strength of the demographically induced housing boom. They encourage fixing up and building on what we have. Attached and multifamily dwellings become more cost-competitive because of their smaller size and lower heating costs per square foot. Energy costs lead to higher density development to facilitate bus use, locate residences closer to jobs, and otherwise reduce automobile use.

The importance of energy costs and housing shifts is small compared to the existence of the technologies that promote lower density. More densely developed forms can take shape outside of central cities. Moreover, the high costs of energy can only accelerate the movement to areas where heating costs are low, as long as heating costs tend to dominate air-conditioning costs in the energy use of the homeowner. This means continuing declines for cities in the Northeast and Midwest.

Energy itsellllllf will change patterns of economic development. Some industries will find it increasingly profitable to move to where the energy sources are. The growth of energy development, concentrated in the South and West and in sporadic areas throughout the country, will create new local economic opportunities, while the consuming states will continue to face difficulties in responding to high costs.

The effects of these forces will be overlaid on top of a new climate in the national economy, creating a complex environment posing new challenges in the formation of development strategies.

The national economic outlook

The stagflation that characterized the 1970s is giving way to a period of increased economic opportunity in the 1980s. National policies that seek to deal more decisively with problems of inflation and productivity are only one contributing factor. The responses of the private market to high energy costs in conservation, development, and distribution are already showing signs of making a major contribution to unwinding the problems we have faced. New energy-related technologies are developing rapidly and prospects are great for a major capital boom in energy-related activities that will stimualte the economy and improve productivity. In these ways the effects of energy on the economy are switching from strongly negative to strongly positive. At the same time, the nation is in the midst of a computer revolution with potentially far-reaching implications. Counterproductive regulations are being modified, and the economy is learning to live with inflation.

The service industries, once thought of as a stagnant sector, dragging down the national rate of economic growth, are now emerging as a major source of innovation and a leading sector in economic development. Although many of the productivity gains in services may not be measured by conventional means, there are already indications of large productivity gains in service industries, and much more to come.

The economy has been held back by declining labor skills as the result of a large influx into the labor force of youth and often inexperienced women. Now, however, it is able to take advantage not only of increased experience through age, but also the accumulation of skills that comes with increasing attachment to the labor force, plus reduced barriers to the kinds of work that women can do and their opportunities to learn.

These factors have already become quite important in contributing to the

STRATEGIES FOR ECONOMIC DEVELOPMENT 145

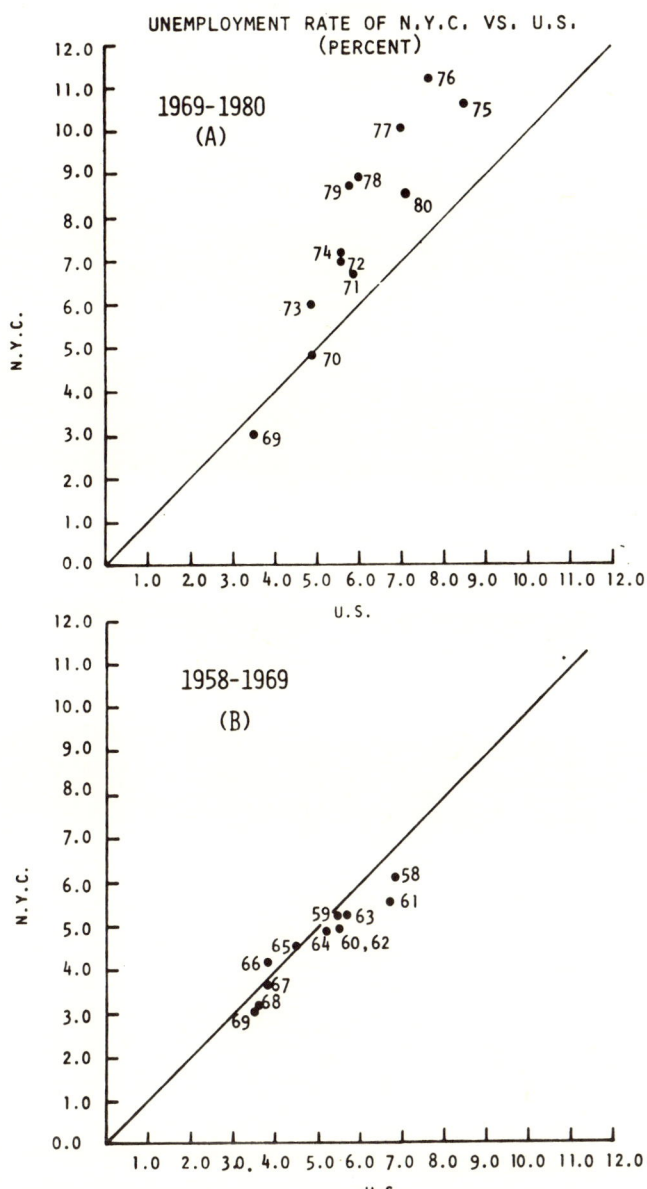

Figure 1

Figure 2

DIFFERENCE BETWEEN N.Y.C. AND U.S. UNEMPLOYMENT RATE
VS. U.S. UNEMPLOYMENT RATE
(PERCENT)

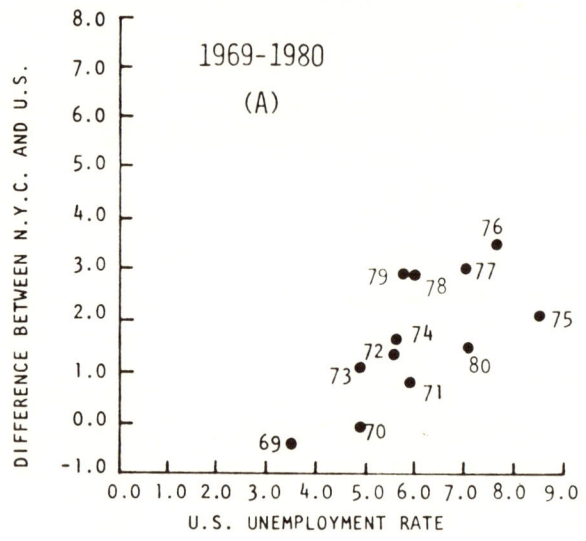

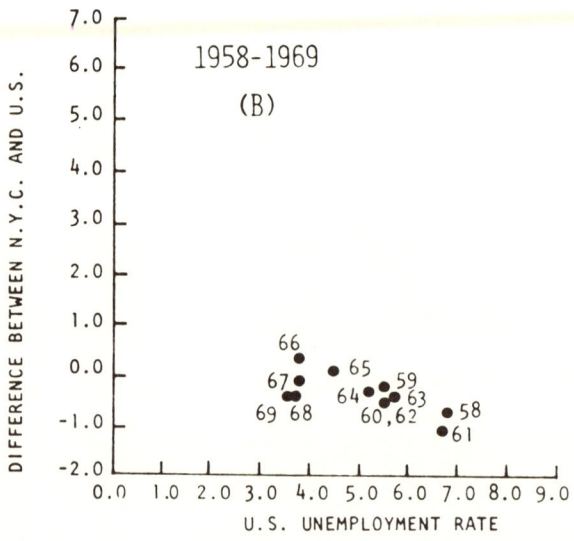

progress of the economy. One piece of evidence indicating just how important they have become is that the size of the decline in productivity during the 1980-81 recession was considerably less than what would have been expected in a downturn of such magnitude. The difference represents a "hidden productivity increase" indicative of the rapid growth that lies ahead. The many developments that are coming together, both fortuitously and in response to the problems we have faced, will produce an economic boom lasting into the mid-1980s. Moreover, there are an impressive series of developments that could contrubute to economic growth sustained at a rate of around 3% for a decade or more afterward.[2]

Some relationships between New York and the nation

One way of assessing the extent to which New York City has tended to follow the national trend is to compare unemployment rates over time. Panel B of Figure 1 indicates that for many years the New York City unemployment rate was lower than the national average (below the 45-degree line of equality). Marked changes occurred in the 1970s, as shown in panel A. This shift can be better understood by plotting the difference between the New York and the national average unemployment rate for each of the periods, as in Figure 2.

During the years 1958 to 1966, the difference between the New York City rate and the U.S. rate tended to be small when the national unemployment rate was high. The unemployment rate in New York was cyclical, but somewhat less cyclical than in the rest of the country, as indicated by the downward slope in panel B. Beginning in 1967 the pattern reversed itself, as panel A demonstrates. Increases in the national unemployment rate were associated with a rising difference between the New York rate and the national rate. Previously, the New York rate increased only half a percentage point for each one-point rise in the national rate. Since 1967 a percentage-point increase in the national unemployment rate has been associated with a rise of 1-3/4 points in New York City. When unemployment declines, it falls more rapidly in New York, too. However, only at an unemployment of around 4% is the New York unemployment rate equal to the national unemployment rate.

A major factor in the unusually low unemployment in New York City during 1967-69 was the very rapid growth of government spending through 1970. The rise in unemployment thereafter in part reflects the much slower growth and cutbacks in government employment in New York which were large in response to the fiscal crisis. A future easing of fiscal pressures could allow the relationship between New York City and U.S. unemployment rates to return partially to the earlier level.

New York City experienced a decline in population of 0.75 million in the 1970s. The sharp decline was encouraged by the particularly high level of the cost of living — a gap with other cities that kept on increasing into 1974. But the large increases in unemployment tempered the rate of growth of prices and moved prices back more into line with other areas. Examining the 1958–69 period, in Figure 3, we see that there was no relationship between the difference in unemployment rates in New York City and the nation, and the difference in each year's rate of growth in Consumer Price Index. For 1969-80, however, a strong relationship was

Figure 3

DIFFERENCE BETWEEN N.Y.C. AND U.S. UNEMPLOYMENT RATE
VS. CONSUMER PRICE INCREASE
(PERCENT)

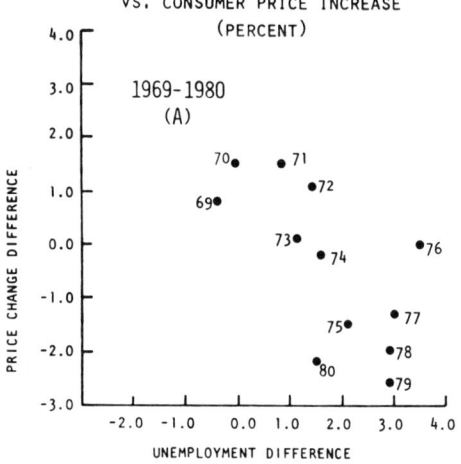

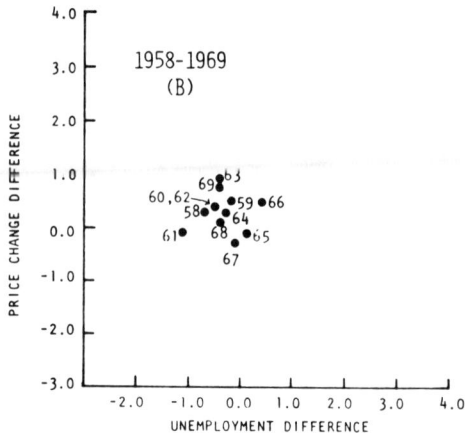

NOTE AND SOURCE FOR FIGURES 1-3

SOURCE: U.S. PRESIDENT, EMPLOYMENT AND TRAINING REPORT OF THE PRESIDENT 1978, TABLE B-29; NEW YORK STATE DEPARTMENT OF LABOR; AND U.S. DEPARTMENT OF LABOR, BUREAU OF LABOR STATISTICS.

NOTE: FIGURES FOR NEW YORK CITY UNEMPLOYMENT RATE PRIOR TO 1972 ARE BY PLACE OF EMPLOYMENT RATHER THAN BY PLACE OF RESIDENCE. BEGINNING IN 1974 THEY ARE BASED ON AN IMPROVED METHODOLOGY USING THE CURRENT POPULATION SURVEY.

Figure 4

NONAGRICULTURAL WAGE AND SALARY EMPLOYMENT: PERCENT CHANGE FROM PREVIOUS YEAR, U.S. AND N.Y.C. 1959-1980

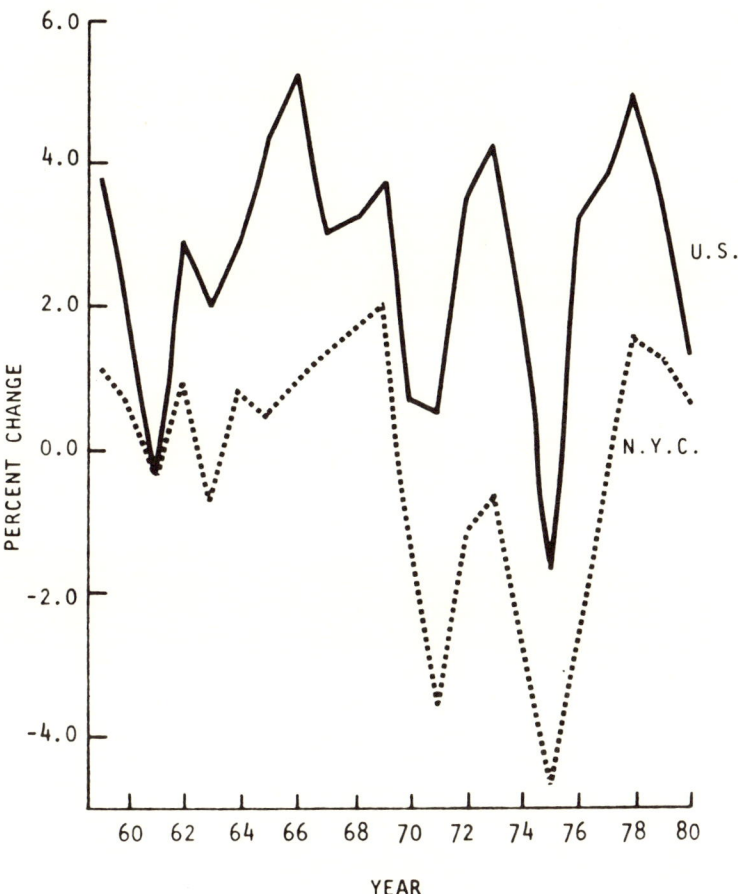

SOURCE: U.S. DEPARTMENT OF LABOR, EMPLOYMENT AND TRAINING ADMINISTRATION, EMPLOYMENT AND TRAINING REPORT OF THE PRESIDENT, 1980; AND NEW YORK STATE DEPARTMENT OF LABOR.

established in which the years New York City's unemployment rate exceeded the national level by the greatest amounts were the ones in which the rate of growth of prices in New York City were most below the national average. There is a true "Phillip's Curve" for cities in which price movements reflect pressures on prices caused by unemployment. The ability to get prices back into line was quite dramatic in some years, but progress in becoming more competitive suffered setbacks with each of the major increases in oil prices.

The effect of changing patterns of government spending, vulnerability to energy-cost increases, and other factors, can be seen in Figure 4 in the year-to-year percentage changes in nonfarm wage and salary employment. The slide in employment in New York City between 1968 and 1971 was especially pronounced. However, the recovery after 1975 was as sharp as in the rest of the economy.

During the years since the mid-1960s, the proportion of the U.S. population employed has increased dramatically. New York City, however, experienced no such increase (Figure 5). If it had, employment in the city would currently exceed its present level by half a million jobs. It is incredible that a city with such proximity between jobs and residential areas and a highly developed transportation system should not be able to accommodate the rapidly growing labor force of women and youth more readily than other areas. Even catching up for the lag in the past would be a major source of gain in the years ahead.

There has been a good deal of talk about downtown revivals in major cities — recovery of office real estate markets, theaters, hotel occupancy, etc. There are many causes, including lower air fares, the post-1973 drop in the dollar, and the high costs of new construction. But it is necessary to place these downtown revivals into perspective. Renewal has been concentrated in the central business districts, with little extension to other areas. Many urban residential communities and neighborhood business areas are continuing to deteriorate.

Furthermore, the downtown revival occurred during a strong cyclical upswing. There is no reason to believe that anything like the recent strength of the downtown areas will continue if the economy grows slowly along a trend. New York City has had a pattern since the late 1960s in which the level of employment was virtually constant during cyclical upswings, but declined sharply during downturns. However, the expected pattern of strong national growth may be very helpful in extending development and in allowing the benefits of renewal to expand from the core to the outer reaches of the city.

Strategies for economic development

The growth of cities was predicated on strong advantages for firms in the same business locating near each other, for firms in allied businesses working closely together, and for economies available from large-scale integration of economic activity. The new technologies of transportation and communication have increasingly made it possible to obtain the same gains that were formerly obtained through these agglomeration economies in more dispersed arrangements. The city is faced with the high labor costs that were justified by agglomeration economies, without

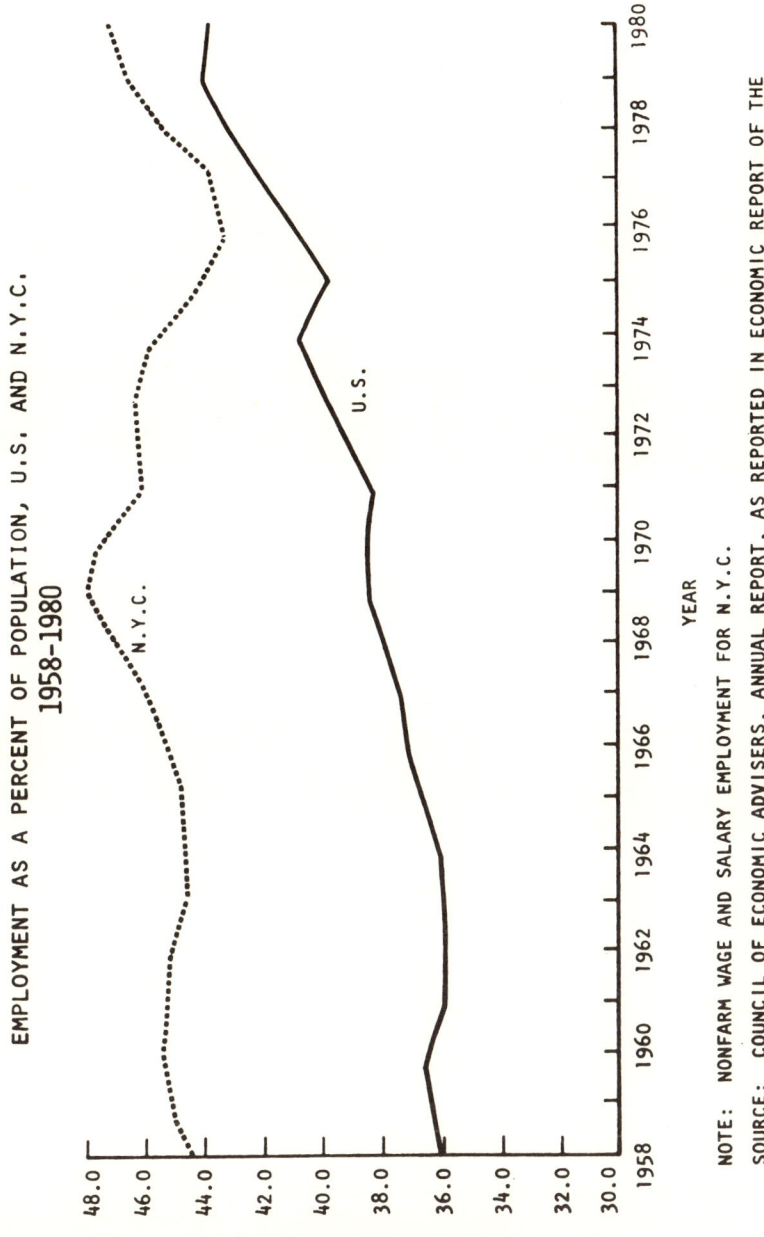

Figure 5

the same productivity advantages from dense configurations, and with high productivity increasingly possible in competitive areas. At the same time, the city faces problems of aging physical plant, bureaucratized public and private organization, and high tax rates. Not only are other parts of the country developing mature industrial structures and technological bases that can compete with New York City, but the glue that binds the city is increasingly coming apart. The greater desire for low-density lifestyles, and the ability to interact with economic units without being nearby, is placing the city in the difficult position of being unable to afford its high costs and unable to offset them by productivity advantages of highly desired physical and economic arrangements.

Many strategies have been suggested for economic development of New York City. Although it is clear that the city must find ways to compete more effectively, what comes across clearly is that no single strategy will suffice. The *national center strategy*, which was the core of the *Plan for N.Y.C.*,[3] cannot be the exclusive focus of development, since its effectiveness is diminished and more selective in a world of greater economic maturity elsewhere. The elimination of the physical transfer of stock certificates no longer requires that Wall Street firms be adjacent to one another. Back-office credit-card operations can be located anywhere in the country, and tax havens can lure banking activities. But New York continues to have specialized advantages and may do very well in the competitive press for interstate banking.

A strategy of improving the residential environment and encouraging *residential development* can also be a useful component or program to improve the city. With declining population, the city need no longer encourage large-scale housing production, but it must avoid creating a climate in which new single-family housing units are discouraged.[4] The city also will have to deal far more effectively with crime and delivery of services in order to keep residential areas viable.

The emphasis on *infrastructure development* and internal renewal which has been the focal point of the Koch Planning Commission is long overdue. With improvements in the city's financing, increased capital-budget levels may permit significant gains. The 1978 extension of the federal investment-tax credit to structures is of large benefit to the city in encouraging private capital spending. But the problem is huge, and will take decades to deal with. Increased efforts at infrastructure development can contribute to avoiding a deterioration in the quality of life, and many jobs can be created along the way.

The city also can benefit from a strategy of *improved competition* with other parts of the country. Reduction in the New York State personal income tax and state business taxes are an important component of an effort to improve competition. The city has made significant strides toward reducing the costs of government, but tax rates in New York remain enormous compared to other areas. Congestion costs, union pressures, and bureaucratic impediments abound, and improved competition will require additional changes. Furthermore, as long as salaries can no longer be justified by the high productivity of the system as a whole, salaries will have to continue to increase at a slower rate than the national average in order to close the gaps in the cost of living and the cost of doing business.

There is a tendency to assume that the natural level of equal competitiveness is one in which the cost of living in New York City is equal to the cost in the nation or in other cities. That need not be the case. If the city continues to have substantial diseconomies as a result of government bureaucracy, congestion, and other factors, to the extent these factors are not fully reflected in the price index, the cost of living may have to go below that of other areas for the city to compete equally. For the city to hold onto its population poses even greater difficulties. Residents may require higher salaries than elsewhere to induce them to stay in an area with high crime, or in which the existence of poor schools requires large expenditures for tuition in private schools. The problems are system-wide, they interact, they are large, and will continue.

With the decline in manufacturing jobs, the city has increasingly emerged as a service economy. There has been an unstated but quite impressive attempt to use *service industries as a basis for economic development*. This is seen in the attempt to encourage tourism, through the "I Love New York" campaign, the growth of show tours, the World's Fair, Op Sail, and other activities. It is seen in the development of a banking-free trade zone, a reinsurance pool, and a convention center. Much more systematic efforts are required to develop service-industry-based strategies for economic development.[5]

The city needs *an energy strategy*. The appalling costs of electricity generated by Con Edison has been a subject of constant controversy, and requires some resolution. The city also needs a strategy for benefiting from the development of energy resources. If significant findings of oil or natural gas should be made in the Baltimore Canyon, the Brooklyn piers may be suitable for the extensive onshore storage and development facilities. But this will require removing subsidies and corruption, which are enough to scare away any developer.

Finally, the city needs a systematic strategy for becoming an *international center* to an even greater extent than in the past. Internationalization has moved ahead rapidly with the growth of travel of foreigners to the United States, encouraged by the decline of the dollar over the last decade. It has been advanced by the rapid growth of business travel, with the increasing interaction among countries as national boundaries become easily crossed. The large Japanese and Middle Eastern communities in New York are a reflection of this development. The city has always been a center for international finance, and it is aggressively trying to retain that role. But it no longer is able to be a center for the movement of physical goods because of the barriers to port modernization. International banks are increasingly being passed by foreign banks. We need to ask ourselves why, and what can be done to allow the international role of New York City to help lead it to greater progress.

What do you do when you are losing your glue? Five responses suggest themselves as being particularly critical in the city's striving for a new strategy of economic development: (1) The city can change tastes toward the density levels or toward living in the city. The "I Love New York" campaign illustrates the kind of imagination that can be brought to this task. (2) The city can seek to reduce costs and improve amenities. A large jail-building program will not reduce costs. But court improvements, which assure that people who commit 200 crimes per year have a reasonable probability of going to jail, will allow tremendous efficiencies from the present facilities. (3) The city can find ways of reducing its vulnerability to shocks, such as international oil-price increases and surges in interest rates. One solution is to have the city and the state do a kind of counter-cyclical financing of their own, building up reserves during periods of prosperity which can then be applied to deficits in welfare and Medicaid during periods of recession. The accumulation of funds in the unemployment insurance trust funds is one such vehicle. Another possibility is for the federal government to require the city's matching shares of program costs to vary with the business cycle. The reduced welfare benefit rates through years without cost-of-living adjustments lower the number of eligibles and contribute to reduced cyclical vulnerability of the city budget from Public Assistance and Medicaid. (4) The city can also seek to gain a new comparative advantage, developing services in areas like insurance and

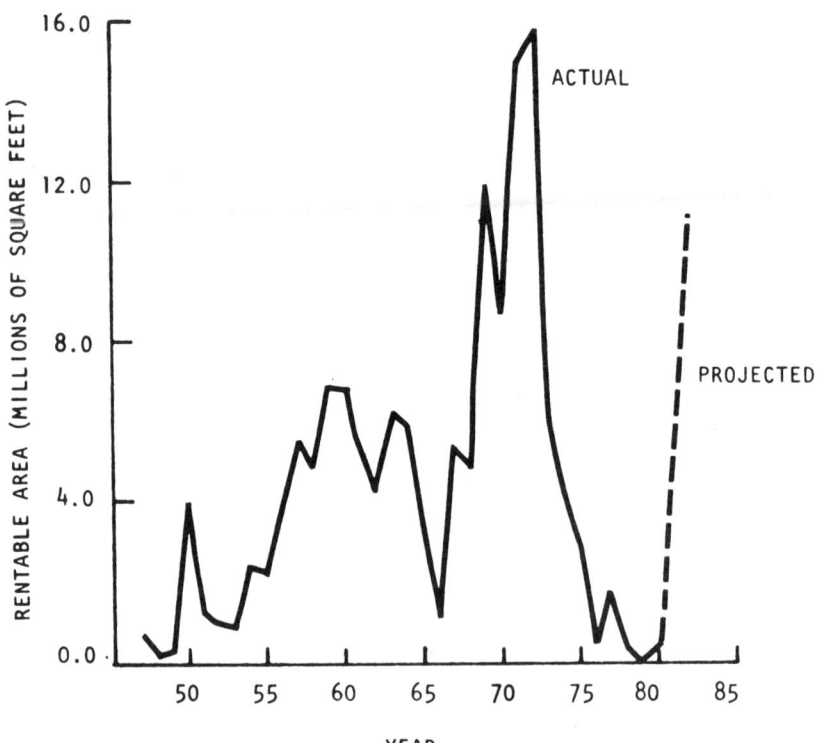

Figure 6

COMPLETED OFFICE SPACE IN NEW YORK CITY 1947-1980, WITH PROJECTIONS TO 1982

SOURCE: CARTER B. HORSLEY, "OFFICE MARKET ADJUSTING TO INFLATION," NEW YORK TIMES, MARCH 1, 1981, SECTION 8, p. 1.

interstate banking to beat the competition. Other regions will imitate the services if they are successful, and the constant development of new services building on past successes will be required. (5) Finally, the city can grow with the new innovators. The influx of foreign-born population, the emerging black middle class, the energies of an increasingly liberated female population, provide tremendous possibilities for the growth of new businesses and the creation of jobs, and for stimulating the competitive climate in a way that makes a wide range of economic activities healthier and more vibrant.

The downtown revival that New York and other major cities have gone through in the last several years, illustrated in Figure 6, is an indication of what can be accomplished with sustained efforts. This need not be a speculative boom-bust as occurred in the 1960s, and need not be confined to the central business district. The city has an opportunity in a period of strong economic development, and having gained from the experiences of the 1970s and early 1980s, to emerge as a strong competitor, drawing on talents and opportunities from many directions, and choosing a sophisticated set of strategies for economic development in tune with the challenges that lie ahead. Those who seek to be honest about what's right and wrong with the city and seek constructive change may take as their motto: "I love New York, especially when it's efficient."

Notes

1. David Harrison, Jr., and John F. Kaln, "Commulative Growth and Urban Density Functions," Discussion Paper No. 75, Harvard University Program on Regional and Urban Economies, February 1979.
2. Irving Leveson, *The Economic Future of the United States* (Boulder, Colo.: Westview Press, 1981).
3. New York City Planning Commission, 1969.
4. Jane Newitt, "Plain Talk About Cities and Suburbs," Hudson Institute, 1981.
5. Irving Leveson, *The Modern Service Sector,* Husdon Institute RM # 83, January 1980.

13

THE FUTURE OF MANHATTAN

Boris S. Pushkarev

Manhattan is often viewed as just one borough out of five or, at most, as the downtown of the City of New York. In fact, it is the downtown of a region of 19 million people, and that region's major economic reason for existence. It still provides more than one out of five jobs in the region and one-quarter of the region's income. Some two-thirds of the region's exports to the rest of the world originate in Manhattan; these are predominantly exports of business and financial services. Manhattan thus belongs not just to the region and to the United States, but also to the world at large. They all have a stake in its future, but the City of New York, obviously, most of all.

Basic decisions about the City of New York hinge on a view of Manhattan's future — business decisions about investment in office buildings, apartments, and productive equipment; government decisions about infrastructure investment, be it the third water tunnel, pollution control, new subways, or rail access; private decisions on where to settle and to pursue a career.

Yet, when decision-makers guess at Manhattan's future, they are also decreeing it in part. A projection of decline will not lead to growth-enabling investment and is thereby likely to preclude growth. A projection of growth will not assure growth, but it will make it at least more likely.

Inevitably, any look at the future must start with what has gone on before. This exploration begins with a series of newly assembled historical statistics, seeks to understand the rather dramatic changes of the recent past, and then discusses some outside forces that are likely to impact Manhattan — and the centers of other major urban areas for that matter — in the future. This latter part reflects a series of interviews and seminars with experts held by Regional Plan Association in 1977 – 80. Needless to say, the author of this paper rather than the numerous persons contacted is responsible for the opinions presented here. The study focuses on Manhattan's economic core — the central business district south of 60th Street — and all subsequent data refer to that area alone.

Past development

The Manhattan central business district (CBD) grew to roughly its present size

THE FUTURE OF MANHATTAN

Table. 1.
Estimated Persons Entering Manhattan CBD on a Weekday (24 hrs.) by Mode, 1920 - 1979
(Hub-Bound Travel). (in thousands)

Year	NYCTA	PATH	Rail	Ferry	Trolley	Bus	Auto	Total estimated	Total previously published
1920	1,084	138	197	100	140	8	176	1,843	
1921	1,117	147	194	100	150	12	203	1,923	
1922	1,188	153	200	101	160	16	234	2,052	
1923	1,291	160	210	102	155	20	270	2,208	
1924	1,369	162	217	103	161	24	307	2,343	2,343 RPA
1925	1,450	166	247	106	160	28	349	2,506	
1926	1,540	168	253	108	150	32	392	2,643	
1927	1,643	172	265	107	140	36	419	2,776	
1928	1,718	170	267	103	130	40	448	2,876	
1929	1,816	172	282	101	120	44	480	3,015	
1930	1,801	163	274	95	108	48	484	2,963	
1931	1,716	147	251	90	97	52	500	2,853	
1932	1,624	128	216	85	88	56	516	2,713	2,697 RPA
1933	1,718	115	194	80	84	68	528	2,787	
1934	1,773	116	197	80	80	80	540	2,866	
1935	1,871	116	198	78	76	92	552	2,983	
1936	1,927	120	210	78	72	104	564	3,075	
1937	1,944	121	212	80	68	116	576	3,117	
1938	1,920	106	197	78	65	128	588	3,082	
1939	2,015	102	210	76	62	138	604	3,207	
1940	2,068	101	206	68	59	150	619	3,271	3,271 RPA
1941	2,062	102	205	67	55	155	648	3,294	
1942	2,240	112	243	65	51	190	480	3,381	
1943	2,240	126	285	60	47	225	430	3,413	
1944	2,212	117	289	58	43	261	470	3,450	
1945	2,279	109	292	57	39	295	530	3,601	
1946	2,432	99	293	58	34	300	638	3,854	
1947	2,403	104	289	51	29	295	645	3,816	
1948	2,288	101	283	48	24	290	657	3,691	3,691 RPA
1949	2,020	96	254	46	21	283	678	3,398	
1950	1,986	84	233	45	18	277	700	3,343	
1951	1,955	77	224	41	15	271	720	3,303	
1952	1,936	66	213	40	12	265	741	3,273	
1953	1,902	61	211	40	9	259	762	3,244	
1954	1,910	59	206	38	6	253	783	3,255	
1955	1,906	60	202	37	4	247	805	3,261	
1956	1,911	59	207	36	3	243	828	3,287	3,313 RPA
1957	1,890	50	202	36	-	243	835	3,256	
1958	1,830	52	199	36	-	243	840	3,200	
1959	1,833	55	193	36	-	243	845	3,205	
1960	1,858	55	178	36	-	243	850	3,220	3,349 RPA
1961	1,875	56	179	36	-	246	860	3,252	
1962	1,893	51	179	36	-	249	870	3,278	
1963	1,873	49	177	36	-	252	880	3,267	3,290 TSRPC
1964	1,887	49	182	36	-	246	890	3,290	
1965	1,867	43	176	34	-	240	905	3,269	3,364 RPA
1966	1,800	49	175	34	-	239	915	3,212	
1967	1,800	61	176	34	-	250	925	3,246	
1968	1,804	63	175	34	-	256	935	3,267	
1969	1,882	67	176	34	-	257	940	3,356	
1970	1,774	69	176	34	-	255	925	3,233	
1971	1,684	69	172	34	-	256	914	3,130	3,167 TSRPC
1972	1,602	71	170	33	-	244	920	3,040	
1973	1,562	65	168	31	-	232	931	2,989	3,014 TSRPC
1974	1,534	68	170	30	-	230	884	2,916	2,977 TSRPC
1975	1,468	69	171	31	-	232	895	2,866	3,008 TSRPC
1976	1,402	72	179	26	-	220	877	2,776	2,852 TSRPC
1977	1,414	73	189	26	-	233	924	2,859	2,862 TSRPC
1978	1,478	74	195	27	-	228	926	2,928	2,870 TSRPC
1979p	1,535	78	208	27	-	236	923	3,007	

p - preliminary; for sources see next page.

Sources, Table 1:

Insofar as possible, the table is based on the concept of "annual average weekday traffic," not "specific weekday in October," as most previously published Hub-Bound data; "October weekday" is generally the same or slightly higher than "average weekday," but occasionally displays random fluctuation. All actual counts are shown in **boldface**, estimates are in regular typeface.

The PATH figures shown are actual "average wekday" counts. Most NYCTA figures are estimated; for. the period since 1956, the estimates are based on a linear relationship between October cordon counts and annual average weekday systemwide trips; this eliminates overcounts in the 1973-76 period. For earlier years, NYCTA annual trips are used as a basis for interpolating between cordon count years. A similar procedure is used to estimate rail trips; the Tri-State 1963 count is used for scaling down raw conductors' counts used without adjustment by RPA in 1956 and 1960.

Ferry, Trolley and Bus trips are graphically interpolated between known years, with the help of partial indicators such as PA Bus Terminal weekday and TA annual trips. Auto entries are calculated by assuming first a consistent trend in vehicle occupancy (leaning on PA trans-Hudson data) and applying it to a graphically smoothed-out curve of motor vehicle entries. Partial indicators (PA and TBTA crossings) are used to help interpolating between Hub-Bound benchmark years. Generally, the rail transit data are deemed most reliable, the auto estimates—least reliable. All series, however, display year-to-year consistency with annual indicators which is not always present in previously published counts.

For previously published data, see: *Hub-Bound Travel 1978,* Tri-State Regional Planning Commission Interim Technical Report 1205 & 1206, January 1980, and prior reports; *Hub-Bound Travel 1960,* Regional Plan Association Bulletin 99, December 1961 and prior reports; interpolation is based mostly on unpublished data files from the Port Authority of New York and New Jersey.

---

during the century of precipitous industrialization between 1830 and 1930. The complexity of the U.S. economy increased enormously during the period, requiring a large and highly differentiated meeting place or ''social brain'' for the central exchange of the needed financial and managerial information. Trade and financial activity connected with the dominant port linking North America to Europe provided the foundation on which this center of finance and economic management was built. The port also offered opportunities for producing goods, and people coming to the CBD to work in factories were for a long time the largest single group. With a population of 10 million gathered within 25 miles of the CBD by the end of the period, it also became a huge retail marketplace and, helped by the concentration of wealth, a focal point of the arts.

The early history of CBD growth has been extensively treated elsewhere, notably in the 1960 New York Metropolitan Region Study by Harvard University. For the most recent thirty to sixty years of CBD history, however, little-known statistical series are now available which can better illuminate the dynamics of its development.

The travelers to the CBD. Because a downtown is basically a meeting place, an appropriate way to measure its size is by the number of people who arrive there in the course of a weekday. Such *Hub-bound Travel* counts have been available, sporadically, for the past six decades. They are estimated on an annual basis in Figure 1 and Table 1.

It is clear that the steep momentum of Manhattan's growth, carried forward from the 19th century, was first broken by the crash of 1929, just as the number of daily CBD entries hit 3.0 million. By 1935 Manhattan travel had recovered from the Depression and resumed its growth, albeit at a slower pace, toward an all-time high in 1946. Coincidentally, the entire New York region peaked, as a share of the nation's population, in the 1940s. Then followed a decline, a wearing off of the short-lived wartime and postwar bulge. By 1951, Manhattan CBD entries were back to the level of 1941, about 3.3 million, and stayed at that level for nearly two decades, until 1969. This prolonged period of stability came to an end with the

THE FUTURE OF MANHATTAN

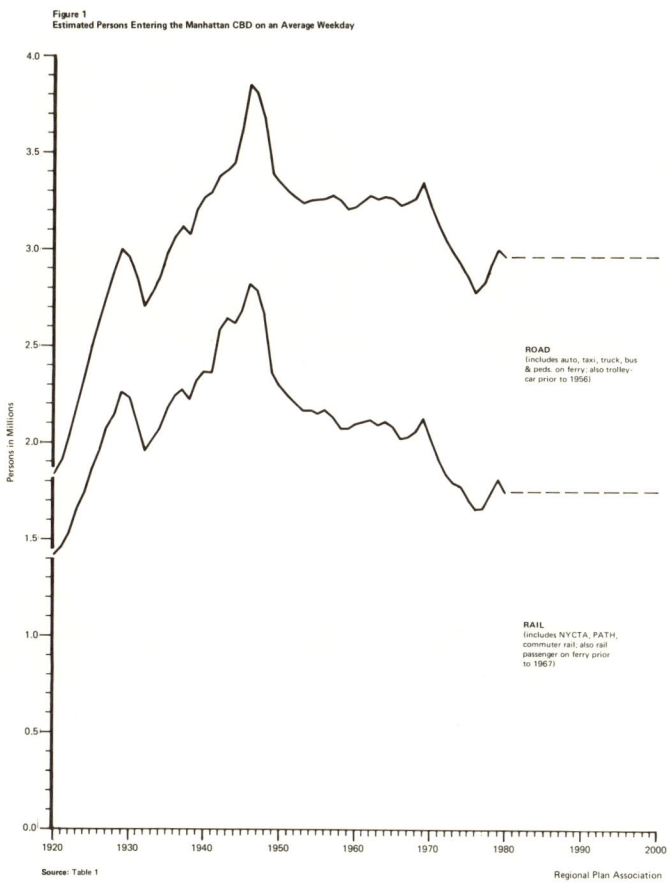

Figure 1
Estimated Persons Entering the Manhattan CBD on an Average Weekday

ROAD
(includes auto, taxi, truck, bus & peds. on ferry; also trolley-car prior to 1956)

RAIL
(includes NYCTA, PATH, commuter rail; also rail passenger on ferry prior to 1967)

Source: Table 1   Regional Plan Association

traumatic decline that began in 1970 and bottomed out in 1976 with CBD entries down to less than 2.8 million. The recovery of 1978–79 pushed weekday entries over 3.0 million again.

While total CBD entries stayed stable for most of the years after World War II, entries by rail (subway and commuter railroad) did experience a gradual erosion, dropping from 70% of the daily total in 1949 to about 60% in 1979. The recovery of 1978 was unusual, in that both subway and rail trips increased between 4% and 5%

Table 2
NYCTA Turnstile Registrations Within the Manhattan CBD (75 Stations)
(by calendar year)

Year	CBD Annual Turnstile Count	Systemwide Annual/Weekday Ratio	CBD Estimated Average Weekday Turnstile Count (000's)	CBD Fraction of Total Turnstile Registrations	Total System Annual NYCTA Ridership (000's)
1956	562,972,647	294.4	1,912	.4197	1,363,674
1957	550,290,466	293.9	1,872	.4179	1,339,380
1958	518,572,346	293.6	1,766	.3992	1,322,975
1959	519,522,500	294.0	1,767	.3988	1,328,958
1960	542,324,381	293.7	1,847	.4120	1,348,921
1961	544,328,935	292.8	1,859	.4103	1,359,915
1962	556,321,852	293.0	1,899	.4124	1,383,517
1963	541,081,693	293.4	1,844	.4108	1,356,817
1964	552,589,036	296.8	1,877	.4115	1,383,225
1965	541,515,517	294.4	1,839	.4128	1,353,067
1966	511,857,201	284.3	1,800	.4196	1,262,943
1967	532,695,523	293.0	1,818	.4228	1,302,572
1968	538,616,856	295.3	1,824	.4253	1,305,854
1969	540,318,751	295.1	1,831	.4250	1,343,270
1970	509,642,015	294.8	1,729	.4258	1,257,569
1971	480,720,775	293.8	1,636	.4223	1,196,876
1972	455,986,022	292.2	1,566	.4212	1,145,129
1973	438,073,506	291.2	1,504	.4213	1,101,414
1974	429,969,451	295.9	1,453	.4240	1,099,970
1975	407,351,280	295.4	1,379	.4215	1,053,933
1976	395,318,664	297.7	1,328	.4271	1,010,497
1977	399,372,694	296.4	1,347	.4354	998,253
1978	418,372,807	297.4	1,406	.4366	1,042,730
1979	434,494,882	297.8	1,459	.4389	1,076,148

Source: New York City Transit Authority *Transit Record*.

Note: p = preliminary estimate.
Turnstile registrations (column 1 and 3) declined faster than total ridership (column 5) in the 1969-1976 period because of the increase in Senior Citizen, weekend half-fare and other non-turnstile passengers.

Table 3
Floorspace, Resident Population and Nonresident Accumulation in the Manhattan CBD, Selected Years

	Nonresidential Floorspace, mil. sq. ft.				Office Vacancy Rate	Residential Floorspace mil. sq. ft.	Resident Population	Peak Nonresident Accumulation
	Office	Mfg./Whsg.	Other	Total				
1900	33	117	114	264		225		
1910	44	145	122	311		230		
1920	74	175	132	381		200	1,028,000	
1924					7.5%			
1930	112	218	144	474	5.0%	189	680,000	
1935	138	225	145	508	25.0%	188		
1940	140	220	144	504	17.0%	186	626,757	
1946	142	219	144	505	1.0%	186		
1950							632,660	
1957	164	205	146	515	2.0%	187		
1960							556,935	1,513,000
1963	199	187	147	533	3.0%	190	550,000	1,540,000
1965							537,000	1,532,000
1970	227	177	141	545	3.5%	199	504,700	1,519,000
1972	267	176	141	584	12.5%	201		1,451,000
1974	275	171	138	584	12.0%	208		1,399,000
1975	276	171	138	585	11.0%	210	466,900	1,378,000
1976							465,500	1,318,850
1977					5.5%		465,500	1,355,800
1978	280	169	140	589	4.5%	215	465,500	1,328,554

Sources: Floorspace: John Stern, Tri-State Regional Planning Commission.
Resident Population: U.S. Census.
Nonresident Accumulation: See Table 1 for sources.

in one year — an increase unprecedented since 1946. Further increases followed in 1979, triggered in part by the gasoline shortage. After March 1980, the three-year recovery of rail ridership was interrupted by the subway strike, a fare increase, and employment declines induced by the recession.

Daytime and nighttime population. The more recent *Hub-bound Travel* counts, which indicate entries and exits by hour, make it possible to calculate the accumulation of travelers in the CBD at any hour of the day. This accumulation reaches a peak around 1:00 P.M. and represents a number substantially lower than the number of entries, because many persons entering travel through, or otherwise spend a relatively short time in, the CBD. The peak daily nonresident population of the CBD was over 1.5 million in the mid-1960s, dropped to 1.3 million in 1976, and rebounded to 1.4 million by 1979. To ascertain the total daytime population, Manhattan CBD residents must be added to that number.

According to the U.S. Census, the resident population of the CBD exceeded one million in 1920; it dropped about one-third by 1930, stayed rather stable until 1950, and then resumed a much slower decline, averaging about 1% annually. It is

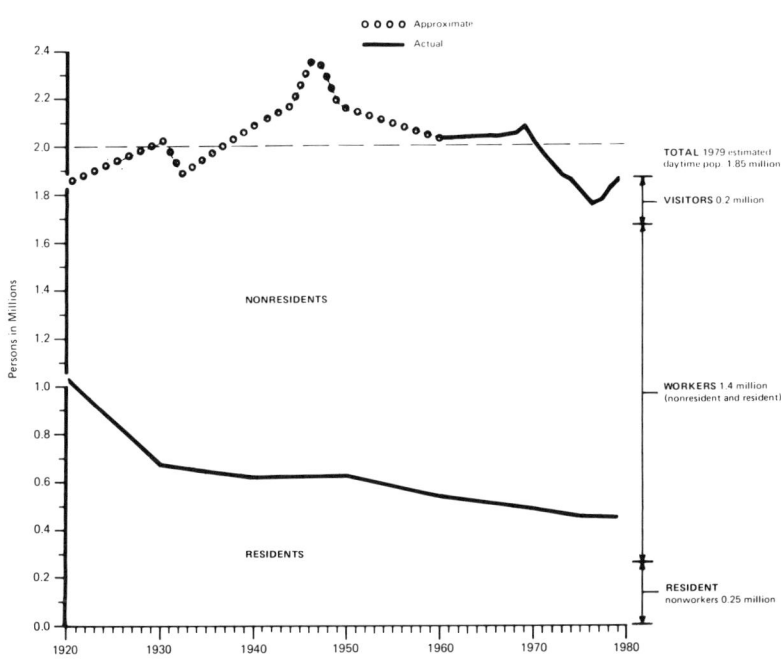

Figure 2
Estimated Daytime Population in the Manhattan CBD

Regional Plan Association

now about 0.45 million, for a total daytime population estimated at 1.85 million in 1979.

The total daytime population of the Manhattan CBD for the past six decades is plotted in Figure 2, and the supporting data are shown in Table 3. The plot reveals that if residents are added to the nonresidents, the fluctuation in total population becomes rather modest: *except for the high in the five postwar years and the low in 1976–77, Manhattan's daytime population was within 10% of 2 million for the entire sixty-year period.* In the early years, when Hub-bound travel grew fast, the resident population was dropping fast; to some extent, the influx of commuters merely compensated for the decline in residents. In the later years, the 1969–76 decline stands out, just as the Depression and World War II, as a major event against a basically stable background.

Building floorspace. The history of building floorspace in the Manhattan CBD over the past six decades differs markedly from the population history, as evident in Figure 3. While resident population was declining sharply in the early decades, there was only a minor attrition of the residential housing stock. Since 1960, as residential population declined slowly, there was a noticeable increase in residential floorspace, created both by new construction and by conversion from other uses. These trends resulted in a dramatic increase in residential floorspace per resident — from under 200 square feet per person in 1920 to roughly 340 in 1960 to some 460 square feet today. Declining household size and increasing real income per person were behind this trend.

Nonresidential building floorspace consists of manufacturing-warehousing, miscellaneous nonresidential uses (which include institutions, such as hospitals and universities, retail, and a variety of other commercial uses) and office floorspace. Both the manufacturing-warehousing and the miscellaneous categories expanded sharply between 1920 and 1935, and have been declining gradually ever since. By contrast, the office component increased sharply between 1920 and 1935, remained static until the late 1940s, and then started an accelerating growth, which peaked in the early 1970s.

In the quarter-century between 1950 and 1975, some 130 million square feet of office floorspace were added to the CBD, almost as much as in the preceding three-quarters of a century, and more than the existing stock of downtown Chicago and Los Angeles combined.

This new office construction was "out of synch" with the CBD's daytime population three times in the past sixty years. The momentum of the building boom of the 1920s continued until 1935, despite the sharp decline in the demand for floorspace caused by the Depression. Therefore, the office vacancy rate in the Manhattan CBD rose from 5% in 1930 to 25% in 1935. The resulting shock caused a standstill in new construction, which brought office vacancy rates down to 1% in 1946 and 2% in 1950. The immediate postwar peak in daytime population did not trigger any new construction. Rather, a new building boom gathered momentum slowly in the 1960s and peaked in the early 1970s just as a new precipitous decline in the CBD daytime population set in. The office vacancy rate in the Manhattan CBD rose from 3.5% in 1970 to 12.5% in 1972; builder bankruptcies were frequent in the following years, just as they were forty years earlier, and the office

THE FUTURE OF MANHATTAN

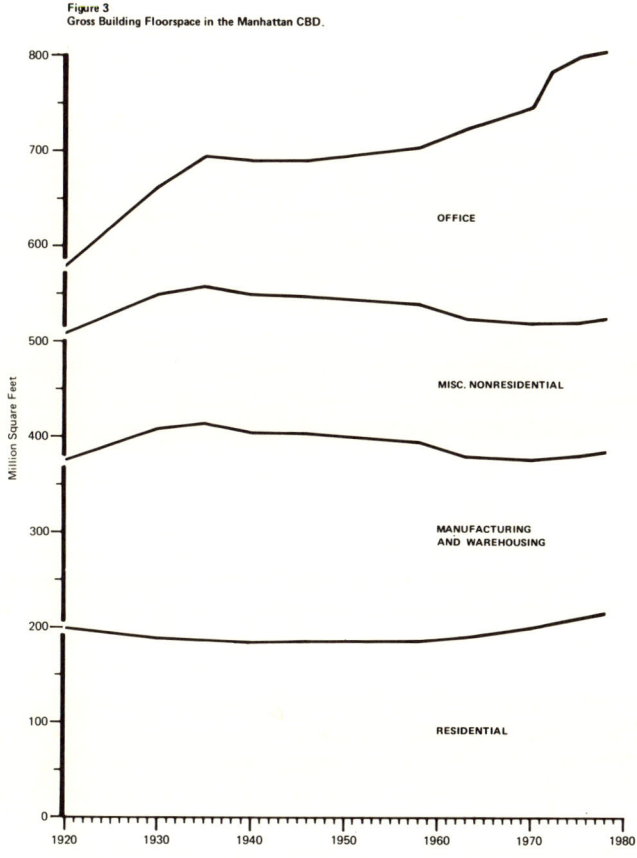

Figure 3
Gross Building Floorspace in the Manhattan CBD.

Regional Plan Association

vacancy rate did not come down to a more normal 5% until 1978. By that time, a new cycle of office-building construction was about to start.

These cyclical swings aside, there was an underlying trend of more nonresidential floorspace per person, just as there was a trend of more residential building floorspace per resident. Between 1960 and 1979 alone, total nonresidential floorspace per person present in the CBD at noontime (excluding nonworking residents) increased from 295 to about 360 square feet. Only a small part of this is attributable to vacancies; most of it is due to greater spaciousness within buildings. The prospects for future construction in the CBD hinge in large part on the question whether this trend toward greater indoor spaciousness will continue, or whether space requirements per person will stabilize. The past increase in floorspace per person of 13% per decade for residences and 11% per decade for nonresidential buildings may not be sustainable in the long run.

Workers. By far the largest component of the CBD daytime population consists of workers. As indicated in Figure 2, their number around noontime is probably about 1.40 million at present; in addition, there are almost 0.25 million nonworking residents, and some 0.20 million visitors of all kinds — businessmen, students, shoppers, tourists, for an estimated 1979 peak daytime population of 1.85 million, referred to earlier.

Interestingly, the estimated number of workers present in the CBD at noontime in 1979 is only about 10% below the level of 1970; the latter year, in turn, was about 2% below 1960. These figures, derived by subtracting nonworking residents and a constant percentage of visitors from the peak daytime population, are commensurate with U.S. Census data, which also suggest a 2% decline in Manhattan workers between 1960 and 1970. For both years, the number of workers actually present in the CBD at midday was about 15% below the Census figure of some 1.8 million workers "traveling to work at least once during the Census week" because of absences, night shifts, and so on.

The 1960 and 1970 Censuses revealed a notable difference in the place of residence of Manhattan workers. As Table 4 shows, the number of Manhattan workers residing in New York City dropped by 80,000 between the two dates, while that residing in the suburban counties increased by 33,000. Undoubtedly, the 1980 Census will show a much more drastic decline in commuters from within New York City and some continued increase in suburban commuters. In 1970, only 21% of Manhattan workers commuted from outside New York City. In the long run, the radius of commutation may tighten if costs of long-distance travel increase greatly. On the other hand, there is the countervailing trend of fewer workdays on the job, which makes long-distance commuting more palatable.

Employment. Census data on workers by place of work are available only once in a decade. For year-to-year monitoring of economic activity, economic statistics must be relied on, which deal with the concept of "job positions" rather than workers. The principal annual series, showing employment by county, is the U.S. Census *County Business Patterns*; however, its definition excludes a number of employment categories (see note to Table 5); another series the monthly U.S. Department of Labor's *Total Nonagricultural Employment* has fewer exclusions, but covers only New York City as a whole, not Manhattan. The coverage of both

Table 4
Manhattan Workers by Place of Residence, 1960 and 1970

	RPA 1960	TSRPC 1960	TSRPC 1970
1. Manhattan	722,610	695,698	579,096
2. Brooklyn	365,320	359,600	380,077
3. Queens	346,660	341,500	369,778
4. Bronx	283,640	280,200	256,673
5. Staten Island	26,330	26,133	37,786
New York City	**1,744,560**	**1,703,131**	**1,623,410**
6. Nassau	113,730	113,000	101,219
7. Westchester	74,460	73,200	71,683
8. Suffolk	19,120	19,000	29,675
9. Rockland	6,080	5,927	12,318
10. Orange	930	943	2,281
11. Putnam	1,030	946	1,483
12. Dutchess	520	493	620
13. Ulster	250	n.a.	435
14. Sullivan	100	n.a.	195
New York State	**216,220**	**213,859**	**219,909**
15. Bergen	61,780	60,900	62,441
16. Hudson	35,840	36,000	38,066
17. Essex	18,850	19,100	17,696
18. Union	13,080	12,870	13,207
19. Monmouth	5,940	5,877	13,795
20. Middlesex	6,370	6,247	12,206
21. Morris	6,340	6,400	8,800
22. Passaic	7,590	6,000	7,095
23. Somerset	1,900	1,863	3,650
24. Mercer	1,070	n.a.	1,502
25. Ocean	790	n.a.	1,610
26. Hunterdon	530	n.a.	519
27. Sussex	300	n.a.	667
28. Warren	100	n.a.	133
New Jersey	**160,480**	**158,047**	**181,387**
29. Fairfield	17,710		
30. New Haven	660		
31. Litchfield	190		
Connecticut	**18,560**	**16,190**	**20,201**
(Out of Region)	(4,270)	n.a.	(4,000)
TOTAL MANHATTAN	**2,133,090**	**2,095,497***	**2,048,907**
CBD ONLY	**1,856,800**	**1,814,700**	**1,745,510****
Estimated workers present in CBD at 1:00 p.m.	1,580,000	1,580,000	1,550,000

Sources: Derived by RPA and TSRPC from the U.S. Census *Journey-to-Work*.

* Adjusted by 7,600 for counties not available (n.a.). Aside from this difference in defining the Region, the difference between 1960 RPA and TSRPC data arises from different procedures in allocating workers who did not report their place of work.

** The difference in 1960 and 1970 "CBD Only" figures may be due in part to allocation procedures; the "Total Manhattan" data are more reliable.

Table 5
Estimated Employment in the Manhattan CBD by Activity, 1950 - 1979

Year	RPA Total Jobs (in thousands)	Office	Production	Retail	Miscellaneous	TSRPC Total Jobs Estimate
1950	2,230	725	820	450	235	2,225
1951	2,212					
1952	2,181					
1953	2,177					
1954	2,131					
1955	2,183					
1956	2,140					
1957	2,120					2,240
1958	2,085	750	715	420	200	
1959	2,055					
1960	2,065					2,165
1961	2,115					
1962	2,160					
1963	2,140	800	650	450	240	2,125
1964	2,110					
1965	2,105	805	595	435	270	
1966	2,120					2,124
1967	2,145					2,146
1968	2,200					2,171
1969	2,255	910	570	460	315	2,230
1970	2,220					2,201
1971	2,120					2,064
1972	2,070					2,009
1973	2,035	830	490	415	300	1,964
1974	1,965					1,920
1975	1,895					1,870
1976	1,845					1,820
1977	1,825	770	400	385	270	1,812
1978	1,860	800	400	385	275	
1979	1,920					

Sources: Total employment for benchmark years is based primarily on the number of jobs shown in U.S. Census *County Business Patterns,* a source available for New York County beginning with 1964; added to this are jobs in government, railroad, self-employment, domestic and unpaid family positions. Following the U.S. Census Journey-to-Work data, approximately 87 percent of New York County employment is allocated to the Manhattan Central Business District (CBD). Employment between benchmark years is interpolated following the U.S. Bureau of Labor Statistics "Total nonagricultural employment" series. The estimates for years prior to 1956 are based on RPA data prepared for the *Metropolitan Rapid Transit Survey* (final report, August 1956, table 10).

Because of dual jobholding and other discrepancies, the number of *jobs* reported here is substantially greater than the number of *workers* employed. For example, in 1970 Manhattan as a whole was reported to have 2,556,400 jobs, but only 2,048,907 workers travelled to work there according to the journey-to-work census.

Estimated composition of CBD employment is shown for four categories: 1. *Office jobs* which include white collar jobs in office buildings; 2. *Production jobs,* which include blue-collar jobs in manufacturing, warehousing and construction; 3. *Retail jobs,* which include those in retail stores and personal services; 4. *Miscellaneous jobs* which include those in institutions, in government services (outside office buildings) and in transportation-communication-utilities (outside office buildings). This category also contains an allowance for statistical discrepancies. The composition is estimated on the basis of industry-occupation correspondence data derived from the U.S. Census of Population and the Tri-State Regional Planning Commission Home Interview Survey; it takes into account the Censuses of Manufacturing and Business.

series varies over time. Thus, Manhattan CBD employment figures, as prepared by the Tri-State Regional Planning Commission (TSRPC), The Port Authority of New York and New Jersey (PA), and the Regional Plan Association (RPA) involve a number of estimates and adjustments. On the whole, the number of "jobs" reported by these agencies is substantially above the number of "workers," because some workers hold more than one job, and because of other discrepancies.[1] These differences are discussed here because they affect the portrayal not only of absolute levels of activity, but also of trends over time. Figure 4 relates the economic series on Manhattan CBD employment to physical data on turnstile entries into the 75 Manhattan CBD subway stations on an average weekday. The latter data (shown in Table 2) are chosen in preference to the Hub-bound travel statistics because they reflect year-to-year changes more accurately.[2]

The decade 1956 to 1966 shows an erratic but reasonably close relationship between CBD subway use and CBD employment, though occasionally increases in ridership are not reflected in employment. The period from 1966 to 1969 suggests a sharp expansion of employment, but that is barely reflected in ridership. While auto and bus use did grow during this period, it was not enough to support such an employment expansion. Overall, between 1960 and 1969 there may have been less of a job boom in Manhattan than economic data indicate.

Between 1969 and 1976, jobs and subway ridership declined dramatically, in step with each other. In 1977, however, subway use increased (only in the CBD, not yet system-wide) while employment indicators continued to drop. The 4.5% system-wide increase in subway ridership in 1978 appeared to be triggered by a modest 1.9% upturn in employment.[3] In reality, the resurgence may have been greater than economic data indicate. In 1979, employment and subway riders increased in step with each other.

These discrepancies notwithstanding, the economic job statistics are the only ones that enable us to analyze the composition of CBD employment — what the jobs are and why they are there — and to relate trends in the CBD to national trends in employment.

Composition of employment. The simplest division of Manhattan CBD jobs is into three groups: (1) blue-collar or production and maintenance jobs in manufacturing, warehousing, construction, and a variety of other fields; (2) white-collar jobs in office buildings; and (3) other jobs, which include retail trade and services, employment in medical and educational institutions, transportation, utilities, and so on. These three categories, which roughly correspond to the three types of nonresidential building floorspace portrayed in Figure 3, are shown in Figure 5.

It is evident that production jobs have been steadily declining in the CBD for the past three decades, and are down to about half their 1950 level. They now comprise only about one-fifth of total CBD employment. Interestingly, their decline halted in 1977. In part, this is a reflection of narrowing cost differentials between New York City and the rest of the world, in part, of renewed building activity, which offers jobs in construction.

The mixed category of "other," nongoods-oriented and nonoffice jobs, has fluctuated over the years in response to economic cycles, but remained relatively stable overall. It is about as large today as it was in 1950. There were shifts, of

Figure 4
Economic Data on CBD Employment (Jobs) Related to Physical
Data on CBD Subway Turnstile Entries, 1956 - 1979

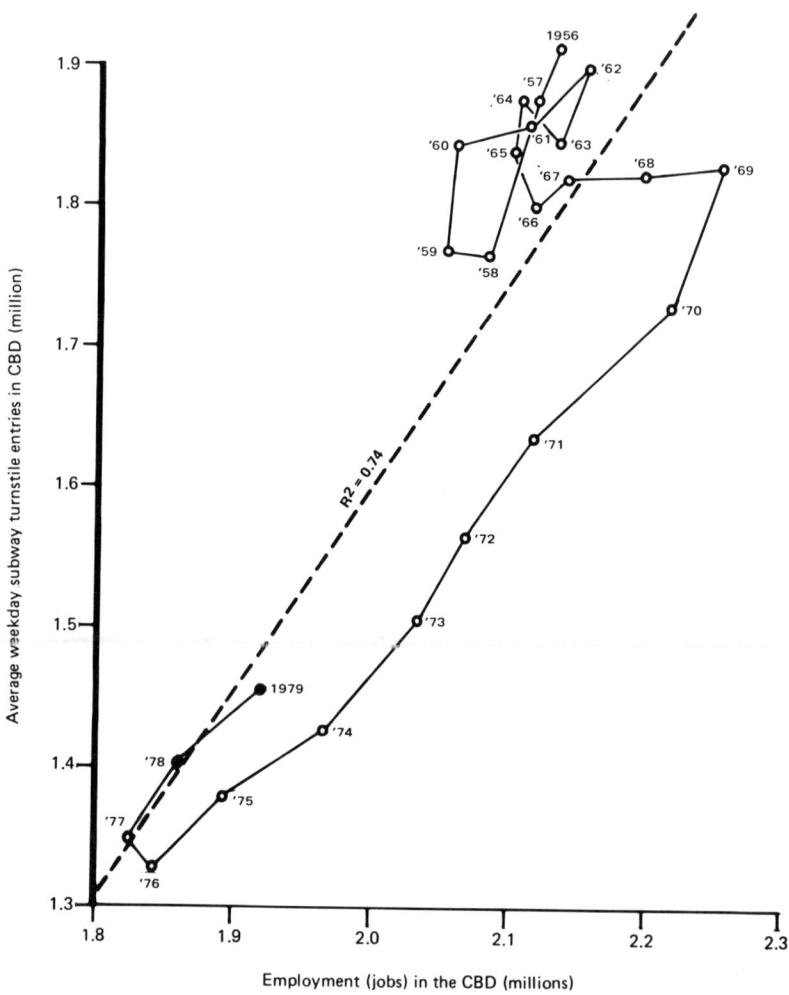

Regional Plan Association

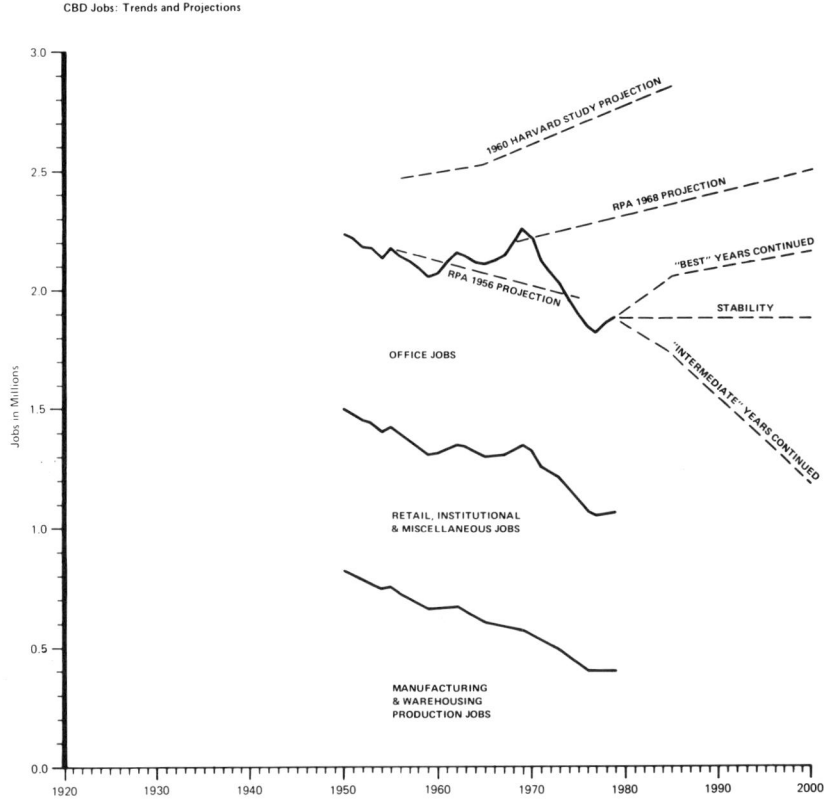

Figure 5
CBD Jobs: Trends and Projections

course, beneath this overall stability, such as declines in retailing employment in the 1950s and 1970s and increases in hospital and university employment in the 1960s. The slight increase in 1978–79 in part reflects tourist-oriented services such as hotels and restaurants. Overall, jobs in this category now comprise somewhat over one-third of CBD employment.

Predictably, office jobs have been the main growth sector of the CBD economy over the past three decades. They appear to have expanded by about 25% between 1950 and 1969, shrank about 15% in the following eight years of regionwide economic decline, but are still significantly above the level of thirty years ago, and represent the main factor in Manhattan's economic resurgence in 1978–79. Specifically, it was mostly the increase in business services — a key national and international function of the Manhattan CBD — that was responsible for this latest increase in office employment. From about one-third of CBD jobs in 1950, the office sector has now grown to represent almost two-fifths.

To anticipate future trends in CBD employment, two approaches are possible. One is to disaggregate these three broab categories of jobs into much finer layers, and to analyze potential developments in each. The other is to look at the relationship between Manhattan CBD employment and national employment in the aggregate.

It is evident from Table 6, which details jobs by occupation, that the Manhattan CBD is far advanced into the postindustrial economy: two-thirds of its jobs are white-collar — professional, managerial, clerical, and sales — and only one-third are manual, blue-collar, and service jobs. With large-scale economic trends pointing toward further growth in knowledge-oriented, information-related activities, and away from goods-producing activities, further increases in white-collar jobs in Manhattan seem logical. However, half of these jobs are in moderate-skill clerical occupations, where inroads by office-automation technology are likely. Conversely, there may be a limit to how far manual jobs could shrink. Less than half of the CBD's blue-collar jobs are in manufacturing production, mostly apparel; the rest are primarily maintenance jobs distributed fairly evenly among a variety of activities.

CBD employment according to major categories of the Standard Industrial Classification is shown in Table 7, and disaggregated further into 41 categorie in Table 8, which ranks the various "industries" according to the size of their employment. The categories enumerated account for 95% of CBD employment; the first eight account for 50%. Among the eight, only the first and the largest, "Miscellaneous Business Services" (10% of all jobs), has grown since 1970 in the face of overall decline, and the outlook is for more growth. "Wholesaling" has been on a long downslide; "Local Government" is set on a course of job attrition (though *federal* employment in Manhattan has declined as well); "Apparel" has been suffering from moveouts and foreign competition; "Banking" is likely to show future growth, but increases in employment may be canceled by labor saving technology; "Printing and Publishing" employment is also likely to be affected by automation; "Securities" face competition from other downtowns and more labor-saving technology; "Insurance Carriers" are likely to decentralize more of their data-processing functions.

There are growth possibilities among the numerous industry branches that account for the remaining half of the employment, but these activities are relatively small. Thus nonprofit organizations, legal services, and "amusement services" — all of which have shown growth since 1970 — are in the 3.3% to 0.7% range of total employment. Restaurants and hotels, another possible growth sector, account for 2.5% and 1.5% of total employment, respectively.

Overall, past trends by occupation and by industrial category suggest continued decline, simply because we are looking at a period of CBD decline. A broader range of possibilities emerges, if one looks at the relationship between CBD employment and national employment in the aggregate.

CBD employment and national employment. As a vital part of the national economy, Manhattan is obviously affected by national economic cycles, both during periods of expansion, and when the economy contracts. Overlaid on top of these are longer-term trends which pertain both to Manhattan's mix of economic activities and to the national share of these activities that it is able to capture at any one time due to its competitive advantage or disadvantage vis-à-vis other loca-

THE FUTURE OF MANHATTAN

Table 6
Estimated Occupational Composition of Manhattan CBD Employment by Industry, 1977

Industry (000's)	Prof/Tech	Manag'l	Clerical	Sales	Prod/Mtn	Services	Total
Agric., For. & Fish	0.4	0.2	0.4	0.1	--	--	1.1
Mining	0.7	0.4	1.4	--	--	--	2.5
Construction	2.6	3.5	2.9	0.3	24.1	0.3	33.7
Manufacturing	34.5	44.5	88.8	17.6	155.9	2.0	343.4
Transportation	7.0	9.6	21.6	2.2	29.8	3.3	73.6
Communications	5.8	9.5	30.7	1.3	12.8	0.8	60.8
Utilities	1.5	0.5	3.8	--	3.8	0.2	9.8
Wholesale Trade	14.6	23.0	60.0	29.3	26.5	3.3	156.5
Retail Trade	6.0	13.5	24.7	31.8	12.8	43.8	132.6
Finance, Insur, RE	45.7	51.9	206.3	22.4	2.2	7.0	335.4
Services	127.3	51.4	126.5	9.6	37.0	132.1	484.0
Government	30.3	7.6	43.1	--	45.0	65.7	191.9
Total	276.4	215.8	610.1	114.6	349.9	258.5	1,825.1
Percent of total	15.1	11.8	33.4	6.3	19.2	19.2	100.0

Note: Based on application of NYC OES taken by 2-digit industry in mid '70's; CAOs separated out before industrywide averages applied; CAO occupation mix based on weights of industry specific white collar demands. Overall, constructed at 2-digit level industry by occupation.

Table 7
Estimated Employment in the Manhattan Central Business District by Industry, 1963-1977

Industry (000's)	1963	1970	1973	1977	Change, 1963-77
Agric., For. & Fish	0.8	1.0	1.1	1.1	− 2.7%
Mining	2.9	3.0	2.8	2.5	
Construction	77.4	53.3	43.7	33.7	−56.5
Manufacturing	501.7	447.2	407.0	343.3	−31.6
Transportation	)	110.8	83.9	73.6	
Communications	)170.7	80.0	66.2	60.8	−15.5
Utilities	)	10.2	10.1	9.8	
Wholesale Trade	260.1	234.0	186.6	156.5	−39.8
Retail Trade	173.3	186.0	159.3	132.6	−23.5
Finance, Insur., RE	339.0	396.6	359.8	335.4	− 1.0
Services	469.5	497.8	493.9	484.0	+ 3.1
Government	144.6	200.1	220.6	191.8	+32.6
Total	2,140.0	2,220.0	2,035.0	1,825.1	−14.7

Source: Regional Plan Association

Table 8
Rank Order of Estimated Employment in the Manhattan CBD by Industry, 1977

Rank	Industry	Estimated Employment (000)	Percentile
1	Misc. Business Services	170.6	10.0
2	Wholesale Trade	156.5	
3	Local Government	141.6	25.0
4	Apparel	122.2	33.0
5	Banking	100.2	
6	Printing & Publishing	85.2	
7	Securities	76.4	
8	Insurance Carriers	68.2	50.0
9	Communications	60.8	
10	Nonprofit Membership	59.9	
11	Medical & Other Health	53.2	60.0
12	Misc. Services	50.8	
13	Real Estate	50.1	
14	Restaurants	46.6	
15	Legal Services	37.0	70.0
16	General Merchandise	33.5	
17	Federal Government	33.0	
18	Misc. Manufacturing	31.0	
19	Educational Services	29.0	
20	Chemicals	24.3	
21	Hotels	22.9	80.0
22	Insurance Agents	21.4	
23	Transportation Services	21.3	
24	Water Transportation	21.1	
25	Apparel Stores	20.9	
26	Special Trade Contractors	19.8	
27	Misc. Retail Stores	18.4	
28	State Government	17.3	
29	Motion Pictures	16.0	
30	Amusement Services	13.6	
31	Air Transportation	12.7	
32	Household Services	12.1	90.0
33	Electrical Equip. Mfg.	11.3	
34	Credit Agencies	11.0	
35	Trucking	10.4	
36	Textiles	10.3	
37	Transportation Equip.	9.8	
38	Personal Services	9.3	
39	Petroleum	8.0	
40	Holding & Other Invest. Co.	7.8	
41	Heavy Contract Construction	7.7	95.0
	Other 27 Industries	91.9	100.0
	Total	1,825.1	

Source: Regional Plan Association

tions. To separate out these factors is by no means easy.

Manufacturing production employment nationwide was expanding rapidly until the 1930s, yet in Manhattan this type of employment began to decline as early as 1918, a result of technological change in production and distribution which favored a more decentralized pattern of factory and warehouse location. Retailing employment nationally continued to expand in the 1950s, yet in Manhattan it dropped 25% between 1948 and 1963, largely a consequence of growth in auto-oriented suburban shopping centers. And while white-collar office employment has been on the rise nationally for the past hundred years, Manhattan could only be expected to capture a rising share of it for a limited period of time, as happened with manufacturing and, later, with retail trade. Eventually, this share would have to decline.

The decentralization of office employment within urban regions has been traditionally linked to population dispersal and improved automobile access, in a manner similar to the decentralization of manufacturing and, later, retailing. Between urban regions, wider access by commercial and private jet and the computer-telecommunications technology may have helped to decentralize offices to "little Manhattans" in the downtowns of Houston, Washington, New Orleans, Boston, Pittsburgh, Dallas, Atlanta, or Seattle (these eight grew the fastest in office floorspace in 1970–75). The sharp reduction in the costs of transporting people and information over long distances has apparently made it possible to have Manhattan-like exposure to information in numerous major CBD's in the nation and in their environs. Also, the growth of population and income in the various regional capitals, as well as the growth of government in the national capital, seems to have created "critical masses" supportive of a wide range of business services and cultural activities.

All these forces, however, have gathered momentum gradually over the past two decades. They fail to explain the sharp ups and downs of Manhattan CBD employment during this period: the expansion before 1969, the nearly 20% decline in the following eight years, and the resurgence in 1978–79. Previous big changes in the fortune of the Manhattan CBD, portrayed in the historic charts, were clearly linked to major world events: the Depression of the 1930s and World War II. *The great decline of 1969–76 cannot be linked to any such visible event.*

True, the beginning of this decline coincided with the national recession of 1970, and the turnaround of 1977–78, with a vigorous nationwide expansion of employment. Yet, in previous years, such cyclical changes have made only minor ripples in Manhattan. So, business cycles likewise fail to explain the events of the past decade. Explanations are reduced to subjective terms such as "overexpansion" of activities related to the stock market and to local government in the late 1960s, "overreaction" to this "overexpansion" in the early 1970s, and the notion that the decline had to "self-correct" itself eventually.

How changes in Manhattan employment responded to changes in national employment is portrayed, year by year, for the 1963–79 period in Figure 6. The response has varied greatly from year to year, so that one can speak of the "best years," the "worst year," and the "intermediate years." In the "best years," a 1% national growth in employment was enough not to cause any CBD decline;

Figure 6
Annual Change in Manhattan CBD Employment Related to Change in National Employment

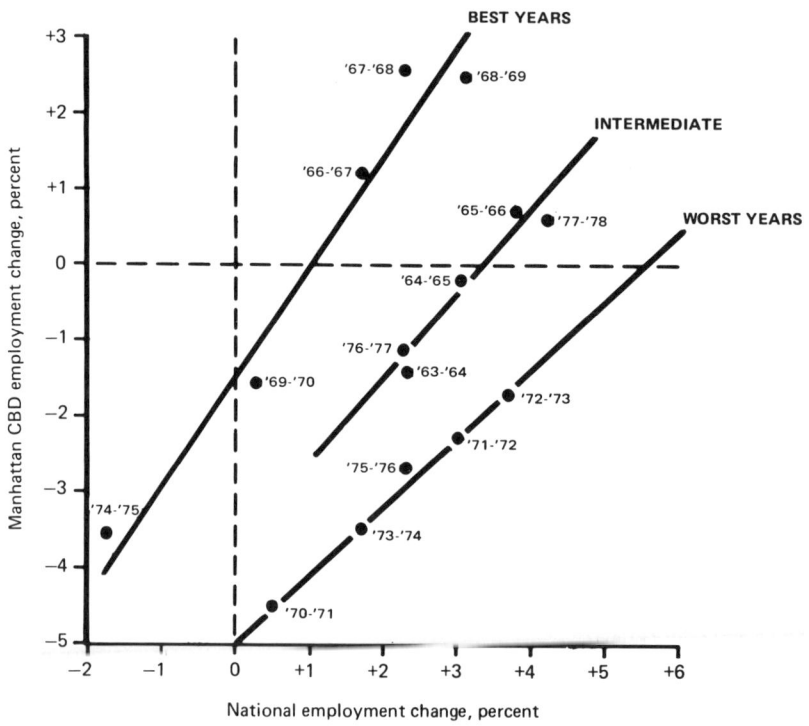

Regional Plan Association

higher national growth produced increases. The periods 1966– 67, 67– 68, 68– 69, 69– 70, and 74– 75 are in this group. While the former four do reflect an overheated wartime economy, the latter period of the "energy recession" fits on the same curve; that is, Manhattan, possibly due to its energy-conserving nature, was affected by the national cutback in employment proportionately less than in most other years. Significantly, the first quarter of 1979 also fits the pattern of the "best years." Compared to the rest of the nation, Manhattan's position in the recession of 1980 also remained quite favorable.

In the "worst years" it would have taken an improbable 5.5% national growth in employment just to have stability in the CBD; in fact, major declines occurred, as in 1970– 71, 71 – 72, 72– 73, 73– 74, and 75– 76. Some of these periods (such as 1971– 73) showed a respectable national growth to which the CBD failed to respond.

The "intermediate years" include 1963– 64, 64– 65, 65– 66, but notably also

1976–77 and 1977–78. During these periods about a 3% national growth in employment was enough not to cause any decline in the CBD; in fact, either modest growth or modest declines took place.

Overall, one can see a pattern where Manhattan's comparative advantage vis-à-vis the rest of the nation improved in the late 1960s, turned abruptly for the worse in 1971, stayed dismal for six years (with one exception), showed much improvement in 1976–78, and rose to the level of the "best years" in the first quarter of 1979. Comparative advantage is defined here as the ability to capture a portion of national growth in employment. Historically, Manhattan's employment tended to be rather income-elastic, and therefore its comparative advantage tended to be better in periods of fast national economic growth than in periods of slow growth.

The range of future possibilities. Any statistical speculation about the CBD's future employment hinges on whether one assumes it will have a comparative advantage typical of the "best," the "intermediate," or the "worst" years, and on the assumptions that are made about the national growth in employment.

The national upswing in employment in 1979, which triggered the first increase in Manhattan jobs in nearly a decade, was, at 4.25%, unusually high. National projections suggest roughly a 2% average annual growth in employment through 1985, and 1.2% thereafter. The reduced growth rate reflects, in large part, the changing age-composition of the population.

According to the "best years" relationship in Figure 6, this would result in 1.5% average annual increases in CBD jobs through 1985, and about 0.3% thereafter, suggesting that *in two decades, Manhattan CBD jobs could very well rebound to 2.16 million, a level characteristic of the early 1960s.*

By contrast, a return to the "intermediate years" relationship between CBD and national employment would spell renewed major declines in the CBD, given the meager national growth projected. The CBD would decline 1.5% annually through 1985, and about 2.5% thereafter, producing a rather implausible loss of 700,000 jobs by the end of the century. A prolonged return to the "worst years" relationship would produce an even greater decline, spelling the end of Manhattan early in the next century.

Such implausible outcomes suggest that the relationship between the CBD and the national economy in the future may well be different from the patterns shown in Figure 6. Renewed decline is possible, but it is likely to be less severe than that suggested by the "intermediate years" curve. Between the possibilities of continued growth and renewed decline, one can also visualize the variant of an essentially stable CBD. The basic stability of Manhattan's daytime population through the past tumultuous six decades may turn out to be a better predictor than the ups and downs in particular shorter periods.

One lesson from the sixty-year history of Regional Plan Association projections is that they were often linked too closely to trends of the recent past *(Regional Plan Association News* 97, pp. 39–34). Three such projections for the CBD are shown in Figure 5. One, from 1956, predicted 1975 employment within 3%, but could not foresee the growth of the 1960s. Another, prepared during this growth period in 1968, could not foresee the imminent decline and was about 19% too high. The

1960 New York Metropolitan Region study by Harvard University, which foresaw a bright future for the CBD, did not make any explicit CBD projections, but it did state that "the city's projected increase of half a million jobs or so between 1956 and 1985 will occur largely in Manhattan's central business district."[4] The roughly 380,000 CBD job increase during this period, implied by the study data and shown in Figure 5, turned out to be furthest off the mark, largely because the study's notions of past CBD employment were also greatly exaggerated. Its implicit 1975 projection turned out to be 42% too high.

Abrupt changes in Manhattan's comparative advantage vis-à-vis the rest of the nation in the recent past are not easy to explain, and make the future seem very unpredictable. The range of possible projections is huge. Still, it seems that changes in the outside world cannot fail but influence this comparative advantage in the future, in fairly predictable ways. It is to these prospective changes that we now turn.

Forces on the horizon

Like any major downtown, the Manhattan CBD essentially lives in two different worlds simultaneously. One is the immediate world of the surrounding urban region, with its mundane issues of housing cost and transportation convenience, with its fiscal crises and labor problems. The other is the wider global world, with rapidly changing technology, shifting markets, changes in availability of resources, changes in the constellation of political and economic power, changes in fashions and in more deeply held values. Increasingly, the global world tends to influence the local world, and must be looked at first.

Demographic change. The most fundamental coming change in the structure of the U.S. population is that, between 1980 and 1995, the number of people between 15 and 29 years of age will shrink from 30.4 million to 25.8 million, even as total population expands. This is likely to have a number of positive effects on urban areas, including reduced youth unemployment and crime, more advancement opportunities for disadvantaged youths, greater job choice for college graduates. It is also likely to open more opportunities for immigrants — legal or illegal. Immigration from abroad has traditionally given new strength and vitality to New York City and Manhattan in particular, and is likely to continue in the future, given the economic and demographic conditions in the Third World. Latin Americans, Chinese, Indians, and Pakistanis — many with strong entrepreneurial inclinations — can be seen among future immigrants.

Current trends toward later marriages, fewer children, smaller households, more two-wage-earner households, greater labor force participation by women, and greater variety of life-styles and living arrangements are likely to continue, and are likewise favorable to urban living. So far, the trickling back to the cities process has been limited to selected neighborhoods, but it does not have to become widespread to have a large impact on cities. Truly urban neighborhoods (those with densities of over 10,000 people per square mile, where auto use is significantly curtailed) contain little more than one-tenth of the nation's population; if only one-tenth of the remaining population wished to move there, they would be overwhelmed. Admittedly, the situation is less favorable in the New York Region, where over 40% of the nation's higher-density housing stock is located; slack demand here — expressed in housing abandonment, even as housing prices in "desirable" neighborhoods soar — may continue for some time.

The racial turnover that so profoundly changed the core of the New York Region around Manhattan in the previous two decades abated sharply in the past decade: Between 1970 and 1976 the proportion of blacks in New York City's population increased only from 21.1% to 23.7%. While neighborhood racial segregation remains rather extreme, during these six years 3.8% of the region's black population did move from the region's central cities to suburban areas (*Regional Plan Association News* 104). Even if the racial tolerance of white suburbanites does not increase at all during the next two decades, by the year 2000 some 36% of the region's blacks will be living in the suburbs, compared to 20% in 1976. This will alleviate residential segregation.

Economic forces. With more than three-quarters of the world population living outside the economically advanced nations, the potential for world economic growth is immense, even if economic expansion in the advanced nations decelerates. There are both institutional and environmental constraints to this growth, but their level — much debated — cannot be foreseen, because future inventions cannot be foreseen. What *can* be foreseen is that the world economy will be getting much larger, much more complex, and much more interdependent; the command posts of this economy — the world cities — will gain in importance as a result.

The gains will obviously be shared by a number of world cities — including those in the most rapidly growing Third World nations. Some international trade and finance functions may be shared by regional capitals in the U.S. — for example, Miami in relations with Latin America, or San Francisco in relations with Asia. Still, it is unlikely that the primacy of Manhattan as a world city will be fundamentally challenged in the foreseeable future. The reasons have to do with its size, its favorable global location, its polyglot population (as one Frenchman put it: foreigners like to come to New York precisely because it is unlike the rest of the United States), the resulting absence of a language barrier as exists, for example, in Tokyo, and the fact that it is the major face to the outside world of the U.S. economy, which is increasingly international.

This is leading to an increasing aggregation of advanced corporate services in Manhattan, especially those with an international orientation. All major U.S. accounting firms — regardless of where they are headquartered — have their international operations in Manhattan, and legal and financial services are similarly specialized. Conversely, foreign firms that have dealings with the U.S. find a Manhattan presence increasingly essential. These are lasting trends — quite apart from such transient phenomena as the undervaluation of the U.S. currency due to persistent trade deficits, or the influx of scarce capital as a result of political upheavals abroad. As a Japanese businessman put it, "We are here because this is the center of world communication, and because this is the center of finance."

International forces aside, office work, or white collar jobs performed in office buildings, represents the most rapidly growing economic activity in the United

States; because office jobs are eminently suited to city centers, they offer a chance to provide a new economic base for deteriorating central cities nationwide.[5] Despite a huge infusion of capital into white-collar activity — in the form of electronic computers and calculators, "smart" typewriters, photocopiers, and new telecommunication devices — the growth in white-collar employment in the U.S. in the 1970s shows only a slight, relative deceleration compared to the 1960s. Of the roughly 20 million new jobs that the national economy is expected to generate by 1990, some 14 million are likely to be in white-collar occupations. Service occupations are also going to grow, as is the increasing "gray-collar" component of technicians servicing the new office machines.

If current trends continue, the bulk of the new white-collar jobs is likely to locate in southern and western states, but Manhattan and other major old downtowns of the Northeast are likely to share in the benefits of this growth. In the first half of the 1970s, downtown office construction per capita of the regional population in Boston and Pittsburgh, as an example, outpaced that of several southern and western cities (including Dallas and Atlanta), and even supposedly less glamorous downtowns, such as those of Philadelphia and Baltimore, registered noticeable office growth.

Much has been made of the fact that in the first half of the 1970s, fully half of the nation's metropolitan areas with populations of over one million lost inhabitants, a situation without precedent in earlier decades. This loss, however, was in part due simply to declining birth rates, in the face of continuing strong migratory movements. "If employment, gross personal income, and per capita income are examined, one finds that on the whole the larger metropolitan areas were *growing* economically, not declining."[6] The New York Urban Region was the only major exception.

Conditions were worse in the core cities of large metropolitan areas, where, during the 1960s, declines in manufacturing employment were compensated by increases in service unemployment, but in the 1970s, the latter also began to decline, except in selected regional capitals (Atlanta, Denver, San Francisco, Washington), causing an overall loss in city jobs. In some ways, Manhattan's "great decline" of 1969–76 was merely an exaggerated manifestation of this nationwide trend. However, before one jumps to a pessimistic prognosis with respect to the future of white-collar employment in downtowns, two facts must be borne in mind. First, downtown or CBD trends are frequently different from those of the entire central city: Downtown growth amid a declining city, or even a declining region (as in Pittsburgh), is nothing new. Second, the reporting and analysis of local economic data tend to be substantially delayed; transit ridership statistics — available on a current basis — suggest that the upswing in economic activity which began in Manhattan in the fall of 1977 was shared by the downtowns of other major metropolitan areas. The events of the first half of the 1970s that hit Manhattan much harder than other downtowns may turn out to be an historic aberration.

Energy technology. Growing availability of cheap petroleum over the past half-century had a profound effect on cities. It encouraged the phenomenal growth in auto travel and in auto-related low-density settlement, but it also improved the living conditions in central cities by replacing coal in home heating, in urban electric generating stations, and on railroads.

Domestic production of petroleum in the United States peaked in 1970 and commenced a gradual decline, despite a huge increase in exploration and doubling of the annual number of wells drilled. Oil imports — foreseen as a painless answer to the depletion of domestic resources in the heydey of technological optimism in the 1960s — approached, for a time, almost half of U.S. consumption, bringing foreign trade deficits, supply interruptions, and dependence on foreign nations. More ominously, for the first time since oil became a major source of energy, its worldwide use is outpacing the rate at which it is being discovered. Seeking to stretch out revenues from a fixed supply of oil in the ground, oil-producing nations have little reason to increase production in the short run.

The current stance of technological optimists is that immense reserves of liquid hydrocarbons are still in the ground in depleted conventional oil reservoirs, which can be reactivated with secondary and tertiary recovery techniques; in heavy-oil fields, which require similar techniques of steam or chemical injections; in tar sands and oil shale, which require mining and heating; lastly in coal, which has been liquefied on a commercial basis in Germany as far back as 1929. However, past cost estimates for all of these techniques have proven notoriously low. Much sharper increases in the cost of conventional oil are necessary to make them commercially competitive. The huge requirements in labor and capital equipment for these processes just do not compare with the *simplicity* of sinking a well and drawing oil. What is more, the processes themselves require large amounts of energy to produce a usable unit of energy. Current coal liquefication techniques require up to three times as much energy in the form of coal as they produce in liquid form. It has been estimated that replacing 10% of the nation's oil output with synthetic fuel may require up to a 50% increase in coal production, with all the attendant environmental and health problems. Oil from shale requires fracturing some 1.5 tons of rock to produce one barrel of oil, and needs large quantities of water, scarce in those parts of the country where the shale deposits are. In short, continued reliance on liquid hydrocarbons will not be easy, and will require serious economic and environmental dislocations. The production of alcohol from organic matter — a form of renewable, solar energy — likewise requires large energy inputs in the form of fertilizer, as well as for distilling; whether it can be achieved on a significant scale without interfering with food and fiber crops, and without a vast, ecologically disruptive expansion of cultivated land remains highly uncertain.

The possibility of an all-electric economy, using hydrogen as an ideal fuel to replace oil, is still technologically distant, awaiting the availability of electricity from permanent solar or fusion power. Neither of these is likely to be cheap, in light of the prospective capital and maintenance requirements of the needed facilities. All of this points to sharply rising real energy prices for an indefinite period of time, and to the fact that there are no alternatives to conservation.

Higher-density urban settlement conserves energy five ways: by reducing the demand for travel, by shifting more of the remaining travel to energy-conserving mass transit modes, by reducing heat loss through building surfaces, by generally shifting consumer demand toward goods and services that are less energy intensive, and by offering better opportunities for resource recovery and cogeneration of electricity in district heating and cooling plants.

Therefore, reduced availability of petroleum from low-cost sources should favor higher-density settlement as a form of energy conservation. Exactly how much reconcentration one can expect on energy grounds depends on how fast energy costs will rise to become a more tangible item in family and business budgets, and on whether rising costs will be augmented by physical gasoline shortages such as occurred in 1974 and 1979. The latter tended to curtail, most of all, travel to dispersed recreation-oriented development, followed by shopping patterns, and then by mode shifts in travel between home and job.

Much will depend, of course, on whether government keeps subsidizing low-density development or whether energy taxes and other government incentives to urban reconcentration are put in effect.

Meanwhile, high-density urban settlement will also be exposed to dangers, because, even though more energy efficient, it has become so dependent on petroleum for electricity and heat in the effort to maintain environmental standards. After all, Manhattan's subways and central steam plants also run on imported petroleum to a large extent (still about 40%, down from 65%), and the possibility of substituting nuclear power for these purposes is, in the current climate, becoming remote. Finding other, environmentally acceptable substitutes — such as methane, natural or synthetic, and remotely produced electricity — is a matter of high urgency.

The passing of the petroleum age challenges the basic physical organization of American life: the spread-out network of settlement, work, distribution, and consumption. Doubling auto efficiency in miles per gallon will be of little help, if it takes twice as many gallons to produce that gallon synthetically. The issue seems to be not whether, but when, the realization takes hold that a return to more traditional settlement forms is in order.

Transportation technology. The shape of today's urban regions and their downtowns has been determined mostly by 19th-century inventions. The railroad — in its several interurban and intraurban forms — made large cities possible to begin with. The elevator provided them with tall buildings. The automobile enabled dispersed low-density settlement around them. The airplane, by contrast — a 20th-century invention — had only a marginal effect on urban form, because long-distance trips are such a tiny fraction of all trips. If anything, the airplane has reinforced the locational advantage of the largest urban regions, those that can offer the most frequent and direct connections to the rest of the world. All of these systems have now reached a plateau of maturity, where quantum jumps in speed and comfort — exemplified by the automation of elevators, the construction of limited-access highways, and the introduction of jet engines — are no longer on the horizon.

Nor do new systems offer much beyond incremental chage. Massive deployment of the helicopter — itself over forty years old — seems out of the question for urban-type travel, earlier visions to the contrary notwithstanding. Automated "light guideway" or "personal transit" systems, which are receiving research and development attention, seem most suited for small-scale applications, such as downtown shuttles. The hopes of their proponents that this synthesis of rail, elevator, and auto technology can one day become the dominant urban travel mode face a huge capital investment hurdle. An immense auto and rail infrastructure is already in place; a whole new capital plant of similar magnitude would have to be built for this new mode of travel. Should this come to pass, urban densities appropriate to this mode would be in the intermediate range, lower than those created by subways or streetcars, but higher than those created by the auto. Ultra-high-speed underground systems, still in the conceptual stage, face the hurdle of a limited market in addition to that of capital cost: Few travel corridors would seem to warrant them, but their effect would be a concentrating one, and their benign environmental characteristics also make them attractive.

In freight transport technology, a dramatic localized impact was made in the past two decades by the containerization of overseas cargo. It has eliminated Manhattan's 300-year-old function as a seaport, opening over 7 miles of pier-studded waterfront to potential new urban amenities and recreational use. This change was not adequately foreseen, for even as one regional agency was building container facilities in those parts of the harbor where ample space was available, another agency continued to build old-time break-bulk piers in Manhattan as late as the early 1960s, and plans to improve lighterage traffic by barge — which has since virtually disappeared — were being formulated by yet another agency. These failures of foresight are pertinent to a related technology — the growing movement of truck-trailers by railroad. Neither Manhattan — a city of 1.4 million by itself — nor the other boroughs of New York City have any facilities to accommodate this type of freight, and progress in providing them has been slow indeed. Ironically, the Harvard Study forecast that piggyback trains will be a major boon to New York City industries.

Overall, the first transport-technology priority on the horizon is increasing the energy efficiency of existing systems, and switching to nonpetroleum-based fuels where feasible, such as with railroad electrification or trolley buses. In the longer run, reductions in excessive mobility are likely, for a small car is not as convenient for long-distance trips as a gas-guzzling recreational vehicle, and an electric car will for a long time be very circumscribed in its radius of operation.

Communication technology. The physical shape of settlement has depended much more on the technology of physical movement of people and goods than on the technology of information transmission. It is very difficult to say whether such a dramatic departure from the previous state of affairs as the introduction of the telephone a century ago had a centralizing or a decentralizing effect. Television, similarly, had profound social effects but, aside from the closing of neighborhood movie houses and the sprouting of rooftop aerials, hardly any physical effects.

As the volume and the importance of information-handling in the economy rises sharply in comparison with goods-handling, vast improvements in information transmission will take place. Two such improvements currently in the foreground are satellite communications and optical waveguides. Satellite communications will make the cost of information transmission independent of distance. Contacting a friend or a computer in a nearby suburb will cost virtually the same as contacting them halfway around the globe. This, undoubtedly, will help out-of-the-way places, which will have the same access to electronic information as major centers of activity. But it will also have countervailing, centralizing effects. For example, as one is able to dial *any* television programs, one will be inclined to dial the most interesting ones, instead of depending on those produced by the local television station. This will enhance the importance of places with the talent pool and the facilities to produce the most interesting programs — places that have an opera house, drama theaters, and so on. Similarly, the electronic interlinking of all the regional stock exchanges is likely to increase total trading and bring additional volume to Manhattan, though not necessarily employment. As for optical waveguides or fiber optics, their main effect is in the tremendous expansion of transmission capacity through fixed channels, such as urban underground conduits. This will greatly lower the cost of local transmission in higher-density areas.[7] Many of them already have broad-band communications networks — such as cable TV — in place, but fail to exploit them for purposes other than entertainment. A more imaginative use of such facilities integrating digital, voice, and visual transmission can give cities a competitive advantage over more remote areas.

Although some of the electronic information may well make some face-to-face contact unnecessary, some may, on the other hand, evoke the need to see things firsthand. The flows of electronic information remain closely correlated with travel flows. In the past, information-transmission expansion has tended to be cumulative, and has substituted for the previous mode only in minor degree: The telephone did not replace mail, even as it made some letters unnecessary, and the movies did not replace theater, even as they closed vaudeville shows. In the future, some people will be working at home in front of computer terminals, and some teleconferencing will take place, but the technological feasibility of such things should not be confused with universal adoption.

Possibly of greater import on the need to gather large numbers of workers in downtowns will be information-handling machinery that further automates clerical and secretarial tasks — word processing, expanding electronic funds transfer, a variety of electronic bookkeeping systems in banking and insurance, eventually computers which take dictation, correct the grammar, translate the letter into another language if necessary, and deliver it via facsimile machine electronically to the addressee. Still, all these are evolutionary improvements, in line with the influx of capital equipment into the office which has been under way for some time and which, as indicated earlier, has only a modest effect on the expansion of white-collar employment.

Two countervailing trends are revealed in discussions with banking executives, as an example. One states that "every function that can be automated will be automated, and every operating job that can be moved out of the CBD will be moved out." Another points out that "banking employment in the CBD may actually expand because banks will be entering new branches of activity, such as managing, bookkeeping, financial, and tax consulting." The two perspectives are not necessarily in conflict — both agree that an upgrading in the level of CBD jobs will take place. Moreover, much of the automation will reduce employment in branches, not in central offices.

Lastly, the institutional framework within which technology operates (such as rate structures and licensing arrangements) must be considered alongside technology itself. For example, the cost of mail delivery within a CBD are a fraction of what they are at dispersed locations, but the difference is not reflected in postal rates, providing one of many subsidies for dispersal at the expense of clustering.

Relations with the surrounding city. The relationship between the Manhattan CBD and the rest of New York City is contradictory in many ways. The CBD does not need a city as large as New York around itself — it could get by with a city about half the size. The city needs the CBD very much — about two-thirds of its economic output is produced there. The prosperity of Manhattan — at least south of 96th Street — is now viewed with some assurance, but most observers remain doubtful about the prospects for the remainder of the city. Continued growth in the CBD would of course reverberate in other boroughs, upgrading housing and local retailing — a process that is taking shape in the "brownstone revival" neighborhoods around Brooklyn Heights, on the Upper West Side, across the river in Hoboken and Jersey City, and is beginning to percolate even into such places as Long Island City, Greenpoint, and East Harlem. Yet, *no amount of foreseeable CBD growth would be enough to pull all of the city's depressed neighborhoods out of poverty.* There, the large unemployable population requires job development — or relocation assistance — efforts quite different from those needed to promote CBD revival. Also, the contrast between the rising skill level of CBD employment and the deteriorating state of so much of the city's housing assures that many of the future CBD workers will continue to seek residences in suburban areas. Most of the 870,000 tenement units of pre-1930 stock are functionally obsolete and probably beyond rehabilitation.

The long litany of complaints about what is wrong with Manhattan as a place of business has less to do with the intrinsic qualities of Manhattan, than with "spillover" effects from the surrounding city, and the disabilities of its government: rundown public spaces, deteriorating infrastructure, dirt and garbage in the streets, pavements in an impossible condition, subway station walls unwashed for forty years, derelicts and prostitutes in the most prominent locations, bad schools, universities turning out second-rate graduates, pervasive fear of crime, weakness of political and business leadership and responsibilities, extraordinarily high taxes and public labor payments in the face of frequently low competence and productivity of public employees. It is also recalled that less than twenty years ago, when New York City had only two-thirds the municipal employees it now has, and they were paid only half as much as they are now in constant dollars, parks were maintained better, subway trains were cleaner, and streets had fewer potholes.

This is not to downplay the reality of the city's purely fiscal problems. To a greater degree than commonly imagined, New York was built as a manufacturing town, and the departure of manufacturing to the South and abroad had caused large parts of the city to lose their economic reason for being. This caused large-scale unemployment and housing abandonment and contributed to social dislocation and fiscal instability. The future attractiveness of the city will depend on its ability to sustain basic municipal services to renew its capital infrastrucure, that is, on its fiscal stability.

Local government expenditures from local sources in New York City in 1975 were roughly double the level of those in the surrounding region; significantly, expenditures per capita for standard urban services (police, fire, sanitation, utilities) were about the same as in the surrounding region; the difference resulted from city expenditures for health, welfare, and housing; for public transportation; for pension payments and interest on debt (three to four times greater than in suburban jurisdictions).[8] The city will not be able to make ends meet unless basically regional and national functions are shifted to the appropriate levels of government.

Yet, changes in political attitudes and institutions will obviously have to go beyond geographic shifts in the tax burden. How likely they are will depend on how necessary they will be perceived to be. For many years, it seemed easier to simply escape from urban problems and to throw money at the poor or at municipal labor unions. Yet, in 1975, when the alternative for New York was bankruptcy, municipal expenditures were curtailed and reforms were initiated. When the suburban escape route becomes less attractive, more reforms may follow, tackling issues of urban education, crime control, and labor relations.

The effectiveness of government at all levels in carrying out any consistent national policy — such as one of recentralization — is hampered by a fragmentation of constituencies, by increasing complexity of the government process, by weakness of managerial authority. Simple principles, such as that no office building should be built away from public transportation, or that each new house built in the exurbs should be taxed for the societal costs it is imposing on the region as a whole, are still viewed as politically inconceivable. But then, so was government regulation of the size of automobiles as recently as eight or nine years ago, when small cars were viewed as virtually un-American.

Notes

1. For the Manhattan CBD, the 1960 TSRPC job totals are, respectively, 19.3% and 13.7% above the Census "worker" totals; for 1970, the excess is 24% and 25%, respectively; the difference is much smaller (about 10% in 1970) in the region ouside the CBD, suggesting that apart from dual jobs, some jobs not physically located in the CBD may be included in the economic statistics, which rely on reports by establishments, not by individuals.
2. Overall, there is a close correspondence between this series and the Hub-bound travel series. The coefficient of determination, or R^2, between CBD subway turnstile entries as shown in Table 2 and persons entering across the CBD cordon by subway, as shown in Table 1, is 0.98; that between turnstile entries and total cordon crossings by all means of travel, 0.95.
3. Subway ridership city-wide is closely tied to events in the CBD because over 75% of all subway trips have either an origin or a destination, or both, in the CBD.
4. Raymond Vernon, *Metropolis 1985* (Cambridge, Mass.: Harvard University Press, 1960), p. 223. See also p. 103 and pp. 234–37.
5. Regina B. Armstrong, "National Trends in Office Construction, Employment, and Headquarter Location in U.S. Metropolitan Areas," in P. W. Daniels (ed.), *Spatial Patterns of Office Growth and Location* (Chichester: Wiley, 1979), pp. 61–93.
6. Thomas Black, *The Changing Economic Role of Central Cities* (Washington, D.C.: Urban Land Institute, 1978).
7. A fiber optic link between Manhattan and White Plains was expected to be in operation by 1981, carrying as much information over 144 strands of glass (each 1/5000" in diameter) as by 1,500 pairs of copper wire. Streams of pulsed laser light, turning on and off 1.54 million times a second, carry up to 672 simultaneous telephone conversations through one glass strand. *The New York Times*, April 11, 1979.
8. Regina B. Armstrong, *Regional Accounts: Structure and Performance of the New York Region's Economy in the Seventies* (Bloomington, Ind.: Indiana University Press, 1980), pp. 209–10.

14

NEW YORK CITY'S FISCAL SITUATION

Herbert J. Ranschburg

To observe, analyze, and evaluate New York City's fiscal situation is now relatively easy. The scarcity of data and the obfuscation practiced by governmental fiscal experts so characteristic of yesteryear has given way to a flood of information handled by men and women of competence. and intellectual integrity. Does that mean that the path of fiscal rectitude is now straight and narrow, hemmed in all along its length by constraints of fiscal propriety? Well, not quite, but the fiscal processes are now so clear and in the open, that obfuscation would become so blatantly obvious that one could question whether anyone would seriously try to perpetrate some major fiscal gimmickry. I am talking only about the City of New York, not about the fiscal bucket-shop characteristics still prevalent elsewhere.

Of course, the city has never had, does not have, and never will have unlimited resources. Consequently, the study of New York City would be part of a basic economics course as a prime example of how painful the allocation of scarce resources can be.

If one accepts prevailing fiscal constraints as basically unchangeable in short run, and *if* one accepts as a fact of life the existing distrubution of power among the city's manifold interest groups, and *if* one assumes that there will be no recurrence of overly creative budgeting and fiscal frolicking, then it can be said that New York City's fiscal situation is salutary, ending toward the goal of fiscal stability. This now appears to be the case, with the city approaching its goal of a fiscal year 1981 budget balanced in accordance with generally accepted accounting principles.

Nobody can tell precisely what future city budgets will look like. Nor should one really care, because a budget at the beginning of the fiscal year and a budget at the end of the fiscal year are but distantly related; what count are the forces and events that shape the budget between Day 1 and Day 365. And on this topic, I think, some comments are in order.

Over the past five years, New York City, in fact, has been governed by a congeries of interest groups. It is significant that a coalescing of these previously bitterly antagonistic forces in the fall of 1975 represented a thoroughly rational reaction to a perceived danger: a fiscal collapse which conceivably could have engulfed not only the public sector but large chunks of the private sector as well.

The main actors in this municipal morality play came from three different areas.

There were federal participants from the White House, the U.S. Treasury, and the Congress; there were the New York State participants from Albany; and there were the local participants: union leaders, representatives of the Clearing House banks, and a few individuals who speak for City Hall. All agreed on what had to be done: The agreed-upon wage freezes, financial bailouts, and loan guarantees were more than techniques used to pull a mismanaged city back from the abyss of fiscal collapse. They were, in my view, the essence of a novel social contract among those who know that either all or none will prosper.

Regardless of what you may hear about this arrangement breaking down, this is not so. At least in the case of our subway system, strike action has still played the role of the traditional overture to collective bargaining for a new contract for transit employees. Nevertheless, this grand coalition of traditional adversaries will not break down, because nobody can afford that kind of calamity. The rising chorus of blame for all fiscal ills being shifted toward Albany and Washington is a good sign that, at least as far as the local participants are concerned, the power group coalition is still functioning: If, instead, the blame were ever turned inward — that is, among the local participants themselves — then one could justifiably become quite pessimistic about the city's future. This may not be the picture one gets when one reads the standard texts about local home rule and democracy, but the picture I draw is a representation of *recent* fiscal reality. It is also, I believe, an illustrated guide for *continued* fiscal health.

You may then ask whether most of the actions so far taken and expected to be taken are optimal from the point of view of the public interest. My answer is no. I am not talking about legality or accounting standards but about fiscal common sense. To be specific: Ever since 1975, the city has adjusted to inescapable fiscal restraints through a combination of two methods: (1) higher revenues (both higher intergovernmental aid payments and inflation-driven increases in tax yields), and (2) a broad, across-the-board, merciless slashing of the quality and quantity of public services. The first method, once inflation cools down, will come to an end, and the second one, unless terminated, will spell the end of New York City as a viable urban center. In other words; the fiscal crisis has become a service crisis.

There are too many things the city tries to do with the means at its disposal. As a result, we are proudly paying our debts and are avoiding bankruptcy but, perhaps not so proudly, establishing new records in the number of truants in our school system, the number of potholes in our streerts, and the depth of the filth clogging our streets and sidewalks. If we continue on this road, then the next mayor of the City of New York may be no more than an accounts payable clerk; no need to worry about that vanishing species called public services. Let it be to Mayor Koch's credit that he is aware of the risks and that he is proposing remedial action in fiscal year 1982. Whether he will succeed, only the future can tell.

What has to be done — and there is great urgency about it — is to make choices about which local functions ought to be continued — and continued well — and which functions ought to be abolished. Politically, I realize, this may be an invitation to suicide to the office holder who has the guts to start out on that road. The rational thing to do is to plan for fewer services which, while much more costly, will, one hopes, be much better.

To be specific, the City of New York cannot afford transit subsidies, cannot afford hospital subsidies, cannot afford CUNY subsidies. The three-quarters of a billion dollars involved in subsidies are not just money. In terms of opportunity costs, they translate into police not hired, classrooms not covered, fire trucks not manned.

Were I a betting person, I would be willing to bet that a continuation of the aforementioned power-group coalition and a substantial cut in the number of public service functions will make the city's future relatively hazard-free. But I think we owe it to ourselves to go one step further and ask; Is this a rational way to run a federal, three-layer-type system of government? How long shall we cover our rusty ship of state with multibillion-dollar layers of intergovernmental aid paint? A shift from federal categorical aid to relatively unrestricted block grants, as proposed by the Reagan administration, may help recipient units of government by allowing them to concentrate funds in areas of their own choosing. But, going further, there is need for an orderly rearrangement of revenue-raising functions and expenditure responsibilities among all types of government. Most of the current discussion on this topic is slightly disingenuous. One cannot talk about shifting expenditures without at least considering the need for or the desirability of shifting revenue sources in the same direction. Although it was probably not designed to achieve that goal, Proposition 13 has had the effect of facilitating such a shift of revenues and expenditures.

I would be the last one to use the dictates of economic efficiency as a shield behind which a single highly centralized all-powerful governmental structure should be erected. Individual freedoms are too precious to be traded in for regional models of governmental efficiency. Yet, the city's chance for a better future requires that we stop being at the ill-tempered mercy of Albany and Washington budgeteers. There must be a better way, so that the energies of the body politic can be directed toward the solution of real problems, not toward the composition of requests-for-more-aid, otherwise known as political-impact statements.

To close out on a note of good cheer, if Ed Koch up in Gracie Mansion were only to dream in his deepest sleep about doing what passes for proper fiscal practices elsewhere, he would never make it down to City Hall in the morning; he'd be detoured into jail.

So you see, we are really quite well off.

15

NEW YORK IN THE NATIONWIDE SLOWDOWN OF 1980–81

George P. Roniger

New York City's economy stabilized in 1980 after a three-year period of growth, while the nationwide economy flattened out. Private employment in the United States showed only slight growth, 0.5%, in the twelve months ended in January 1981. The city fared somewhat better, with employment rising by almost 1% during the same time period. The business activity index was flat when averaged for the year, but showed considerable improvement in the latter half (5%).

. . . Compared with previous recessions

The city's economy headed into the recession of 1980 from a period of some strength compared with its state in the early part of the two previous recessions of 1970 and 1974. In early 1970, for example, the economy was unbalanced, with an unsustainable overload of activity in government, in finance, and to a lesser extent in construction. In addition, the New York area was losing competitiveness.

In late 1973, the city faced the onset of the most severe nationwide recession of the postwar period in the midst of what would prove to be an underlying downturn of the private local economy that was to last the better part of a decade. Also, local government activity was about to retrench sharply.

In contrast, at the onset of the recession in early 1980, the local economy almost confidently faced the nationwide economic slowdown from a position of modest strength developed over the past two years: a relatively well-balanced economy, and a period of improved price, wage, and tax competitiveness.

The city's cyclical peak

The gains of 1976–79 were sustained by many sectors: business and personal services, finance, construction, retail sales, and the overall tourist and recreation industry. All, of course, gained from the nationwide economic expansion. Beyond that, special factors impinging on the local economy were almost uniformly favorable. Extraordinarily heavy stock market turnover aided the financial sector. Tight housing and office conditions on the upper end of the market provided a modest boost to construction. And the rejuvenation of a number of the city's neighborhoods boosted renovation activity. Retail sales were exceedingly strong, aided by a local tourist boom and apparently also by increased values of art and jewelry. Even local government ceased to be the substantial drag that it had been in the mid-1970s.

Manufacturing did show a somewhat different picture. Employment in this sector stabilized in 1978 for its strongest showing in a decade. But, as nationwide industrial production ceased to grow in 1979, manufacturing employment in New York settled again into a state of erosion. During 1980, manufacturing employment dropped by roughly 3% in both New York City and the nation.

Underlying directions

The underlying trends (exclusive of cyclical fluctuations) have improved significantly in New York in recent years. Differences between local and nationwide rates of change, as measured by employment, have narrowed considerably. In 1976, the number of jobs nationwide rose by over 3%, while the number of jobs in New York City declined by over 2%, for a gap in the two employment growth rates of over 5%. By 1979, that gap had narrowed to 2%. It was below 1% in the twelve months through May 1980 and was eliminated by January 1981. New York City benefited — relatively — over the two years by its meager dependence on hard-goods manufactures and private home construction. But the narrowing of the gap has been fairly well sustained for the entire period since mid-decade of the 1970s.

It may also be some comfort to be reminded that, historically, the city's economy has shown somewhat less cyclical volatility than the overall nationwide economy. This makes intuitive sense; the city's economy is based relatively heavily on the less cyclically sensitive services sector and is less dependent on the most cyclically responsive sectors — durable goods and construction. Our econometric experiments suggest that the cyclical variation of the city's level of private employment around its trend direction is about three-fourths as great as the cyclical volatility of nationwide employment around its own trend. This means that the rate of growth of employment in New York — lower on average than that of the United States — generally comes closer to U.S. changes during recession. It falls further behind nationwide growth during periods of maximum nationwide expansion, when hard-goods output and high construction activity boost the local economies of other places to a greater extent.

The nationwide downturn

The "recession" of 1980 was unusually short, only one quarter in duration, yet it was quite sharp. Moreover, the recovery was anemic. At the close of 1980, gross national product was still 0.3% below the fourth-quarter 1979 level, and industrial production had fallen 1.2% since the previous December. The volume of retail sales exhibited a 5.7% decrease over the twelve months despite the third-quarter rebound. Industrial production, total employment, and real personal consumption expenditures all finished the year below their 1979 year-end levels.

As is usual, the housing and automotive sectors led into the recession. Although the brunt of the cutbacks in the automotive industry fell on the industrial northeastern and north central states, New York City is not dependent on this or the other manufacturing industries that are most volatile. The city, as noted, is somewhat secluded from the gyrations in the housing markets, although it is subject to its own cyclical influences in this sector. But by mid-1980, related, if less dramatic, cutbacks in consumer and business demand depressed the local economy.

Although gross national product registered a 6.5% gain (at an annual rate) in the first quarter of 1981, the year-to-year growth was only 0.5%. January retail sales, March automobile sales, and the quarter's industrial-equipment output were the chief components of the rise. Retail sales ended the quarter on a low note, and real personal income was flat in March. The expiration of auto rebates and weakness in construction and industrial production pointed to slower growth in coming months.

Nationwide, the economy will remain depressed for a period to come by the weakness in purchasing power that already has been sustained since early 1979, and the adverse effect of limited growth in final sales on output and on plans for capital outlays. But, as economic activity remains sluggish, credit demands also have declined and will continue to decline, allowing credit to become more readily available to those who contiue to seek it. Interest rates were expected to decline by the end of 1981 and inflation was expected to abate, as the drop registered in the first quarter of 1981 indicated.

All these were expected to set the stage for the nationwide reexpansion likely to begin in the second half of 1981. But it will take time before the damage is undone and demand for goods and services strengthens substantially.

The economic forecast of Citibank, therefore, envisaged an increase in national output of 2% to 3% for 1981. The lessening of inflation, a decline in interest rates, and stronger housing and machinery and equipment purchases in the second half will spur the modest recovery. Establishment employment nationwide, which grew at a rate of almost 5% in 1978, rose only 0.1% in the twelve months ending in February 1981 and was expected to show growth during 1981. Unemployment rose from under 6% in late 1979 to over 7.5% in the second half of 1980. The unemployment rate was expected to be in excess of 7.5% during the remainder of 1981.

New York did not escape unscathed but still exhibited greater private employment growth than the nation as a whole. The city's manufacturing industries, already weakened somewhat over the past two years, continued to feel the effects of a restrained level of consumer purchases. Total nationwide output of apparel grew by 1.3% during 1980, and consumption expenditures for clothing and shoes rose by a comparable amount. Output of these major New York industries was flat, at best, and employment decreased in both. The 1981 local outlook for apparel was minimal growth, at best. Electrical machinery and equipment output of the nation took a slight dip in 1980, and employment in the industry decreased by over 1%. New York City's electrical equipment industry employment dropped by 9%, showing more volatility than the industry nationwide. The outlook for 1981 was for another downturn with recovery beginning in late 1981. Printing and publishing, the second largest New York manufacturing sector, held up well throughout 1980. In this relatively stable industry, both output and employment were level, and should have picked up later in 1981.

Other sectors felt the pinch, also. The tourist industry apparently slowed down somewhat, as measured by hotel occupancy. For the year, the rate dropped from 81.5 to 78.4, partially due to significant additions to the stock of rooms. As some households reassess their ability and willingness to accept the major financial burden that a city vacation entails, tourism growth will slow. Output of business and personal services also will be dampened — perhaps more subtly — by cutbacks in household purchasing power and weak growth in business profits.

Some constraint was likely to show up later in 1981 in the New York construction sector and also in growth of the financial sector. Both would be delayed reactions to high rates of interest in 1980 and early 1981. Some construction projects that might have been planned, were likely to have been delayed by the recent interest-rate environment and by difficulty in obtaining financing commitments in recent months. Furthermore, the recession dampened enthusiasm for new construction. It severely constrained demand for residential units, and it dampened hotel occupancy. Commercial construction, however, increased during 1980. The employment gains were realized in the first half with decreases occurring in the second half. Permits filed pointed to a continued surge in commercial construction activity, but it was felt that the real estate markets in New York could weaken significantly, if temporarily, as new space came on stream while the overall economy remained sluggish.

Activity and employment in the financial sector were expected to be impinged by the slowdown in the growth of demand for financial services. Some financial intermediaries, furthermore, would require time to adjust to the financial pinch created in their profit statements by the extraordinary cost of funds in 1980 and early 1981.

In sum

The nationwide outlook and the state of the economy of New York City were suggestive of near stability in employment during 1981. Unemployment of city residents, which hit a double-digit rate in March 1981, was expected to hold at levels near 9%–10%. After adjustment for inflation, personal income was unlikely to grow substantially over the coming year. Profits of local business would be sluggish and some would be driven from business by low demand for their products.

Yet, the experience in, and following, the recessions in the 1970s whereby the city lost 130,000 jobs in 1971 and 160,000 in 1975 would not be repeated. In the early and mid-1970s, nationwide recessions acted as catalysts to exacerbate local area vulnerabilites in a number of overextended and competitive sectors — especially finance, real estate, local government, and manufacturing. Longer-term nationwide shifts of people, business, and purchasing power from older urban areas to growing areas of the country created a further drag in New York.

In 1981, in contrast, there was no local economic sector as clearly out of the line of its sustainable level of activity as was the case in the earlier years. The price, wage, and tax position of the local economy was somewhat improved. The movement to the Sunbelt and to the rural areas of the country may have passed its peak.

Ultimately, of course, the nationwide economy would rebound. Given the recent directions of the city's economy, the city might well reenter an expansion phase by 1982.

Contributors

REGINA BELZ ARMSTRONG, Vice-President for Economics, Regional Plan Association
MAURICE B. BALLABON, Associate Professor, Department of Economics and Finance, Bernard M. Baruch College of the City University of New York
MATTHEW P. DRENNAN, Associate Professor of Economics, Graduate School of Public Administration, New York University
SAMUEL M. EHRENHALT, Regional Commissioner of Labor Statistics, Middle Atlantic Region, Bureau of Labor Statistics, U.S. Department of Labor
PEARL KAMER, Chief Economist, Long Island Regional Planning Board, and Adjunct Professor, W. Averell Harriman College for Urban and Policy Sciences, State University of New York at Stony Brook
BENJAMIN J. KLEBANER, Professor of Economics, The City College of the City University of New York
WILLIAM J. LAWRENCE, Associate Professor of Economics, Graduate School of Business, Pace University
IRVING LEVESON, Director of Economic Studies, Hudson Institute
BORIS S. PUSHKAREV, Vice-President for Research and Planning, Regional Plan Association
HERBERT J. RANSCHBURG, Vice-President, Citizens Budget Commission
EDWIN P. REUBENS, Professor of Economics, The City College of the City University of New York
GEORGE P. RONIGER, Vice-President, Citibank, N.A.
MARILYN RUBIN, Associate Professor of Urban Affairs and Policy Analysis, New School for Social Research, and Consultant to the Budget Director, City of New York
THOMAS J. SPITZNAS, Regional Economist, Chemical Bank
THOMAS M. STANBACK, JR., Professor of Economics and Senior Research Associate, Conservation of Human Resources Project, Columbia University
EMANUEL TOBIER, Professor of Economics and Urban Planning, Graduate School of Public Administration, New York University.
ILENE WAGNER, Assistant Director for Policy Analysis, Office of Economic Development, City of New York
MARK A. WILLIS, Senior Economist, Regional Economic Staff, Federal Reserve Bank of New York
DENNIS YOUNG, Associate Professor and Director of Research, W. Averell Harriman College for Urban and Policy Sciences, State University of New York at Stony Brook